AUDIOBOOKS AS ARTIFACTS

LISTENING FOR CLASSIFICATION AND APPRECIATION

DAVID SHEINBERG

First published in 2024
as part of the Books, Publishing, and Libraries Book Imprint
doi: 10.18848/978-1-963049-37-4/CGP (Full Book)

Common Ground Research Networks
2001 South First Street, Suite 202
University of Illinois Research Park
Champaign, IL
61820

Library of Congress Cataloging-in-Publication Data

Names: Sheinberg, David, author.
Title: Audiobooks as artifacts: listening for classification and
    appreciation / David Sheinberg.
Description: Champaign, IL : Common Ground Research Networks, 2024. |
    Includes bibliographical references. | Summary: "Their
    ever-evolving popularity notwithstanding, audiobooks remain a rather
    undertheorized phenomenon. The handful of existing studies have adopted
    an inherently historicist approach, failing to identify or scrutinize
    their aesthetic importance. Thus, rather than regarding them as mere
    recorded 'versions' of existing literary works, this book explores them
    as the unique products of a hitherto undefined genre, namely,
    performance-based aural artifacts. Appropriately, the very act of
    listening to them is rendered a distinct aesthetic experience in its own
    right. If the proof of the proverbial pudding is purportedly in the
    eating, then by surveying a series of case studies, this book aims to
    provide one with comparative close listenings-appropriately analyzing
    and debating their aesthetic properties and merit. Finally, in exploring
    what is identified herein as one's 'informed intuition' and its role in
    the craft of casting audiobooks, this study also proposes a new
    understating of how aesthetic appreciation works in action"-- Provided
    by publisher.
Identifiers: LCCN 2024013072 (print) | LCCN 2024013073 (ebook) | ISBN
    9781963049350 (hardback) | ISBN 9781963049367 (paperback) | ISBN
    9781963049374 (adobe pdf)
Subjects: LCSH: Audiobooks. | Oral reading. | Listening (Philosophy) |
    Narration (Rhetoric)--Philosophy.
Classification: LCC ZA4750 .S54 2024 (print) | LCC ZA4750 (ebook) | DDC
    808.5/4--dc23/eng20240501
LC record available at https://lccn.loc.gov/2024013072
LC ebook record available at https://lccn.loc.gov/2024013073

This book is dedicated to my parents—for their love and unwavering support, for putting me through university, and for putting up with me in general; to the blessed memory of my grandparents, Nechama and Arye Aharonov—for always encouraging, supporting, and, indeed, inspiring me; and to my uncle, Meir Aharonov, may they rest in peace—without whom this would not have been possible.

ACKNOWLEDGMENTS

First and foremost, I wish to thank Common Ground Research Networks for recognizing the due merit of my manuscript and affording me the opportunity to publish with them.

Next, I owe a wholehearted debt of gratitude to Professor Robert Gordon at Goldsmiths, University of London. In seeking a suitable PhD supervisor, Robert proved the only person to have instantly, and quite intuitively, "get it," and graciously welcomed me under his wing. I will forever cherish his invaluable advice, comments, provocative insights, patience, unfailing guidance, and genuine good heart. He is, to all intents and purposes, the epitome of a true *mensch*.

I also sincerely wish to thank my PhD examiners—Professors Matthew Rubery and David Peimer—for their perceptive feedback and encouraging assessments, and for urging me to publish.

For affording me their input, intuitions, and time, I hereby thank Casting directors Claudia Howard, of Recorded Books, Inc., and Patrick McQuaid of ID Audio Ltd. Furthermore, for providing me with helpful advice, information, and insights, I would like to acknowledge Mr. Jonathan Turell—CEO of the Criterion Collection; Ms. Robin Whitten—Editor/Founder at *AudioFile Magazine*; Ms. Michele Cobb—executive director of the Audio Publishers Association, publisher of *AudioFile*, and consultant at Forte Business Consulting; Mr. Jan Paterson—Director of Books and Audio at BBC Studios; and Ms. Mary Thompson—audiobook reviewer for *AudioFile*.

I would also like to convey my heartfelt gratitude to Tony Gregory—for reminding me that I not only *can* but, in fact, most certainly should.

Last and, indeed, not least, I express my heartfelt gratitude to my friend and colleague, Dr. Madeleine Schechter, PhD, whom I first met when seeking an MA supervisor. Madeleine's academic integrity, unrivaled interdisciplinary intellectual infrastructure, and, indeed, her uncompromising rigor, have all established themselves as embedded commands that guide my research and writing. Her telling me, just about a decade ago, "you're in the big league now!" still resonates with me—and makes me strive to prove her right.

TABLE OF CONTENTS

INTRODUCTION

Soundscapes of Childhood

Ray Bradbury's dystopian classic, *Fahrenheit 451,* depicts a not-so-distant future in which reading is forbidden, books are burned by firemen, and any hope for a brighter tomorrow ultimately rests upon a collective of exiles—the "Book People"—who have taken it upon themselves to save books from annihilation by way of committing them to heart. In the graceful and touching penultimate scene of François Truffaut's 1966 cinematic adaptation of Bradbury's novel (a scene that also stands out in communicating a director's own personal "take" on given source material), one finds an old man on his deathbed, reciting passages from his chosen book to his nephew—so that he, in turn, can later take his place and effectively "become" the book. Interesting as it may be to ponder why Truffaut happened to have specifically chosen Robert Louis Stevenson's last, unfinished novel, *Weir of Hermiston* (1896), my own particular interest in this heartfelt scene resides elsewhere. Although, perhaps, overtly sentimental, I find that the very notion of one's being able to supposedly assume, embody, or, indeed, "become" a written text, through speech, evokes a certain quality that is both majestic and haunting.

Audiobooks, too, seem to me to exhibit this particular quality in a rather unique manner. Even as child, I was always captivated by audiobooks, often finding myself listening to various recorded narrations, aural performances, and sound productions on both phonographic records and audiocassette tapes. To this day, I still have in my possession a number of home-made recordings, featuring my own parents' reading stories to the 2-year-old me.

Perhaps that last sentence requires some clarification. After all, I do not in any way wish to imply that my parents were never altogether inclined to actually sit down and read me stories. Quite the contrary: memories of them reading to me rank among my most vivid early childhood recollections. In point of fact, the recordings in question feature my parents not only reading directly *to* me (where my own odd comment or insightful reflection can be heard as an added nostalgic bonus) but also—and perhaps more interestingly—reading *for* me, albeit not in my presence. Recently conducted inquisitive interviews notwithstanding, it remains somewhat unclear just what it was that prompted my parents to go about and introduce such a scheme. One can surmise, however, that this endeavor was certainly *not* designed to occupy their infant child while they happened to be otherwise engaged. Rather, these tapes were, to be sure, a labor of love—created for the benefit of a child with an unmistakable passion for storytelling. For the most part, so it seems, these recordings aimed to serve as an opportunity for me to re-experience and delight in my favorite stories. In addition to their current status as a personal time-capsule, the fact that they were delivered by two individuals who also happened to possess a genuine knack for this particular task no doubt helped sow the seed. Indeed, those recordings—coupled with the garden-variety commercial productions that I used to devour during my early childhood—have surely left their impression, most likely igniting my prevailing passion for the spoken word—so much so, in fact, that at the age of 7-and-a-half, I began creating my *own* cassette tapes.

Perhaps that, too, could benefit further elucidation. Evidently, the 7-and-a-half-year-old me, in what might be perceived of as a clear case of "monkey see, monkey do," had taken it upon himself to record a series of cassette tapes—in which I am heard not only reading stories but also telling jokes and performing musical numbers—all consciously directed at a *designated* (albeit completely absent and imaginary) audience of other children.

While the core reasons for my being engrossed by this endeavor—up to around the age of 13, in fact—are presently contemplated upon in therapy, and although the tapes themselves are now devotedly stored in an offshore safety-deposit-box (with the passcode to which engraved on the inner circle of a fun-size golden ornament, attached to a polar bear, somewhere in Alaska), I ultimately ended up dedicating my PhD dissertation to the exploration of audio-books—not only as a cultural phenomenon but also as a unique *artistic* praxis. This book constitutes the evolution of that study.

"And Is Not That, in a Sense, a Performance?"

In 2006, RTÉ released an eighteen-disk box set entitled *Samuel Beckett: Three Novels*, containing unabridged aural iterations of *Molloy*, *Malone Dies*, and *The Unnamable*—all immaculately performed by accomplished Irish actor Barry McGovern. Originally published between 1955 and 1957 as three individual novels, they are customarily regarded as Beckett's "trilogy." McGovern—who in the mid-1980s had performed a one-man show consisting of selected passages from the "trilogy"—addresses the performative properties that inhabit Beckett's prose:

> Many myths abound about Samuel Beckett. Some of these have to do with the question of performance of his dramatic works, especially the transference from one medium to another. […] Adaptations of prose works are legion—on stage, TV and radio. […] many of these adaptations were authorized by Beckett himself or given his blessing—as was my own one-man show *I'll Go On,* […] produced by Dublin's Gate Theatre in 1985. The prose works were written to be read, not performed in the conventional sense of the word. The early work is written in the third person. But in the great middle period of the late 40's and 50's the voice changes to the first person: the voice of […] *Molloy, Malone Dies* and *The Unnamable*. It always seemed to me that these prose writings cried out to be read aloud. And is not that, in a sense, a performance?[1]

Rather than intuitively surmising that it undoubtedly *is*, one of this book's main objectives is to provide a more elaborate response to this question.

Despite the various available approaches associated with the term, one may not necessarily require an exhaustive explanation of what a "performance" actually is. Indeed, its meaning, I would argue, should be a given. Nevertheless, I fully intend to address the nature of performances in respect of the matter at hand, namely, how to explain just what it is that *makes* a "reading aloud" constitute a performance to begin with. Since some performances may be intrinsically classified as *artworks*, then to determine whether or not (and, indeed, to what extent) a reading aloud might qualify as a putative performance would effectively require one to assign it with a particular aesthetic context—that is, a discrete set of circumstances—insofar as identifying just what it is that *makes* in an artwork. Thus, if an audiobook essentially constitutes a performance that is confined to an exclusively aural medium, I find that it should ultimately be identified as a unique kind of artwork in and of itself.

Audiobooks and Aesthetics

Granted, there is no quibble as to whether or not one derives aesthetic pleasure from audiobooks. At the same time, however, there also seems to be little to

---

[1] Barry McGovern, "It's a Question of Voices….," in [Accompanying Booklet to] *Samuel Beckett: Three Novels*, read by Barry McGovern. (RTÉ, RTE271CD, 2006), 29.

no reference at all to audiobooks as distinct aesthetic *products*—that is to say, artworks, to all intents and purposes—that effectively embody, comply with, and, indeed, adhere to their own unique aesthetics. In this context, my premise is that audiobooks should not necessarily be engaged with or perceived of as a purported substitute for so-called "actual" reading—and, appropriately, I find that the act of listening to them should be understood as a unique aesthetic experience in its own right.

Despite the intense and prosperous proliferation of "aurality"—prevalent in a number of interdisciplinary fields—audiobooks, quite regrettably, are seldom discussed in aesthetic terms and rarely listed among other artistic genres or practice. As Bernard J. Hibbitts explains it,

> Slowly, sound began to have a discernible impact on a variety of different disciplines and undertakings. In linguistics, Ferdinand de Saussure departed from then-conventional academic wisdom to argue that true language was speech, as opposed to some combination of speech and writing. [...] A variety of European and American poets abandoned the visualist analogy between poetry and painting (*ut pictura poesis*) that had held intellectual sway since the eighteenth century and instead began to explore the inherently aural relationship between poetry and music. In Ireland, W.B. Yeats called for a return to "the living voice" in literature. Influenced perhaps by the various anti-ocular, aurally indulgent musings of the nineteenth-century philosophic iconoclasts Søren Kierkegaard and Friedrich Nietzsche, Henri Bergson and Edward Husserl turned to dynamic aural phenomena such as tone and melody for metaphoric antidotes to the prevailing spatialized and visualized—and hence strangely static—idea of time. Sound even had an impact on the visual arts. [...] Other artists like [...] Wassily Kandinsky openly likened the process of painting to musical composition (he would ultimately call some of his efforts "improvisations"). A few artists even ventured into the relatively untested waters of "performance" where sound could be directly manipulated in the context of other media.[2] [excluded footnote references 475–486 from original]

This study sets out to identify audiobooks as the chief expressions of a distinct artistic genre—which, in turn, should also be considered in the broader context of general aesthetic categories. Yet since no aesthetic category actually exists

---

[2] Bernard J. Hibbitts, "Making Sense of Metaphors: Visuality, Aurality and the Reconfiguration of American Legal Discourse," *Cardozo Law Review* 16, (1994): 313–314.

for sufficiently classifying audiobooks as what shall henceforth be regarded as an "aural artifact," I have expressly taken on the challenge of constructing one. (As will presently be made clear, classification is merely part of the equation. What I find as the more serious—and, arguably, more interesting—challenge resides in the realm of evaluation and appreciation).

As Iben Have and Birgitte Stougaard Pedersen have quite rightly suggested, "not all recordings of texts read aloud are audiobooks and [...] a recorded oral tale without a written source is not an audiobook either."[3] Indeed, although audiobooks may not be the sole example of what an aural artifact is, they certainly prevail as one of its principal and "standard" manifestations, whose most prominent counterparts (two of which are routinely associated with the distinguished discipline of media studies) can be found in the wide-ranging realms of podcasts, recorded poetry, and radio drama.

While all three could be regarded both in terms of distinct cultural phenomena and as particular forms of performance—all similarly confined to an exclusively aural medium—I find that they should effectively abide by and adhere to corresponding aesthetic considerations. At the same time, however, analogous as they may appear to be—that is, as putative aural artifacts—they are certainly not identical. Since radio drama, in particular—as the products of what is surely a recognized and well-established genre in its own right—have been researched quite extensively, it is *not* my intention to scrutinize their dramaturgical complexities or analyze the artistry. Nonetheless, and although the core of my endeavor is certainly dedicated to the realm of audiobooks, I have decidedly included an exploration of significant "non-standard" aural artifacts—that is to say, recordings that cannot be tagged as one of the aforementioned prominent types of aural artifacts, yet clearly *can* comply, *mutatis mutandis*, with the same general aesthetic category that I am to presently propose.

Audiobooks in Academic Research

While audiobooks have existed essentially in one form or another since the late nineteenth century—with their inception commonly traced to Thomas Edison's tinfoil-cylinder phonograph recordings from the late 1880s—they remain to

---

[3.] Iben Have and Birgitte Stougaard Pedersen, "Reading Audiobooks," in *Beyond Media Borders, Volume 1: Intermedial Relations among Multimodal Media*, ed. Lars Elleström (Växjö, Sweden: Palgrave Macmillan, 2021), 201.

this day virtually unexplored.[4] There are, however, a handful of noteworthy exceptions, the most essential of which, as far as my own study is concerned, are briefly covered herein:

First and foremost, special attention should also be paid to Matthew Rubery's *The Untold Story of the Talking Book* (2016)—an illuminating, extensive, and well-researched panoramic survey of the manners in which "spoken-word" recordings have captured one's reception over the past 150 years. Although this study certainly cites and alludes to a profusion of recordings that constitute "complex works of art worthy of sustained critical attention in their own right," it does not necessarily attend to what *makes* them "works of art," to begin with.[5] Notwithstanding, the book surely shines through among a mere handful of publications dedicated to outlining the role of the audiobook amid the history of recorded sound, which, as far as Rubery is concerned, begins in verse. By his own admission, "three concerns find their way into almost every chapter: the audiobook's standing as a 'book,' its reception by a bemused public, and controversies over whether listening to books qualifies as a form or reading."[6] While aesthetic concerns seem, for the most part, more haphazardly implied than explicitly addressed, Rubery predominantly attends to the "talking book" phenomenon in respect of its historical innovations and overall social impact on the concept of storytelling—effectively making for an absolutely fascinating and compelling study in its own right.

A couple of years earlier, Rubery had edited *Audiobooks, Literature, and Sound Studies* (2011), which certainly stands out as one of the single most substantial publications to consider not only the cultural significance of audiobooks but also their abiding aesthetic merit—both of which, as this collection of essays demonstrates, have never been properly explored. D. E. Wittkower's essay, for example, is predominantly concerned with questions such as "What is it like to listen to an audiobook?" or "What are we listening to when we listen to an audiobook?"[7] Whereas the former arguably alludes to some kind of purported

---

[4] Citing John Cohen's *Human Robots in Myth and Science* (1967), Lorna Tracy finds that it was, in fact, Giovanni Battista Porta (1542–1597) who had conceived of conserving words in sealed leaden tubes long before Edison's men "had conceived of the possibility of keeping as permanent a record of uttered speech as of words committed to print." Lorna Tracy, "Echoes in a Bottle," *Books at Iowa* 8, no. 1 (1968): 24.

[5] Matthew Rubery, *The Untold Story of the Talking Book* (Cambridge, MA: Harvard University Press, 2016), 5.

[6] Ibid., 20.

[7] D. E. Wittkower, "A Preliminary Phenomenology of the Audiobook," in *Audiobooks, Literature, and Sound Studies*, ed. Matthew Rubery (New York: Routledge, 2011), 216.

aesthetic experience, the latter seems to suggest—or, at least, conceivably support—the need for my suggested aesthetic category.

Similarly significant—and, indeed, unreservedly *essential*—is Helen Roach's *Spoken Records* (1970), whose intuitive insights (and, indeed, insightful intuitions) call one's attention to the importance of *evaluating* these kinds of recordings:

> Educators and students are aware of records as valuable oral complements to the study of drama poetry. Parents are familiar with records as a source of entertainment. But there are all kinds of records available today which would interest many adults if they knew about them. [...] As surprising as some of the inclusions in the repertory of spoken recordings that are now available are some of the omissions. One cannot come to this territory expecting to find what he wants, as is the case for music. [...] Perhaps not surprising in a pioneering field is the fact that many records have not been well done. New listeners have been turned away by poor recordings before hearing others which make for rewarding listening. Some records are indeed works of art. [...] There are basic elements present on any good recording. [...] A frequent case of poor recordings has been failure to adapt to the new medium. Even actors with considerable stage experience have not always made the adjustment.[8]

My own objective in this respect is to establish the necessary framework for not only classifying audiobooks as artworks but also appreciating their inevitable aesthetic properties—which, alas, might otherwise remain unaccounted for.

In this respect, another noteworthy project in the current media landscape—to be sure, unique in its contribution to the discourse about what the future holds for books, as a medium—is Have's and Pedersen's *Digital Audiobooks: New Media, Users and Experiences* (2015). Here, too, the authors outwardly state that "research on audiobooks is rare, and as an everyday phenomenon it is more or less unexplored."[9] As such, Anne-Mette Bech Albrechtslund quite rightly identifies their publication as a thorough, reflective, interdisciplinary, and "densely packed volume which opens up a range of interesting perspectives for different areas within the broader field of media and information studies."[10]

---

[8] Helen Roach, *Spoken Records*, 3rd ed. (Metuchen, NJ: Scarecrow Press, 1970), 9–10.

[9] Iben Have and Birgitte Stougaard Pedersen, *Digital Audiobooks: New Media, Users and Experiences* (New York: Routledge, 2016), 16.

[10] See Anne-Mette Bech Albrechtslund. "Book Review: Have, Iben, and Birgitte Stougaard Pedersen. *Digital*

According to Juan Obregon—similarly explaining that "audiobooks are rapidly gaining popularity with the massive access to digital downloading and streaming services that are taking over all entertainment and culture markets including, of course, literature"—Have's and Pedersen's project certainly highlights the importance of audiobooks in respect of the new type of reading experience it evokes, thereby making it quite clear why "it should no longer be overlooked by both scholarly and popular discussions of digitization of literature."[11] By their own admission—and citing Sarah Kozloff—Have and Pedersen endeavored to discuss the "digital audiobook" through two primary filters, namely, "as a remediation of literature, that is, as another literary format, and [...] as an auditory mediated experience in everyday life [...]—a popular phenomenon that is part of digital, mobile audio culture in a mixed-media environment offering intimacy and sociability."[12]

I, for one, find that it is Have's and Pedersen's keen awareness of the perceptual (and, therefore, aesthetic) issues that the audiobook phenomenon evokes that makes their work stand out—and, explicitly, their suggestion that the audiobook constitutes "a medium of its own"[13] and that "listening to an audiobook could be described and analyzed as a multisensory experience involving multiple media strategies influenced by aesthetic features and styles".[14] One's aesthetic experience, in turn, can be said to be dependent upon such aspects as *where* and *how* one engages with (i.e., listens to) an audiobook. Ultimately, as Albrechtslund explains it, Have and Pedersen "base their analysis on mediatization theory and post-phenomenology in particular, but draw on an interdisciplinary approach including elements from media and sound studies, sociology, aesthetics, and literary theory."[15]

To be sure, to take on an aesthetically oriented, interdisciplinary approach is quite rare and should certainly be embraced. Nevertheless, and although I would conclude that audiobooks should necessarily replace "actual" reading, one could certainly be inclined to adopt the stance taken by Have and Pedersen—for

---

Audiobooks: New Media, Users, and Experiences. New York: Routledge, 2016." *MedieKultur Journal of Media and Communication Research* 32, no. 60 (2016): 236.

[11.] See Juan Obregon's review in *MEDIENwissenschaft: Rezensionen*, Jg. 35 (2018), 10–11.

[12.] Have and Pedersen, *Digital Audiobooks*, 16.

[13.] Albrechtslund, "Book Review: *Digital Audio Books*," 236.

[14.] Have and Pedersen, *Digital Audiobooks*, 24.

[15.] Albrechtslund, "Book Review: *Digital Audio Books*," 236.

whom it seems clear that audiobooks constitute a new *form* of reading, effectively rendering them as *actual* books, to all intents and purposes. In this context, even their most recent project, *The Digital Reading Condition* (2023), a finely-selected collection of essays, co-edited with Maria Engberg,[16] further articulates the interdisciplinary approach one would do well to advocate for a more comprehensive understanding of audiobooks amid one's varying reading conditions, habits, and practices.

Although certain recent studies may have begun subsuming the general field of sound studies under an avowedly aesthetic perspective—e.g., *Saving New Sounds: Podcast Preservation and Historiography* (2021)[17]— most contemporary publications tend to examine the audiobook phenomenon in respect of the publishing industry, effectively focusing for the most part on market trends, modes, and models of digital distribution (i.e., on-demand streaming), consumer-behavior and listener-demographics, product popularity and life cycle, as well as commercial success and critical esteem. Maria Snelling, for example—citing Stewart, Casey, and Wigginton—explains that despite the progressive rise in audiobook sales, "they do not yet bring in the same revenue of print books; all forms of print books bring in over three-fourths of US trade sales every year." Similarly, citing Michael Kozlowski, Snelling notes that people listen to audiobooks nowadays mainly for entertainment or for stimulating the brain.[18]

Some scholars, however, have also decidedly set out to explore both the motivations for and the purported impact of audiobook consumption—explicitly amid the fields of education, pedagogical strategies and practices, learning disabilities, child development, and language acquisition. According to James F. English, for instance, "the audiobook is becoming such a prominent part of the literary media landscape that, as educators, we can no longer ignore it." Asserting that aural iterations appear to be "increasingly influencing" the manner in which students engage with and relate to the novels they study in class, he finds that one needs to ask, "What are the pedagogical implications of the turn toward

---

[16.] Maria Engberg, with Iben Have and Birgitte Stougaard Pedersen, *The Digital Reading Condition* (London: Routledge, 2023).

[17.] As its authors point out, "the questions our authors ask are sometimes technical or aesthetic [...] But they are also cultural and social [...]." Jeremy Wade Morris and Eric Hoyt, eds., *Saving New Sounds: Podcast Preservation and Historiography* (Ann Arbor: University of Michigan Press, 2021), 3.

[18.] Maria Snelling, "The Audiobook Market and Its Adaptation to Cultural Changes," *Springer Publishing Research Quarterly* 37, no. 42 (2021): 642–656, accessed August 22, 2023, https://www.ncbi.nlm.nih.gov/pmc/articles/PMC8489886/#CR15.

audio? What changes might we need to make in our ways of developing and teaching literature classes to include the audiobook in them?"[19]

Nevertheless, as my own study aims to demonstrate, aesthetic considerations certainly merit further serious attention. While it may not necessarily adhere to "academic research" *per se*, I find that *AudioFile Magazine* also serves as a unique exception amid the unique dynamic landscape that audiobooks belong to. Launched in 1992, the reviews it outputs make an explicit point of focusing on the presentation of audiobooks (and other types of "spoken-word" recordings)—and, indeed, on the nature of the *performance* that inhabits them—rather than analyzing or critiquing the written material.[20] As its passionate founder and editor Robbin Whitten explains,

> As you know, as a listener, the performance and the narrator and that listening experience is the whole deal. That's really what is important when you're listening.[21] […] And it's really important, I think, what *AudioFile* does is to help people discover titles to listen to, but also to have that critical review aspect—that's, you know, diverse, because we're working with a lot of different reviewers—but, you know, to sort of reinforce those standards that, you know, the industry embraces, for the most part. But, you know, to be taking about that and to make it possible to have standards within audiobooks. And to emphasize, I think, that this is not print—it's a different format, and these are the things that are different about it— […] that listening experience, that emotional piece that the narrator may bring.[22]

And it is precisely at this point where I choose to turn to the philosophy of arts.

The Philosophy of the Arts and the Role of Aesthetic Theory

Having painstakingly scrutinized the trajectory of conceptual art theories— explicitly since I maintain that audiobooks can be (or, at the very least should be)

---

[19] James F. English, "Teaching the Novel in the Audio Age," *PMLA* 135, no. 2 (March, 2020): 420.

[20] See URL: accessed February 2, 2013, https://audiofilemagazine.com/.

[21] "Interview with Robin Whitten—Founder/Editor of AudioFile Magazine," November 3, 2022, in Cindy Burnett's *Thoughts from a Page* Podcast, accessed November 20, 2022, https://www.thoughtsfromapage.com/interview-with-robin-whitten-foundereditor-of-audiofile-magazine/, 03m27sec–03m27sec.

[22] Ibid., 27min17sec–28min00sec.

regarded as artworks, to all intents and purposes—I elected to adopt the particular mindset of the New Institutional Theory of Art (NITA): that is, the most recent version to date of a theory whose theoretical infrastructure dates back to the mid-1960s.

As will later be articulated in detail, this theory proposes four core "rule-schemes," pertaining to both the context and the necessary given circumstances for all things art, namely, the "what," "why," "who," and "how." Working together, they essentially suggest that certain persons create certain artifacts, in an attempt to convey certain meaningful, insightful notions that they subsequently present before certain other persons. In the absence of these rule-schemes, an artist "would not know what to do, why to do it, nor how to go about doing it." Likewise, an audience would be unable to comprehend what precisely has been presented before them.[23]

A primary premise of this book is that a proper theoretical employment of NITA potentially facilitates the practical formation of new aesthetic categories for different pertinent artistic media. Effectively applying the said rule-schemes to the realm of aural recordings should assist one in ascertaining whether or not— and, indeed, to what extent—audiobooks can be regarded as performance-based aural artifacts, that is to say, the artistic products of a unique general aesthetic category. Furthermore, considering the remarkable abundance of recordings that could—perhaps even *should*—be regarded as aural performances, assigning them a designated aesthetic category of their own seems no less than imperative.

Ultimately, as a classificatory apparatus—drawing on the distinction between "art" and "not art"—my suggested new category constitutes a distinct artistic institution in its own right. As will later be made clear, effectively it *institutes* (i.e., quite literally creates and determines) a particular kind of artistic praxis. In other words, it establishes what counts as an aural artifact, thereby bestowing on audiobooks their artistic identity. Similarly, as an evaluative tool, it prescribes both the implicit criteria and explicit parameters for evaluation and appreciation.

Philosophy into Practice

As will also be further articulated later on, when one engages with an audiobook not only as the performance *of* an original text—in itself a recognized artwork— but also as a singular, idiosyncratic aural artifact in its own right—one should be

---

[23] David Graves, *The New Institutional Theory of Art* (Champaign, IL: Common Ground Publishing, 2010), 40; 44.

able to ascertain its aesthetic quality. Furthermore, as I will demonstrate, when more than one aural iteration (of the same original text) exists, one should also be able to determine which particular version might be deemed aesthetically better.

While the aforementioned "non-standard" recordings could arguably be more easily categorized as special borderline case studies, I find it more appropriate to consider them in terms of institutional categories. Having literally construct-ed a brand-new aesthetic category—explicitly aimed at classifying any and all aural artifacts—one should effectively able to identify the different varying sub-genres that it inhabits. As such, both the "standard" cases (i.e., audiobooks, re-corded poetry, and radio drama) and the "non-standard" manifestations (which this book sets out to unveil) all become so-called "sub-(institutional)-categories" within a larger "mother institution." To be sure, the very fact that one can distin-guish between the various types of aural artifact merely highlights the inherent need for creating the overall category to begin with.

Consequently, in focusing primarily on the realm of audiobooks, I endeavor to fully articulate what an aural artifact is, and, subsequently, why and how it should be both analyzed and aesthetically evaluated. My intention is not to sur-vey the entire spectrum of existing audiobooks but rather to focus my efforts ex-plicitly on the form of the first-person narrative—for which audiobooks seem to lend themselves as the obvious medium. While this should certainly not suggest that third-person narratives are in any way less complex or interesting candidates for analysis and evaluation, I find that engaging with aural iterations of the first person—where an actual human voice speaks directly into one's ears, ostensibly delivering *its* own personal story—can ultimately provide one with an enhanced, and arguably a more rewarding, direct, and immersive aesthetic experience.

Nearly ten years following her directorial debut, *In a World...* (2013)—a com-edy about a female vocal coach who endeavors to work in providing the voice-over for film trailers—American actress–writer–director–producer Lake Bell created the audiobook *Inside Voice: My Obsession with How We Sound* (2022), published by Malcom Gladwell's Pushkin Industries.)According to Bell, the title of her 2013—which she also wrote and stars in—was inspired by the phrase commonly employed by voice-actor Don LaFontaine, who has been cited for having recorded the voice-over for over 5,000 film trailers. Bell came up with the plot after having realized that apparently no notable film trailers, with per-haps one or two exceptions, have effectively employed female voice-over). In her audiobook project, Bell's objective was to take a deep-dive into not only the power of the human voice but also the manners in which one's unique vocal signature can effectively unravel a variety of aspects pertaining to one's identity. Indeed, as Have and Engberg quite rightly indicate, "the presence of a human voice brings intimacy and authenticity and is able to generate first-person-like social attention." Audiobooks no doubt embody this property in their overall aesthetics, and as one customarily listens to them on one's own (i.e., as opposed to a more communal setting), the inherent intimacy in one's listening experience seems further enhanced. As such, according to Have and Engberg,

> When wearing headphones, voices speak directly into the head of the listener. Being there with the host, listening to recordings of real sound environments and actions in the world, and—maybe most importantly—sharing the experience here and now with the host generates another kind of immersing experiences, compared to [Virtual Reality].[24]

By her own admission, these domains have fascinated Bell since infancy. The audiobook itself has listening length that runs approximately six hours, and it features nearly twenty contributors, ranging from linguistics experts to dialect coaches, to poets, and performers. To be sure, and albeit arguably somewhat self-evident in this case, *Inside Voice* is also quite unique in that it exists *only* as an aural artifact and has not, in fact, been published in print. Furthermore—in what effectively serves a rather fresh take on the audiobook as both a distinct medium and, indeed, artform—it should also be noted that in addition to Bell's own personal journey and her exploration of the social aspects associated with one's voice (e.g., how others might judge one based on his/her voice alone, or how many individuals seem to have an issue with hearing a recording of their own voice), Bell's project also provides its listeners with interactive vocal exercises and games.[25]

A Precursor to the Chosen Case Studies

The concrete analysis of my major case studies begins by surveying over fifty audiobook versions of Mark Twain's *Adventures of Huckleberry Finn* (1884)—a quintessential nineteenth-century novel, whose narrator happens to be an adolescent

---

[24] Iben Have and Birgitte Stougaard Pedersen, "Trends in Immersive Journalism," in *The Digital Reading Condition*, eds. Maria Engberg, Iben Have, and Birgitte Stougaard Pedersen (London: Routledge, 2023), 85.

[25] See publisher's URL, accessed August 31, 2023, https://www.pushkin.fm/audiobooks/inside-voice.

boy; subsequently, I explore the more unconventional complexities surrounding the aural iterations of Samuel Beckett's *Molloy* (1955)—a novel that in
itself questions the very concepts of authorship, identity, and narration; finally,
I attend to the pseudo-autobiographical writings of Australian performer–
satirist–author–Dadaist–comedian–artist Barry Humphries (1934–2023)—
texts that credit Humphries' fictional personae as the actual, legitimate authors.

Granted, the profound literary complexities that inhabit Beckett's prose—
and, for that matter, no doubt, Twain's writing, too—steadily exceed those that
one might find in the monographs of the multi-hyphenated Humphries. Yet, as
aural artifacts, their distinguishing aesthetic intricacies are far less unequivocal.
With Humphries, they are all but labyrinthine and borderline-surreal: in delivering the audiobook incarnations in character, each pseudo-autobiographical
novel becomes a *literal* self-portrait—which, in turn, is self-told, delivered,
and, indeed, performed by its own assumed personage. Thus, it is in this context
that these particular audiobooks appear to have ostensibly infiltrated a deeper
level of aesthetic contemplations, conceivably exceeding those evoked by the
aural iterations of Twain's and Beckett's respective narratives.

To one degree or another, all my chosen case studies appear to question the
boundaries of what an autobiography entails, challenging not only the very concept of the first-person narrative but also the arguable validity of the first-person
narrator. Since the direct speech and overall storytelling style in *Huck Finn*, for instance, is conceivably filtered through Twain's own embedded irony, it effectively
evokes questions pertaining to the very nature of autobiographies and the identity
of those who authored them. By the same token, the fragmented speech pattern of
Beckett's narrating protagonists invites queries concerning the very nature of the
narrative form itself. In the same vein, Humphries' in-character delivery appear
to put into question not only the identity of the narrating protagonists but also
their very (non)-existence. Furthermore, as they fundamentally consist in being
both commonplace works of fiction and yet quite literal memoirs of distinct fictional characters, these particular aural artifacts appear to throw interesting light
on whether certain audiobooks might, in fact, negate the original printed work.

Casting Contemplations and the Role of Intuitions

Implications pertaining to the craft of casting can be singled out as a significant
discovery that directly corresponds with this book's approach to aesthetically

evaluating aural artifacts. As Rubery correctly points out, "casting is the single most important decision made by an audiobook publisher. It is a truism that narrators can make or break a story."[26] He explains that to appropriately "fit" a speaker and a given script has always been "a delicate matter," and, as such, the task of "finding a suitable narrator" entails "matching the speaker to the fictional character's [...] audible markers of identity."[27] Indeed, I would argue that assigning a specific text to a particular performer is essentially informed by having already somehow *evaluated*—that is, in one's mind's ear—whether or not, and, indeed, to what extent, that "fit" should yield an aesthetically good putative performance.

In the mid-1950s, prolific Israeli dramatist–director Nissim Aloni (1926–1988) embarked for Paris. There, he had the good fortune of studying with French actor and director Jean-Marie Serreau—a former student of Charles Dullin—while relishing a variety of classic stage productions by both the celebrated *La Comédie-Française* and the renowned *Berliner Ensemble*. In 1963, still inspired by all he had absorbed abroad, Aloni co-founded the short-lived Tel Aviv–based *Teatron Ha'Onot* [the *Seasons Theatre*]. His co-founders were Israeli actor–singer–comedians Yossef (aka "Yossi") Banai (1932–2006) and Avner Hizkiahu (aka "Hizki") (1926–1994). The first play staged in their repertoire was Aloni's own *The American Princess* [*Ha'Nesichah Ha'Amerikait*, in the original Hebrew]. Fundamentally a two-hander, the play consists of a meta-theatrical allegory of sorts, featuring three on-stage protagonists, two of whom are designed to be performed by the same actor, and four off-stage characters who are merely heard but not actually seen.

Full disclosure: while I certainly acknowledged Aloni's inventiveness and witty wordplay—which I was predominantly acquainted with through his works as a translator and sketch-comedy writer—I admittedly did not really "get" the play. At the time, if I'm being completely honest with myself, I recall finding the very task of reading the play excruciatingly strenuous and rather unrewarding. As such, I began doing what one naturally does when confronted with an acutely problematic text: flicking through the pages. It was then that I realized that the play had, in fact, essentially been written for—and, appropriately, originally performed by—Banai and Hizki.

[26.] Rubery, *The Untold Story of the Talking Book*, 5.

[27.] Ibid., 98.

Now, although my then limited acquaintance with the two merely hailed them as highly skilled entertainers who often worked together, I felt confident enough to wittingly re-read the play, while attempting to conjure up and envision—or, rather, en*sound*, in my mind's ear—not only their voices but also the manner in which I intuitively recognized they would have, supposedly, delivered Aloni's text. Suddenly, as if by sorcery, the text began to "work" and make sense. Every word, syllable, pause, dash, and three-little-dots on the printed page appeared to eloquently comply with my intuition of how Banai and Hizki would have performed Aloni's play.

Unbeknownst to me at the time, there was, in fact, an *actual* recording of the play: not long after the original production completed its run of over fifty performances, the playwright–director and his cast of two sat themselves down in a recording studio, intent on releasing an aural iteration of the stage play. (The recording has since been re-released in 2004 on what is now a discontinued 2-disk set, which, regrettably, is about as rare a find as the original vinyl LPs). When I ultimately got my hands on that recording and began listening to the recording, for the first time, I was instantly overwhelmed by an intense sense of *déjà vu*: I felt as if I had already heard it. I also recall being quite in awe of just how that recording appears to crystallize, precisely to what extent Aloni had tailor-made *The American Princess* to fit the distinct cadence, staccato, speech patterns, and overall vocal signatures of Banai and Hizki.

Now, while it is not the aim of this book to articulate the intuitions that are no doubt rooted in the very core of the unique craft of casting—which, regrettably, seems virtually unexplored and quite under-theorized—this book *does* identify a particular inherent quality in the overall process of aesthetic evaluation that implicitly applies to casting too. For want of a better term, I find that this quality can best be described as one's "informed intuition." This, in essence, allows one to match a particular performer—or, in this case, their distinctive vocal qualities—with a specific given text. In this context, and drawing on my own personal experience in matching Aloni's text with what I perceived as the potential putative performance that Banai and Hizki might endow it, I would argue that one's "informed intuition" ultimately constitutes both a cognitive and creative process. As such, one's ability to conceive of an aesthetically good match—even if the match itself does not yet exist in practice—can be linked to one's sense of aesthetic appropriateness: that is, what *should* count as a good artwork.

CHAPTER ONE

A Brief Introduction to the New Institutional Theory of Art: The Internal Logic of What Art Is

"A Great Disturbance in the Force"

In the autumn of 1964, in the midst of the so-called "anything goes" epoch—advocating the modernist notion of creating "art for art's sake"—a young philosopher and art critic, Arthur C. Danto (1924–2013), enters the Stable Gallery in Manhattan to engage with Andy Warhol's most recent exhibition. There, for the first time, he encounters Warhol's *Brillo Box* installation. Supposedly sensing what could, in lieu of a better reference, be surmised as "a great disturbance in the Force," the young Danto—who had since become an influential and distinguished figure in philosophical aesthetics, as well as a revolutionary interpreter of Postmodern artworks—found himself unable to detect any discernible difference between the familiar packaging of Brillo's *actual* scouring-pad product and Warhol's plywood replica. In other words, Warhol's piece exhibited nothing significantly different from—and, as such, was effectively identical to—the *real* Brillo boxes found at one's local supermarket. Intrigued, and almost instinctively, Danto endeavored to decipher that disparity.

All philosophical questions, as far as Danto was concerned, distinguish primarily between identical objects, whose differences—albeit radical—are fundamentally invisible. As such, when confronted with two objects that appear to be exactly alike, one could nevertheless define them in two completely different ways. For Danto, identifying those differences became acute. The prevailing attitude at the time upheld that for an object to be considered a putative artwork, it must possess a certain intrinsic exhibited quality—or, indeed, a set thereof—that, in turn, would be responsible for its particular artistic identity. To be sure, even in recent times, one is somewhat accustomed to associate an object's perceptual and sensate features with what would essentially render it an ostensibly legitimate artwork. It had then occurred to Danto that that which defines "art" had, in fact, absolutely nothing to do with a particular object's so-called "aesthetic properties"—or even, for that matter, with the object itself.

In what posed a predominantly ontological conundrum (rather than an epistemological one), Danto's focus of interest was not so much about ascertaining whether or not (or to what extent) Warhol's *Brillo Box* was, in fact, an artwork to begin with as about being able to identify the non-perceptual differences between "art" and "not art." As such, he concluded that whatever it was that *made Brillo Box* an artwork at all was necessarily indispensable to any and all artworks. In his seminal essay, "The Artworld," Danto not only demonstrates that aesthetic features do not define art but also articulates that that which in fact *does* define art is to be found elsewhere. In his own words, "to see something as art requires something the eye cannot descry—an atmosphere of artistic theory, a knowledge of the history of art: an artworld."[1]

By facilitating a socio-cultural context—that is, a set of given circumstances that the Artworld inhabits, complies with, prescribes, and, indeed, adheres to— Danto's "atmosphere" is effectively generated by a rich, well-documented, and, at times, antithetical heritage of conventions, intentions, and interpretations, all pertaining to the very core of art and art-making. Ultimately, to define a particular object as an "artwork"—despite its uncanny resemblance to an object that, to all intents and purposes, is "non-art"—one requires an aesthetic theory, which, in turn, would prevent one form mistakenly identifying the real object as an artwork.[2]

An "Institutional" State of Mind

In 1958, British philosopher G. E. M. Anscomb established a paramount distinction between two opposite sets of facts that exist in the world, namely, "brute facts" and "institutional facts."[3]

Brute facts, as the phrase implies, are ostensibly inflicted by the world itself. They are, by their nature, nothing more than what they naturally are: cold, feral,

---

[1] Arthur Danto, "The Artworld," *Journal of Philosophy* 61, no. 19 (1964): 580. It should be noted that although Danto evidently employs both "artworld" and "Artworld," I have chosen to adopt the latter—predominantly in order to comply with the form utilized in *The New Institutional Theory of Art* (2010), which, as aforementioned, constitutes the core theoretical infrastructure that has ignited my study.

[2] Danto, "The Artworld," 581.

[3] G. E. M. Anscombe, "On Brute Facts," *Analysis* 18, no. 3 (January 1958): 69–72.

absent of sentiment or emotion, and—drawing on Wittgenstein's *magnum opus*, the *Logico-Philosophical Treatise* (1921)—fundamentally deprived of any kind of meaning, value, or moral code. Being, in point of fact, undisputed facts, there is quite literally nothing that one can do about them and, as such, one is simply expected to accept them.

Institutional facts, by contrast, are man-made and socio-cultural at their core. Nevertheless, being facts, the two are just as irrefutable as their brutish counterparts. The very fact that they successfully sustain their status as facts at all inevitably rests on the particular "cultural institutional system" that both inhabits and generates them, and amid which they operate. Despite what might seem somewhat counterintuitive (being that they are essentially contrived, rather than natural), institutional facts are invariably considered not only more important and meaningful but also more tangible and pertinent than the mere brute facts of the matter.

All socio-cultural institutions (e.g., education, law and order, religion, marriage, games, sports, or—as will presently be established herein—art) are purposefully devised and constructed for preserving what one's particular socio-cultural environment or setting finds most important. As such, they essentially prescribe the manner in which a given institution is supposed to ostensibly "behave": that is to say, they present one with a well-thought-out set of rules and certain acts of conduct, which are certainly not arbitrary—as without them, the particular realm governed by the institution in question simply cannot exist. By this token, they effectively possess the power to render a "thing" into a "something"—predicated on whatever one both desires and determines to valorize. In this context, one's institutions are responsible for not only bestowing a certain something with an identity of its own but also for endowing it with a certain unique set of meanings and values.

Notwithstanding, just as one's culture is prone to change in accordance with whatever one valorizes—e.g., the inclusion, exclusion, or amendment of different ideas, values, and understandings—one's cultural institutions, too, are inevitably not immune to amendments, modifications, and re-envisioning.[4]

---

[4] Spiritual teacher Ram Dass (born Richard Alpert; 1931–2019) had alluded to this notion, intuitively and quite articulately, through what he regarded as one's shifting cultural mythologies. In one of his talks, given in the early 1990s, he speaks, for example, about the sense that society and culture seem to him to be "between storylines," living amid a period of transformation, in which one basically sees fit to abandon the "dysfunctional myths" that have thus far dominated one's life, and instead *feel* one's way into "new mythic identities"—that is, "new stories"—which, in turn, would effectively "justify" or endow one's existence with a "functional meaning." I find the following talks, in particular, make for a fascinating listening, and especially in the context of one's ever-evolving cultural institutions and the meanings with which they provide us all: accessed December 12, 2022, https://www.youtube.com/watch?v=bJ0lA8KtQhk; and https://www.youtube.com/watch?v=vivNOuDDqSE (from 14min22sec onwards).

A Note on the Institutional Definition of Art

While Danto had quite successfully articulated why it is that aesthetics—or, indeed, "beauty," for that matter—do *not* make artwork an artwork, American philosopher George Dickie finds that Danto had failed to explicitly identify what in fact *does*. This is certainly an important distinction. As such, in Dickie's account of art as a cultural institutional system in its own right, he identifies that artistic praxis shares a similar authoritative power in granting certain objects their identity as artworks. Nonetheless, as Dickie recognized full well, this can arguably only take effect amid the particular confines and atmosphere of Danto's Artworld—which, as far as Dickie was concerned, should be understood as a paradigmatic representation of an instrument for reconciling between brute and institutional facts.

In this respect, whereas Danto's interest seemed to focus on the power of the Artworld to award a completely different status unto two supposedly different objects that possess the exact same aesthetic properties, Dickie seemed to engage the two sets of simultaneously undisputed facts that all artworks inevitably inhabit. In other words, if Danto was concerned predominantly with discerning the given circumstances that assign two identical objects each with an independent identity of its own, Dickie was primarily invested in discerning the given circumstances that assign a single object *two* completely independent yet simultaneously valid and pertinent identities.[5]

In brief, Dickie began developing his "institutional" definition of art in 1969, re-working its various revisions well into the 1970s. His objective was to establish a panoramic, comprehensive, and, indeed, definitive theory for any and all artworks. Despite explicitly focusing on classification—having surmised that neither evaluation nor appreciation necessarily corresponds with or adheres to what actually *makes* an artwork an artwork—Dickie *does*, in fact, appear to implicitly allude to aesthetically *good* artworks.[6] Indeed, as the later evolution

---

[5.] In this respect, the fact that Marcel Duchamp's seminal artwork, *Fountain*, for instance—the infamous overturned porcelain urinal, signed "R. Mutt 1917"—counts as a legitimate artwork, to all intents and purposes, is, in essence, an "institutional" fact. Appropriately, when extracting the piece from the context of the Artworld, one is ultimately left with the "brute" fact of the matter—which, in turn, renders the object as nothing more than a rather ineffective urinal. In the same vein, one can understand and experience Jackson Pollock's *Convergence* (1952) as a divine depiction of the human spirit, and, *simultaneously*, observe the very same painting as merely a large canvas riddled with spritzes and blots of paint that look as if they might as well have been produced by either a sugar-rushed or a mentally-unfortified 4-year-old with a tendency for over-dramatics. The latter, albeit an intentionally exaggerated account, effectively instantiates a rather common "brute fact" that can be applied to the majority of such paintings.

[6.] George Dickie, *Evaluating Art* (Philadelphia, PA: Temple University Press, 1988), ix.

of the institutional approach to art quite clearly demonstrates, the notion that an object may be legitimately (i.e., both theoretically and practically) classified as an artwork to all intents and purposes, does *not* necessarily and by all means entail, determine, or secure its status as an aesthetically *good* artwork. When engaging with aesthetics, therefore, there is arguably no escape from distinguishing good artworks from those that would ultimately be deemed aesthetically flawed.[7]

Audiobooks, too—as I intended to demonstrate herein—can be similarly evaluated: that is to say, the (institutional) fact that a particular recording can be identified and *defined* as an aural artifact—indeed, an artwork in its own right—does not guarantee that its aesthetic quality is necessarily good.

The *New* Institutional Definition of Art

Although ultimately published in 2010, artist–philosopher–musician David C. Graves began developing the NITA since as early as 1994. Originally co-mentored by noted Israeli philosopher and linguist Asa Kasher—alongside the source and authority, that is, Dickie himself—Graves attributes NITA to their collaborative efforts. By his own admission, they did not set out to "reinvent" what art is purported to be but rather, quite simply, to describe what it actually is.[8] For the most part, NITA explicitly challenges—while, at the same time, clearly makes sense of—the overwhelming "anything goes" spirit that seems to have led one somewhat astray for over half a century, effectively expecting one to accept virtually *anything* as art, almost categorically and without thinking twice. Put simply, NITA makes it abundantly clear that although indeed "anything goes," surely "not everything works."[9]

Adopting the perception of art as a "constitutive" socio-cultural institutional system—and drawing on Dickie's interlocking clauses—NITA proposes a humble,

---

[7.] Borrowing Ruth Lorand's analogy, just as one's definition of a "citizen" fundamentally includes persons who do not obey the law, one's definition of "art" should effectively apply to bad artworks. See: Ruth Lorand, *Al tiv'a shel omanut* [On the Nature of Art] (Tel-Aviv, Israel: Dvir Publishing House, 1991), 161.

[8.] David Graves, "Art and the Zen Master's Tea Pot: The Role of Aesthetics in the Institutional Theory of Art," *Journal of Aesthetics and Art Criticism* 60, no. 4 (Autumn 2002): 351n18. In this context, it should be noted that American philosopher and aesthetician Robert Stecker points out in a rather lengthy footnote that he is acquainted with but a single instance that had pursued the institutional definition beyond the point Dickie has taken it, namely, Graves' then recent PhD dissertation—which, for Stecker, showed promise as being "marvelously useful in such matters as interpreting artworks." Robert Stecker, *Artworks: Definition, Meaning, Value* (University Park: Pennsylvania State University Press, 1997), 69n2.

[9.] Graves, *The New Institutional Theory of Art*, 37.

yet complex, set of four basic rule-schemes: "R1–R4." Together, they form the universal tenets of what art is; individually they consist of self-contained elementary components, without which art cannot exist. To attain a comprehensive understanding of each individual rule-scheme is ultimately dependent on—and, indeed, necessitates—fully grasping each of the other three. Explicitly, "R1–R4" pertain to the artwork, the artist, the designate audience, the particular realm in which the artistic practice takes place, namely, the Artworld itself:

> **R1:** A practice counts as an *Artworld-system* if, and only if, it is a framework for the presentation of artworks by artists to an Artworld public.

> **R2:** An object counts as an *artwork* if, and only if, it is an artifact created by an artist, and presented to an Artworld public, within an Artworld-system.

> **R3:** A person counts as an *artist* if, and only if, he or she participates with understanding in the creating of an artwork, to be presented it to an Artworld public, within an Artworld-system.

> **R4:** A set of persons counts as an *Artworld public* if, and only if, its members are prepared in some degree to understand an artwork, created by an artist, which is presented to them in an Artworld-system.[10]

"R1–R4," *in nuce*, imply that certain persons create certain artifacts—by way of which, as will presently be made clear, they attempt to convey some meaningful and insightful notion—and they present these artifacts before certain other persons. Without them, a putative artist "would not know what to do, why to do it, nor how to go about doing it."[11] An assumed audience would likewise be unable to comprehend either what they have been presented with or how to interpret it as art to begin with. By governing the given circumstances for myriads of artistic praxes, goals, and activities—thereby not only facilitating distinct parameters but also determining the means for successfully abiding them—the four tenets, "R1–R4," effectively suggest what putative products one can (or, indeed, perhaps *should*) generate.

Consequently, as a schematic definition, NITA is virtually restriction-free. Its all-inclusiveness, however, only springs into action as one observes the rules

---

[10] Ibid., 40.

[11] Ibid., 44.

of the game. While "R1–R4" provide and prescribe the necessary minimum requirements—that is, an object, an artist, a designated audience, and an Art-world at large—they simultaneously are completely indiscriminate insofar as what explicitly those requirements necessarily are. This is to say, they convey nothing specific about what counts as object, who may be considered an artist, or who might be included as a member of his/her/their audience.

In what I consider to be an inspired stroke of "pluralistic fascism"—for want of a better term—NITA effectively grants license to a truly, madly, deeply infinite variety of artistic forms, praxes, endeavors, and product. As such, practically anything can count as an object, and, indeed, anyone can be either an artist or an audience. At the same time, in light of the plenitude of existing and ever-evolving artworks produced by the contemporary Artworld, the restrictions that NITA *does* in fact prescribe, all eventually adhere to the Artworld at large. The cogitable paradox notwithstanding, it must be understood that although NITA basically facilitates complete artistic freedom—while simultaneously all but enforcing a significantly strict set of practical responsibilities and abundantly clear rules of conduct—its crucial insight ultimately concludes that the fact that anything *can* work does not necessarily entail that everything indeed *should*.

All artworks should essentially be understood not only in the context of their own particular constitutive praxes but also in respect of their inner workings amid the confines of the Artworld—whose institutional structure gives birth to a variety of so-called "sub-(institutional)-categories." These, in turn, pertain to a magnificent myriad of artistic genres and different media, and essentially derives from—and, indeed, both adhere to and comply with—the general set of rules governing the larger institutional system.

At the most rudimentary level, the rule-systems govern the "medium-based" institutions, effectively deploying the choice and use of a particular medium: e.g., painting, sculpture, the theatrical stage, literature, music, film, etc. Although the rules that govern this level are more specific than "R1–R4"—imposing their constraints on the "material" aspects of an artistic praxis and the putative artwork it produces—they are nevertheless similarly non-restrictive in granting one an abundant spectrum of different possible materials. Overall, medium-based insti-tutions predominantly attend to the "what?" aspects of an artwork: that is to say, what kind of artifact is an artist to make, and what materials he or she will employ.

Next, the level of the "Big Theory" institutions, effectively ordaining the so-called "ideological" aspects of artistic praxes (including, yet certainly not restricted to political principles, religious inclinations, and philosophical credos).

In other words, they essentially generate all of one's garden-variety "isms": e.g., Realism, Romanticism, Idealism, Impressionism, Expressionism, Cubism, and so on. For Graves, they all represent "a very general attitude of the practitioners of the system regarding what they hold to be the nature of art (or of their art)." As such, this level distinguishes all the notions, ideas, and theories that are Artworld-relevant from those that are Artworld-external (e.g., theories that assign philosophical, psychological, or sociological meanings to artworks and art-making), regardless of the extent to which they might mutually influence and inform one other. Overall, Big Theory institutions predominantly attend to the "why?" aspects of an artwork: that is to say, why make art, to begin with, and, indeed, why create and utilize artifacts as a means of doing "what one wishes to do."[12]

Finally, the level of the "working theory" institutions brings together the material with the ideology, thereby putting the "big theories" to (artistic) praxis. As such, it both facilitates and generates different artistic genres and endeavors: Action Painting, Epic Poetry, Film Noir, Spaghetti Western, Progressive Rock, Radio Drama, etc. Overall, it is here that one engages with the key "how" aspects of an artwork, that is to say, how one should employ one's chosen medium to embody that which one wishes to convey. For Graves, these aspects "are geared to answer that key question, providing one of the most fundamental principles of art criticism and evaluation, that of technique."[13]

While one might consider art-making a predominantly intuitive process, here, evidently, artists are required to comply with and adhere to a specific set of (sub-institutional) rules, and—by *actually* practicing them—ultimately create unique and distinct artworks. NITA thus appears to re-establish the notion of "embodied meaning" as a *logical* conclusion—rather than as a theoretical assumption—effectively rendering it as the distinct logic of a discrete "structured institution", namely, Artworld at large.[14] As Graves himself explains it,

> The difference between the institutional theory and any other theory of aesthetics, is that the standard theory [...] assumes that art is embodied meaning. That assumption is false, as an assumption, for the only true assumptions one may

---

[12] Ibid., 52–53.

[13] Ibid., 53–54.

[14] Graves, "Art and the Zen Master's Tea Pot," 345. For further reading in this particular context, also see Madeleine Schechter, *Semiotics and Art Theory: Between Autonomism and Contextualism* (Würzburg, Germany: Königshausen & Neumann, 2008), 17–18.

make about a work of art is that it is an artifact created by an artist to be presented to a public in some Artworld system. Any further assumptions regarding the nature of the artifact have all been proven false, by the Artworld itself. Which is why the aesthetic theories failed to define art conclusively. [...] We defined art quite conclusively in purely institutional terms, and assumed only as much: an artifact created by an artist, and so on. As we focused upon art as a cultural practice, we got our reward for our theoretical diligence: the institutional theory *showed* us what art is, when actually and properly practiced. The very structure of the institution showed us that art is a matter of embodied meaning. The logical difference is absolute—we did not assume that art is embodied meaning, we *concluded* it. [emphasis in original][15]

Artistic Beauty and the Internal Logic of Artworks

In his eloquently concise definition of artistic beauty, Graves concludes that "a particular object is deemed beautiful, when, and to the degree that, it embodies and exhibits the internal logic of its own world."[16] The premise informing this notion seems simple enough: that is, at the very core of all artworks, there essentially inheres a unique, palpable, and unmistakable "internal logic" of their own—which, as a purportedly inherent "lawfulness" of sorts, is quite indispensable to one's aesthetic experience. Thus, when engaging with artworks, one is ostensibly assigned the minimum responsibility of making sense of what a particular artwork's so-called internal logic is, or, indeed, what it should be. Next, one should determine whether or not—and, indeed, to what extent—that particular artwork successfully embodies and exhibits its own unique internal logic. In Graves's own words,

> Following Wittgenstein of the Tractatus, that the only necessity that exists is logical necessity, this paper argues judgments of correctness and incorrectness in cultural practices like art or the law are, essentially, logical judgments. The paper suggests that logical understanding itself is the ability to understand necessity. Hence, tautologies are not merely propositions that are true on all instantiations of

---

[15] Graves, *The New Institutional Theory of Art*, 86.

[16] David Graves, *"Lir'ot shki'a ve'lamut"* [To See a Sunset and Die], *Odyssey—A Journey through Ideas*, no. 4 (July 2009): 34.

their variables (in basic PC), the point is that they are necessarily true. Likewise, the conclusion of a logically valid argument is not merely true if the premises are, it is necessarily so. This concept of necessity—we could say the concept of necessity; as there is no other—is exhibited by our logical calculi, but it is understood by sense. It is a deep-seated and fundamental intuition which senses logical force per se, thus construed as necessity. This basic sense of necessity that logic affords us is then carried over to other cultural endeavors. Any field governed by a system of rules will bear its own unique internal logic. In fact, that internal logic is precisely what makes the system a system. Hence, all such cultural practices, like art, the law, games etc., will, in a crucial respect, behave the same way: logically. When one is engaged in the practice of such a field, be it painting a cubist picture or making a move in chess, that very same "intuition of necessity" that logic expounds is at work. It is offered, then, that an aesthetic judgment, for instance, as to the correctness or incorrectness of a particular feature in a work of art is, in essence, a logical judgment.[17]

Conceivably, any internal logic is principally responsible for constructing a given system's governing framework. A system that lacks a distinct internal logic would thus be unable to fulfill its purpose, and, as such, could be deemed redundant. An internal logic, therefore, appears to endow institutional systems with something that the rules alone cannot provide.[18] At the same time, since one's socio-cultural institutions may well be subject to change—appropriately modifying the very framework that both presides over and prescribes the particular praxis they purportedly protect—any internal logic should ultimately champion and facilitate a "mercurial elasticity" of sorts, thereby licensing their freedom to potentially comply with any newly adopted set of values or frames of reference. This, to my mind, is also what makes the notion of internal logic quite altogether indispensable to evaluating artworks.

---

[17] David Graves, "Logic and the Sense of Necessity," in *Book of Abstracts*, the 15th Congress of Logic, Methodology- and Philosophy of Science (aka CLMPS) 2015, 225, accessed April 30, 2024, http://philomatica.org/wp-content/uploads/2013/01/CLMPS_LC_book-of-abstracts-29.7.2015.pdf.

[18] The rules of a particular game, for instance—an institutional system in and of itself—can only specify what the particular goal of that game is, effectively prescribing what possible legitimate moves a player is permitted to make. Yet simply attaining an understanding of the rules, of any game, is clearly not enough. To *actually* play—that is, to "get" the point of a game—requires of one something beyond the mere setup prescribing the rules: namely, one must identify the proverbial "spirit" of the game, which is an inherent tenet of its internal logic.

Beauty Is *Not* in the Beholder

Despite what one has learned (or, perhaps, for some, unlearned) from postmodern-ism and its various derivatives (which may conceivably prompt one to challenge the notion that there exists but one way to grasp a particular lawfulness), NITA seems to have successfully equipped one with "clear theoretical mechanisms for carrying the major activities involved in theorizing about art: how to classify a work of art, how to interpret a work of art, and how to evaluate a work of art."[19] This, in essence, is why I find that one can potentially apply NITA to any given artistic genre. Similarly, as Graves' elegant conception of beauty quite tellingly hits the nail on the head, it, too, might extend well beyond the ostensible confines of the Artworld and be applied to almost any field that is governed by a system of rules. Indeed, as an overarching socio-cultural system—that both inhabits and in itself consists of an elaborate amalgam of signs and putative meanings—the Artworld effectively constitutes one the West's most ancient, and surely well-documented, cultural realms as "a world unto itself."[20] As such, it arguably becomes one's duty to acquaint oneself with just how this realm actually works.

Evidently, this notion goes against the commonly held maxim about art assert-ing that beauty is ostensibly in the eye of the beholder. Albeit a widely popular preconception, and despite resonating with the Latin phrase *de gustibus non est disputandum*—supposedly awarding it some intrinsic sense of profoundness—it is, in fact, a gross misconception. Put simply, its massive general appeal notwith-standing, and while it may very well tell one a thing or two about the implied beholder, it ultimately conveys absolutely nothing about what the beholder actu-ally beholds. This is not to say, however, that a beholder—or, indeed, his or her experiences—should in any way be rendered unimportant or irrelevant. Quite the contrary. As designated audience, the beholder counts as a crucial constituent in the definition of art. As such, he or she would need to carry out their institutional responsibility, namely, as NITA suggests, be "prepared in some degree to under-stand" precisely what it is that they happen to be beholding—rather than question whether or not (or to what extent) it merely happens to be to their liking. Of course, while everyone is entitled to his or her opinion—and despite the manner in which it might inform, influence, or broaden one's overall understanding of

---

[19] Graves, *The New Institutional Theory of Art*, 57.

[20] Ibid., 17.

a particular work—the question of one's personal preference simply does not determine an artwork's aesthetic quality. Consequently, as a theory about art, its deficiency lies precisely in having nothing whatsoever do to with art.

To fully appreciate any artwork, one should embark on a journey in an attempt not only to identify what kind of artwork one has been present with (e.g., its particular style, genre, and context) but also to ascertain *why* one has been presented with that artwork to begin with, that is, to decipher the core ideas and insights that an artist aimed to instill into his or her artwork. For the most part, artists should be able to justify not only their chosen medium but also the particular aesthetic tools they adopt and employ. They should similarly be able to account for the manner in which their artwork conveys (or attempts to convey)—either explicitly or implicitly—whatever it is that they endeavor to communicate or "say" to their designated audience. Artworks could thus be conceived as vehicles for communicating ideas that could not otherwise be expressed. Artistic praxis, at its core, is appropriately rendered a form of inter-subjective communication.

Conceivably, both the notion of internal logic and that of art as "embodied meaning" seem to reside amid the Artworld's sub-(institutional) categories and, in particular, the "working theory" level. As such, each artistic style, genre, or movement can be said to embody, comply with, and, indeed, adhere to a distinct and unique internal logic of its own. Ultimately, when setting out to establish whether or not—and, indeed to what extent—a particular artwork successfully exhibits the internal logic of its own world, one is appropriately required to seek (and, hopefully, find) what that internal logic actually is. To do so, however, one cannot rely on pure rational analysis or inductive reasoning alone.

An Intuition to Be Reckoned with

Throughout the seventeenth and eighteenth centuries, empirical science and analytical thinking had generated an almost unprecedented popularity among scholars, scientists, and the general public alike. Drawing on the influential intellectual infrastructure laid out by such eminent thinkers as Sir Isaac Newton and René Descartes, the general atmosphere at the time seemed to surmise that one can employ science to explain every single phenomenon that one happens to cross paths with. Soon enough, Science—as an agency of sorts, in its own right—not only categorically opposed anything ostensibly non-scientific (e.g., art and other such so-called unimportant and frail disciplines) but also began brewing an overwhelming desire to effectively monopolize every given field of study.

At the same time, however—and despite its proven potential first and foremost in explaining, preserving, and prolonging one's life expectancy—there will always remain certain fields or phenomena in the world that fall into the category of that which *cannot* be explained, deciphered, or, indeed, defined by modern empirical science. (Consider, say, attempting to ascertain a particular restaurant's purported pretentiousness. Indeed, there is no such thing as a "pretension barometer" as "pretentiousness" cannot *really* be measured). Intuitions, in this respect, have routinely been associated with one's *knowing* something to be true, to all intents and purposes, while lacking the ability to explain precisely why. As such, intuitions have also customarily been dismissed as nothing more than a "hunch" or a "gut feeling." Science, on its part, conceivably has no idea what to "do" with them and can neither understand nor cope with their so-called inner workings. Notwithstanding, while one cannot, alas, empirically substantiate intuitions (i.e., as actual, objective truths), one should not necessarily regard them as less true than something one *can*.

Intuitions alone, of course, are certainly not enough. In this context, if one accepts that all cultural institutions and praxes can be said to "behave" *logically*—thereby complying with, and, indeed, adhering to some overall "intuition of necessity"[21]—then to grasp that logic, making sense of it, is conceivably rooted in one's innate, universal cognitive ability to *sense* not only necessity and appropriateness (or, indeed, the lack thereof) but also structure, meaning, relationships, and interconnectedness. Thus, I would argue that one is conceivably able to link the notion of internal logic to what might be identified as "informed intuition": that is, a logical conclusion that is contextualized through concrete, firsthand experience and informed, to varying degrees, by certain insights and conclusions that one attains via theoretical analysis.[22]

To aesthetically evaluate artworks, therefore, that is, to *see* them, in both senses of the word, requires one to analytically deconstruct and understand their

---

[21] Graves, "Logic and the Sense of Necessity," 225.

[22] Although arguably self-evident, it should be noted that just as intuitions can be no less accurate than empirically-proven things, certain intuitions may also be quite inaccurate—or, rather misleading, and, indeed, wrongly informed. As Arthur Koestler, for instance, puts it, "both the poet and the scientist know by bitter experience how many of the apparently happy discoveries of intuition have to be rejected. The diver into the unconscious mostly returns to the surface with nothing but a handful of mud. It remains to be explained how it comes about that he does sometimes return with a pearl." Arthur Koestler, *Insight and Outlook: An Inquiry into the Common Foundations of Science, Art and Social Ethics* (New York: Macmillan, 1949), 335.

purported meaning, and, at the same time, to *actually* see with one's own eyes that particular meaning at play. By the same token, to *know*—intuitively—that a particular artwork is *necessarily* good, requires one to possess not only a certain degree of theoretical knowledge about that particular artwork but also a deeper understanding of whether or not (and, indeed, to what extent) that artwork should well be deemed a good example of its own particular kind. It is precisely in this respect that NITA thus re-contextualizes the question of aesthetic value as a matter of inherent appropriateness, effectively equipping one with an easy-to-use practical how-to guide, that is, "how to classify a work of art, how to interpret a work of art, and how to evaluate a work of art."[23] Ultimately, while successfully demonstrating that artworks do *not* necessarily have to be aesthetic—and, indeed, that beauty does not axiomatically define art—NITA advisedly concludes that artworks most certainly, to all intents and purpose, *should* be aesthetic.[24]

---

[23] Graves, *The New Institutional Theory of Art*, 57.

[24] Ibid., 87.

CHAPTER TWO

Aural Artifacts: The Distinct Products of a Hitherto Undefined Aesthetic Category

Listening into the Audiobook Phenomenon

Although by the late 1960s a varied range of audio recordings could be found amid different collections of academic libraries, it seemed, alas, quite altogether impossible to detect which particular type of recordings one might find in a given collection—since, at the time, virtually no effort had been invested in discerning between musical and non-musical recordings.[1] Edison—whose wax cylinder invention made such recordings possible, to begin with—had initially conceived of two kinds of potential consumers for the material he wished to capture, namely, (a) one who seeks to relax at home after a long day's work and (b) one who is either blind or visually impaired.[2]

On the one hand, Edison certainly seems to have had an implicit designated *audience* in mind, appropriately identifying the potential of his invention to enhance the enjoyment that one attains from listening to a book narrated by an "elocutionist" as opposed to the "average reader." He thus recognized that certain persons appear to possess the ability to endow words "with the finest grade of feeling and accent."[3] On the other hand, rather than concerning himself with the preservation of live musical performances, Edison is cited to have been more interested in the notion of capturing and immortalizing the voices of "great men" for the sake of posterity.[4] As such, he conceivably cared not a whit about the potential arthood these recordings might embody and exhibit.

---

[1] Tracy, "Echoes in a Bottle," 25.

[2] Rubery, *The Untold Story of the Talking Book*, 37–38.

[3] Ibid., 35; 37.

[4] Tracy, "Echoes in a Bottle," 24.

Rarely regarded as something more than a form of entertainment, questions pertaining to the status and identity of audiobooks as so-called *real* books reside at the very core of critical reactions they seem to inevitably draw. Consider, for instance, George Guidall's heartfelt letter, submitted to the *New York Times* in 2011, conveying his frustration as a veteran audiobook narrator:

> To the Editor: Discussing the popularity of audiobooks, James Parker notes that they "are on the rise" ("The Mind's Ear," Nov. 27). But are they "on the rise" because they've just been discovered, or is it that *The New York Times* has finally conceded their importance after years of denying them the status they deserve? Having narrated more than 900 unabridged novels over the past 20 years, I can attest to the fact that audiobooks long ago rose to achieve a most respected place in the minds and ears of those who appreciate the narrative art form along with the beauty of classic literature. Letters thanking me for bringing Proust, Dostoyevsky, and Cervantes to life; for "telling" the stories of Tony Hillerman, Wally Lamb and Lilian Jackson Braun; and for heightening the experience of books previously read speak to a facet of audiobooks' success that seems to have been overlooked: the relationship generated between narrator and listener. The relationship is based on an unspoken intimacy, matching empathy and the emotional honesty the narrator provides. It's not a fad. It's not something with which to pass the time, although it helps. It's an art form and, when well executed, should be appreciated as such. GEORGE GUIDALL[5]

Conceivably, the fact that one customarily engages with the exact same text in both the original printed book and in its aural iteration facsimile seems to have sparked ample heated debates between lovers of print versus lovers of audiobooks—each defending their own personal choice and, to a certain extent, a deep-rooted and well-groomed ideology.

Overall, the prominence of the written word—being visual and thus, conceivably, eternal—seems to have assumed an overwhelming reverence and, for the most part, a commonly accepted authority. The spoken word, however—and despite its intrinsic connotation (at least in certain circles) with the creation of the world—might be characterized as ephemeral and fugacious, thereby arguably rendering it both tenuous and unreliable.

---

[5] George Guidall, "Letter to the Editor: The Minds Ear," *New York Times,* December 23, 2011, accessed August 20, 2022, https://www.nytimes.com/2011/12/25/books/review/the-minds-ear.html. For further insights, see URL: accessed August 31, 2023, http://www.georgeguidall.com/library-appearances/.

This may well be the reason why, as Rubery observes, "readers who express discomfort toward hearing printed books read aloud seldom express the same unease toward reading oral scripts in print."[6] He finds that it is arguably the novel's long-standing "association with print" that had "set it apart from other genres originally intended for aural reception."[7] As Snelling similarly points out, citing Eileen Hutton,

> There's a misconception that the hardcover is not only superior but that audiobooks are cheating the print book. Some feel they don't retain as much information when they listen than when they read; others feel that listening is more pleasurable, especially if it is a common practice.[8]

According to Sara Knox, critics and listeners alike quite vigorously dispute the notion that listening to audiobooks, as opposed to reading, constitutes "a more passive interpretive activity [...] precisely because the interpretive act of voicing has already been surrendered by the listener."[9] In 2011, for instance, annoyed by John Schwartz's *New York Times* essay that had alluded to the act of listening to audiobooks as a kind of reading, one Ms. Amy Stodola, of Harrisville, N. H., wrote to the editor—asserting that enjoyable and stimulating as it may be, "listening to audiobooks is no more a kind of reading than riding a train is a kind of walking."[10]

A Note on the Written Word vs. the Spoken Word

Although, to a large extent, the prevailing hierarchy still clearly lends itself to printed books, the fact that reading and listening constitute considerably different and discrete *aesthetic* experiences simply cannot be understated. Calling attention to inherent, long-established "anti-audio prejudices" that the discipline of literary studies evidently holds against the audiobook phenomenon, English explains that

---

[6] Rubery, *The Untold Story of the Talking Book*, 35.

[7] Ibid., 38.

[8] Snelling, "The Audiobook Market and Its Adaptation to Cultural Changes."

[9] Sara Knox, "Hearing Hardy, Talking Tolstoy: The Audiobook Narrator's Voice and Reader Experience," in *Audiobooks, Literature, and Sound Studies*, ed. Matthew Rubery (New York: Routledge, 2011), 128.

[10] Amy Stodola, "Letter to the Editor: The Mind's Ear," *New York Times,* December 23, 2011, accessed August 20, 2022, https://www.nytimes.com/2011/12/25/books/review/the-minds-ear.html.

These intertwined and mutually reinforcing prejudices are (1) that listening is a shortcut, a timesaving hack, a lazy way to get through a book while performing other tasks such as shopping or working out at the gym; (2) that listening is superficial, a kind of skimming by ear that limits comprehension and undermines the pedagogy of close reading; and (3) that listening is an impediment to genuine literary experience, that its specific attractions—having mainly to do with the skills of a performer—are ancillary to the text itself and hence represent a distracting detour away from authentically literary response.[11]

At the same time, English quite rightly elucidates that "whether taken separately or as the coordinated elements of a disciplinary common sense, these antipathies are unwarranted," later adding that there is no "empirical basis for the belief that listening is somehow a superficial or unrigorous substitute for 'actually reading' a book."[12] In the same vein, as Rubery explains it,

The alleged passivity of audiobook reception is largely responsible for suspicions that it is "not really reading." […] The defensiveness of audiobook listeners is evident in their frequent apologies for listening to rather than reading a book. […] A nostalgic preference for the material book underpins the discomfort many readers feel toward an act of reception involving no tangible manuscript. Listening to a book is not a sensuous experience in the same way as is holding a book in one's hands, with the heft of its binding and the texture of its pages. The proximity of the audiobook to the printed book is unsettling because it threatens the very identity of reading in a way that is not true of other forms of adaptation easily set apart as secondary to the printed text.[13]

I, for one—as will be both reiterated and demonstrated throughout—certainly find that *listening* to audiobooks should ultimately be perceived of as a unique aesthetic experience in its own right. As such, in the particular context of this study, the act of reading a book need not be perceived as a supposedly more important, serious, or highbrow endeavor than the act of listening to an audiobook. By the same token, the latter need not be dismissed as passive or easier task, nor

---

[11] English, "Teaching the Novel in the Audio Age," 424.

[12] Ibid.

[13] Rubery, introduction to *Audiobooks, Literature, and Sound Studies*, 11–12.

as an undertaking that might supersede reading. Rather, it should fundamentally be considered in respect of its own terms.

Decidedly insisting on employing the word *reading* to describe the manner in which one engages with audiobooks, Have and Pedersen explain that "reading an audiobook takes place in a triangulation between everyday practice, specific technological formats/conditions and specific aesthetic or modal literary experiences of reading."[14] Furthermore, they also reject the purported passivity of audiobook listening—emphasizing that not only can this activity "be just as captivating and gripping" as actual reading but that being a *different* kind of activity, it, "therefore requires different methodological approaches than the analysis of a traditional reading experience."[15]

To be sure, just as viewing screen or stage adaptation of a literary work does not necessarily substitute for engaging with the original work that particular adaptation is based on, listening to an audiobook, too—as a general rule—does not excuse one from ostensibly enduring the burden of reading a book for oneself. In this respect, any concern that audiobooks might, alas, render reading obsolete—purportedly providing idle persons an "easy way out" by excusing them from properly engaging with *actual* books—seems to me not only overtly patronizing but also quite preposterous.

Where the Rubber Meets the Road

To consider audiobooks as more than mere aural iterations of written texts, ostensibly lifted from the printed page and subsequently delivered unto a recording device, I find that one requires a designated aesthetic category that would set the context—indeed, the given circumstances—amid the confines of which, they can be *classified* as distinct products of the Artworld. Subsequently, one should also be able to both evaluate and appreciate their aesthetic nature.

Yet, as established *ab initio*, no such category has been defined hitherto. Indeed, as Rubery points out,

> Despite the audiobook's subliterary reputation, most audio publishers consider themselves to be champions of the book who have found a way to help people

---

[14] Have and Pedersen, "Reading Audiobooks," 204.

[15] Ibid., 209.

read even more of them. In their eyes, they make books accessible to people with busy schedules, long commutes, and print disabilities who would not otherwise be able to read them. There is no doubt in their minds that audiobooks are first and foremost books, and their editing decisions often reflect this philosophy. Publishers seeking to untether audiobooks from other books are a recent development. Only in the last few years have publishers begun to experiment in earnest with alternative forms of storytelling that treat the audiobook as an independent art form in its own right or as one that no longer needs a printed source to justify its existence.[16]

It is only in the concluding chapter of his illumining, predominantly historicist, and, indeed, thoroughly researched study that Rubery begins to postulate what I consider to be the aesthetics of audiobooks:

> So far my account of the talking book's history has concentrated on its fidelity to the printed book. The last chapter, however, tells the other side to this story. It considers how the convergence of formerly distinct media has encouraged publishers to reconceive audiobooks as something other than a replication of print ones. Instead, companies like Audible—the world's largest audiobook retailer—have begun promoting audiobooks as an independent art form in its own right, one that can do things other books cannot. Whereas publishers traditionally have encouraged a neutral, restrained style of speaking in order to avoid distracting attention from a book's words, many of today's publishers encourage actors to perform.[17] […] Hence, this chapter investigates how audiobooks use human voices, celebrity readers, sound effects, musical scores, and other devices to distinguish themselves from books and even to compete with radio, television, film, and other digital media. Such experimentation reflects a growing confidence among publishers in the audiobook as an art form in its own right instead of a derivative version of the printed book. In fact, many publishers no longer care whether their recordings are considered "books" at all.[18]

As will presently be elucidated, by establishing an appropriate aesthetic context— that is, a given set of institutional circumstances—the general aesthetic category I propose herein is not restricted to audiobooks alone. Rather, it effectively determines whether or not—and, indeed, the extent to which—any so-called

---

[16.] Rubery, *The Untold Story of the Talking Book*, 4.

[17.] Ibid., 245.

[18.] Ibid., 246–247.

"recorded text" or "spoken-word" recording might count as an "aural artifact": that is to say, an artwork, to all intents and purposes.

As an overall "mother institution," it prescribes the criteria and parameters not only for the standard and predominant instances (e.g., audiobooks, recorded poetry, radio drama), but also the so-called "non-standard" phenomena (e.g., *audio-vérité*, commentary tracks, or narrations of long-form journalistic publications). As such, it effectively concretizes all potential "sub-(institutional)-categories" that ultimately adhere to a shared aesthetics, and, indeed, comply with a kindred internal logic—which, in turn, can account for a variety of aesthetic questions: e.g., what kind of artworks can aural artifact be said to be? How is an audience expected to engage with and experience them? Do all texts merit an aural iteration? Who might count as the "artist" in this endeavor? (i.e., the person or persons featured on the actual recording—or rather the director, sound engineer, producer, or casting director) and what makes an aural artifact aesthetically good?

A New Aesthetic Category

Having scrutinized the workings of NITA, and following my attempt to delve into the overall institutional structure of the Artworld at large, I find that one is able to extend the reach of the aforementioned four core rule-schemes ("R1–R4"), thereby utilizing them in order to quite literally *create* new aesthetic categories and, indeed, artistic genres—which, in turn, would effectively constitute unique Artworld systems in their own right, appropriately complying with and, indeed, adhering to their own rules and parameters. As Graves himself points out, "this humble set is where it all begins."[19]

Appropriately, what follows is my proposed application of "R1–R4," which together constitute the inner workings of what I consider to be the "Institution of Aural Artifacts"—that is, an Artworld system, and, indeed, a *new* general category:

[R1] The *praxis* of aural artifacts counts as an exclusive Artworld-system (that is, a distinct aesthetic category in its own right) if, and only if, it establishes a particular framework that governs the creation and presentation of aural artifacts by performing artists for the benefit of a designated audience—all amid the confines of a predominantly aural medium.

[19.] Graves, *The New Institutional Theory of Art*, 40.

[R2] An audio recording counts as an *aural artifact* if, and only if, it has been either created or/and presented by performing artists, for the benefit of a designated audience, amid the exclusive confines of a predominantly aural medium.

[R3] A person counts as an *aural performing artist* if, and only if, they participate with understanding in either the creation or/and presentation of aural artifacts, for the benefit of a designated audience, amid the exclusive confines of a predominantly aural medium.

[R4] A set of persons counts as the *designated audience for aural artifacts*—insofar as their capacity as a particular sector of the Artworld public—if, and only if, its members are prepared to take upon themselves a degree of responsibility to engage with, understand, consume, and experience an audio recording as an aural artifact—which has been either created or/and presented for their benefit, by an aural performing artist, within a particular Artworld system, amid the exclusive confines of a predominantly aural medium.

As an ostensible caveat—or rather, as a brief elaboration, of sorts, *vis-à-vis* my proposed R3—it should be noted that in addition to the person or persons whose voice is featured on the recording, the overall authorship of any given aural artifact may well belong to more than a single aural performing artist—all working collaboratively, for a common creative objective including, but not restricted to, e.g., the roles of the director, producer, sound engineer, or casting director. Implicitly, it should also be pointed out that an aural performing artist would customarily, albeit not necessarily, prove to be a *professional* performer.

Audiobooks as Adaptations

As far as Rubery is concerned, the definition of audiobooks can be said to reside somewhere between performance and adaptation.[20]

I, for one, most definitely tend to agree: all audiobooks, in one way or another, may be identified as a hybrid of sorts—that is, consisting of an iteration, interpretation, and, indeed, an adaptation, all rolled into one. While complete and unabridged recordings conventionally prevail nowadays as the gold standard, a good case in point is the *abridged* recordings that once used to roam wild. Originally, abridgments were conceived of for two main reasons, namely, cost-effectiveness and economizing shelf space. If producing a single unabridged

---

[20.] Matthew Rubery, introduction to *Audiobooks, Literature, and Sound Studies*, 13.

audiobook required retailers to spread it over, say, fourteen cassette tapes—the standard-issue format of the day—then they could certainly not expect a consumer to pay fourteen times the price of what a single cassette tape used to cost. Retailers, in effect, preferred providing a larger variety of abridged audiobooks—usually spread over two or four cassette tapes—rather than selling a limited number of individual 14-cassette box sets.

Arguably prevailing as something of a sub-section of the audiobook genre—that is, in itself a sub-(institutional)-category of aural artifacts—abridgments might more easily be categorized as adaptations than as unabridged audiobooks. As the original written text is not only transformed into the spoken word but also ostensibly tampered with, abridgments appear to form a somewhat easier target for criticism. One could argue, for instance, that their apparent existence as a seemingly incomplete representation of the original literary work essentially prevents one from experiencing the *actual* work, thereby potentially affecting one's ability to evaluate and appreciate it. One might even go so far as to say that the very act of shortening an existing complete work essentially amounts to "butchering" the original book. Possible moral implications aside, and although one might clearly be inclined to sympathize with these general sentiments, I find that the phenomenon of abridgments, as an ostensibly "watered-down" version of an original work, should nevertheless *not* become a matter of concern.

Cost-effectiveness and shelf space notwithstanding, one is sure to come across certain abridgments that were purposefully created amid the particular context of the Artworld. In fact, quite a significant number of authors have not only approved and facilitated the abridged audiobook version of their own work but have also themselves actively made the assumed necessary cuts and edits. Some authors have even narrated the abridgments themselves, effectively endowing them with the so-called ultimate mark of approval.

This, I find, demonstrates that authors no doubt understand that listening to audiobooks should not pose an alternative to reading—and, furthermore, that certain works, as aural iterations, may even convectively *require* some so-called "watering-down." As such, that an audiobook happens to be abridged should therefore *not* revoke its status or identity as a legitimate aural artifact—or, indeed, as a candidate for appreciation.

Audiobooks as Performances

The element of performance—as the second attribute that Rubery affords audio-books—is, to my mind, no less than crucial. Indeed, as my proposed application of "R1–R4" aims to illustrate, it certainly constitutes a defining feature of any aural artifact.

Evidently, however, the spectrum of what is considered the praxis of "performance" continuously broadens and progressively evolves. Since its inception, in fact, scholars and artists alike have proposed a variety of explanations, understandings, and interpretations pertaining to what a performance actually is. On the one hand, scholars such as Marvin Carlson regard performance as an anti-discipline, arguing that it "resists conclusions, just as it resists the sort of definitions, boundaries, and limits so useful to traditional academic writing and academic structures."[21] On the other hand, certain scholar-practitioners (e.g., Richard Schechner) have even gone so far as to argue that essentially anything and everything can be perceived or studied as an ostensible performance. This approach, however, conceivably goes well beyond what might be regarded as theatrical performance in that it predominantly invests in identifying aspects of performativity in a variety of fields that are not necessarily artistic.

Consequently, one could argue that the meaning of the term should essentially be a given: that is, a performance constitutes a human behavior, consciously created or designed for a designated audience—thereby aiming to manipulate or influence the viewer by drawing attention to the doer. (Human behavior in itself is predominantly not self-conscious. While certain behavior may include a performative aspect, it would nonetheless customarily be analyzed using anthropological terms. As such, I find that one could also potentially consider terms in respect of the distinction between brute and institutional facts). Put simply, identifying a particular behavior *as* performance requires the appropriate context.

According to Hilde Hein, performances constitute an "aesthetic phenomenon of primary significance," and, as such, warrant an aesthetic category of their own. She finds, for instance, that since "every social institution and every intellectual system of the modern era has accommodated itself to change as a fundamental value," one could very well benefit from re-examining "the classic categories of aesthetics by bringing to bear upon them the dynamic elements of the category of

---

[21.] Marvin Carlson, *Performance: A Critical Introduction* (London: Routledge, 1996), 206.

performance."[22] Her insights, I find, seem to evince an inherently "institutional" quality—explicitly when considering audiobooks as aural artifacts in terms of performance. Hein's notion, for instance, of the "appreciator-critic,"[23] strongly resonates, to my mind, with the aforementioned "candidate for appreciation." Furthermore, in what clearly highlights the unique role of the performer—effectively supporting their key position in my proposed application of "R1–R4"—Hein argues that

> The new trends within the arts pose a challenge to standard aesthetic categorization, suggesting that new categories might well be adopted, categories which place the role of performer in primary perspective. [...] I suggest [...] that innovations in art invite us to reconsider the old art forms as well as the new in the light of aesthetic categories which are more oriented toward process and activity than those of the past. This may enable us to rectify the incongruity referred to above between the layman's conception of art as something essentially performative, and that of the aesthetician who views performance as a derivative artistic function. It may also permit us to gain new insight and understanding of works of art of the past in much the same fashion that conceptual revisions within science and philosophy have consistently rewarded historical inquiry in those areas. Aesthetics, like philosophy and like the arts [...] is cumulative in the sense that it feeds upon its own history which, in turn, is constantly replenished from the store of contemporary experience.[24]

Appropriately affirming their status and identity as artworks in and of themselves, an argument could be made that each and every performance conceivably embodies a unique and distinct internal logic of its own—which, in turn, both complies with and adheres to the different sub-(institutional)-categories provided by the Artworld at large.

In the same vein, it is interesting to note that Peter Kivy finds that the very act of *reading* literary works constitutes a certain type of performance in its own right. This, to my mind, is quite an intriguing notion, one that—in explicit

---

[22] Hilde Hein, "Performance as an Aesthetic Category," *Journal of Aesthetics and Art Criticism* 28, no. 3 (Spring 1970): 384.

[23] Ibid., 382.

[24] Ibid., 386.

consideration of the audiobook phenomenon—seems to both highlight and validate the aesthetic experience involved. As David Davies explains,

> Kivy's bold thesis in this very engaging and stimulating monograph is that lit-
> erature in general—not just drama or even poetry but also the novel—should be
> viewed as a performance art, analogous to music, where the instances of works
> through which they are appreciated are performances enacted by readers. [...]
> Furthermore, Kivy argues, silent readings of novels are analogous to perfor-
> mances of musical works "in the head" by score readers. Performances of literary
> works "in the head" can be seen as expressive "soundings" that, as in the case
> of "soundings" of musical works by score readers, embody an interpretation of
> the overall sense of the work. Given that the silent reading of a novel can be
> viewed as a performance, Kivy further maintains, this is how it should be viewed:
> literature in general, including the novel, is properly viewed as a performance
> art. [...] Kivy's compelling presentation of the case for a performative element
> in literature may serve to awaken us to the significance of such aspects of liter-
> ary experience, even if [...] the case for viewing literature as a performance art
> requires further argument and elucidation.[25]

Now, it should also be noted that drawing on modern semiotic theories—and
particularly the distinction made by Patrice Pavis between a "written text" and
a "performance text"—it could be established, *in nuce*, that virtually every text
simultaneously assumes two ostensibly separate identities.[26] As a "written text,"
a text exists as a scenario for performance, inherently containing instructions for
a performance—thereby determining, at least in part, what the performance text
should consequently be. In other words, by effectively prescribing the purported
guideline and implicit suggestions for a putative performance (i.e., rather than
explicit instructions), written texts might be perceived of as an ostensible blue-
print or an arguably incomplete working script—and, as such, they may well be
subject to change. Appropriately, when engaging with a written text, attention
should also be paid to the varying socio-historical connotations it is associated

---

[25] Davies, David. "Book Review: *The Performance of Reading: An Essay in the Philosophy of Literature* by Peter Kivy." *Journal of Aesthetics and Art Criticism* 66, no. 1 (Winter 2008): 89–91.

[26] For further reading see, e.g., Patrice Pavice, *Theatre at the Crossroads of Culture* (London: Routledge, 1992), and *Contemporary Mise en Scène: Staging Theatre Today,* trans. Joel Anderson (New York: Routledge, 2013). Also recommend is, e.g., David Osipovich, "What Is a Theatrical Performance?" *Journal of Aesthetics and Art* 64, no. 4 (Fall 2006): 46.

with, the pertinent scholarly theories and criticism it has been subjected to, as well as its past performances (if any) and potential possibilities (or conceivable limitations) in terms of future productions.

At the same time, as a "performance text," it inevitably absorbs and integrates a director's conceptual commentary or so-called "take" on the written text's internal logic and embodied potential for realization. It is, in effect, both influenced by and dependent on one's reading of the written text as a candidate for a particular production—that is, merely one among a range of possible versions (all of which, at least potentially, constitute artworks in their own right).[27]

The perpetual interaction that purportedly prevails between them thus surely involves varying degrees of interpretation, editing, or remediation. If, therefore, a text's two identities would inform, contribute to, and serve as the various constituents associated with a particular text's overall internal logic as an artwork, then an audience, in turn (and in virtue of their "institutional" role), is essentially assigned the responsibility to both ascertain and identify what that internal logic supposedly is and subsequently evaluate whether or not, and the degree to which, it is actually exhibited amid a putative performance. This is not to say that if a certain performance does not happen to constitute a so-called perfectly "faithful" rendition of the written text it derives from, then it should, *ipso facto*, be deemed aesthetically flawed. Quite the contrary. Some performances quite intentionally set out to create their own ostensibly deconstructed "take"—effectively creating and substantiating a somewhat different internal logic. An audience is thus required to be mindful of just *that* in order to properly evaluate such cases in their own terms. Notwithstanding, and perhaps especially when engaging with a single performed iteration of the same original written text, one's challenge conceivably remains to detect (or, at the very least, contemplate on) which versions can be said to count as the good examples of their own particular kind.

It is, to my mind, in this context that one should also consider the phenomenon of recorded poetry readings. Although it is not the focal point of this study's

---

[27] At first blush, this distinction seems akin to the classic distinction between types and tokens. (See appendix for a more detailed annotation). A deeper investigation, however, would reveal that this approach essentially considers written texts to embody a particular and unique range of various possibilities for their fullest realization as potential performances. As such, and drawing once again on Graves' definition of artistic beauty, a performance text should arguably embody and exhibit the internal logic of the written text (or, at the very least, certain essential aspects thereof). To slightly paraphrase a quote attributed to American actor Jason Robards: if it is not on the page, it has no place on the stage.

exploration, these recordings certainly adhere to the same overall "mother institution" (i.e., the general aesthetic category I propose herein). Thus, in identifying
them as aural artifacts to all intents and purposes, they cannot be ignored:

In his introduction to *Close Listening: Poetry and Performed Word* (1998)—
an engaging and hugely influential collection of seventeen essays, all written
especially for this singular publication—American poet and scholar Charles
Bernstein argues that

> In a sense, this collection presents a complex, multilayered response to a quite
> simple, and common, response to a poetry reading, as when one says: "I under-
> stand the work better hearing the poet read it. I would never have been able to
> figure out that the poems would sound that way." (This is not to discount the
> significance of performances by poets that seem "bad" for one reason or another
> or may make one like the work less than on the page, nor to distract from the
> significance of the performance of a poem by someone other than its author.)[28]

Similarly, according to Peter Middleton,

> What we can conclude [...] is that written poetry has always been read aloud
> by both authors and readers, long before the advent of the contemporary poetry
> reading, which is now such a dominant feature of poetic practice. [...] Sometimes
> called rhetoric, sometimes elocution, oral reading, even orthophony, the training
> of public speaking with written texts including poetry, is the missing part of the
> story of poetry readings.[29]

In the same vein, Peter Quartermain maintains that

> There is a wide and inevitable disparity between how we hear the poem when
> we read it silently, and how we sound it, saying it aloud; the poem performed
> in the head is an imagined poem in the world of sound. [...] The inner speaking
> we hear as we read is not the voice we hear when we outwardly speak, and the
> noises we make when we read a poem aloud are never the noises we think the

---

[28.] Charles Bernstein, introduction to *Close Listening: Poetry and the Performed Word* (Oxford: Oxford University Press, 1998), 6.

[29.] Peter Middleton, "The Contemporary Poetry Reading," in *Close Listening: Poetry and the Performed Word*, ed. Charles Bernstein (Oxford: Oxford University Press, 1998), 279.

poem makes. Maybe the variation has to do with the familiarity of the poem, or the fixity of our interpretation, or the frequency of our performance.[30]

What I find most illuminating about the insights and intuitions that *Close Listening*, as a whole, appears to advocate ultimately resides not only in the notion that one is able to better understand a poem through its performance but also in the implied existence of so-called "bad" performances. In this respect, the distinction between the printed word and its performed equivalent can also be associated with the idea of there being a particular manner in which the written text *should* be spoken. As Wittkower explains it,

> In the written word, the particular modes of relevance of one word upon another are not communicated through grammatical roles alone but also take place through the occult actions of punctuation marks. In the spoken word, similar signals are given through precisely timed pauses and changes in tone. The commas used to offset modifying or explanatory clauses, such as those surrounding this aside, are intended to be heard differently, and to construct meaning differently, than those within a list. The colon indicates content: that which follows it loops back upon and superimposes on that which precedes it. The modifying or explanatory clause—set off by commas or em dashes, like this—is lowered in pitch relative to the primary "timeline" of the sentence. Some words are emphasized in volume or enunciation in order to signal to the listener that these words are essential to the retrospective reconstruction of the meaning of the sentence in question. Words in subordinate clauses and noun phrases are run together subtly in order to indicate their unification as objects distinct from other "moving parts" within the overall claim. Parentheticals are uttered sotto voce (at half voice, like this).[31]

In Search of the Internal Logic That a Text Inhabits

In his fascinating comprehensive exploration of the influential theories concerning Western dramatic acting and performance praxis from the nineteenth century onward, scholar-practitioner Robert Gordon chronicles a panoramic and comparative survey, which not only articulates their individual socio-historical

---

[30.] Peter Quartermain, "Sound Reading," in *Close Listening: Poetry and the Performed Word*, ed. Charles Bernstein (Oxford: Oxford University Press, 1998), 221.

[31.] Wittkower, "A Preliminary Phenomenology," 221.

evolution but also illuminates the manner in which they all inter-connect. Gordon puts forward six definitive categories, all of which, to my mind, are aesthetic at their core. The manner in which he contextualizes and concretizes these categories ultimately endows each of them with a distinctive internal logic of its own. He associated each individual category with a discrete style of acting and particular genre of performance. All six categories also conceivably correspond amid what can be identified as a larger institutional framework.[32] Put simply, Gordon quite eloquently demonstrates that one should be sensitive to the different types of texts one works with. By way of illustration, acting in a play by Chekhov, for instance, while following a praxis that is linked with Brecht, would, alas, not be the way to go. (Albeit a legitimate artistic choice, which would certainly necessitate some well-thought-through reasoning and justification. For the most part, however, this could conceivably be compared with playing, say, a game of baseball, while adhering to the rules of hide-and-seek). Alternatively, one could also consider different known approaches and praxes associated with the same particular text or given genre; e.g., while John Gielgud or Laurence Olivier may have once been considered the unrivaled masters of the modern Shakespearean domain, when comparing their approaches to those of, say, the Royal Shakespeare Company or, indeed, Kenneth Branagh, one can begin to consider the extent to which each approach appropriately adheres to, complies with, and, ultimately, best serves the purported internal logic that Shakespeare's works abide by.[33]

---

[32] Robert Gordon, *The Purpose of Playing: Modern Acting Theories in Perspective* (Ann Arbor: University of Michigan Press, 2006).

[33] Consider, e.g., the opening monologue British theatre director and teacher John Barton (1928-2018) introducing the unique nine-part TV masterclass *Playing Shakespeare* (1984)—originally inspired by two-part 1979 *South Bank Show* special dedicated to the Royal Shakespeare Company—in which he addresses the inherent necessity of living and breathing for understanding how to perform Shakespeare's text: "The best guide, I think, to playing him [Shakespeare] for the actors comes from Shakespeare himself, who was an actor. And it's in Hamlet's "advice to the players"—and it can't be quoted too often. [...] I believe that one speech goes to the very heart of it. [...] I believe that in the Elizabethan theatre, the actors knew how to use and interpret the "hidden direction" Shakespeare himself provided in his verse and his prose. [...] There are few absolute rules about playing Shakespeare, but many possibilities. So, [...] we want [...] to show how Shakespeare's own text can help to solve the seeming problems in that text. Of course, much of it is instinct and guesswork. We will try to distinguish between what is clearly and objectively so and what is highly subjective. [...] We shall concentrate on finding out how Shakespeare's text *works*. Of course, what we say is bound to be personal. We don't believe there's only one way of doing Shakespeare—that way madness lies. Out of the infinite number of questions which come up when we work on him, we have picked the ones that seem to us the most important. Another actor or another director would rightly stress things differently, or violently disagree with us, or raise points which we leave out because he felt they more important. [...] You, the audience, are quite as important in all this as our actors—both now, and in the theatre. If we don't *reach* you, we fail. [...] It's so easy for an audience not to listen—particularly with a knotty and difficult text. I may be cynical, but I don't believe most people really listen to Shakespeare in the theater unless the actors make them do so. I certainly don't. [...] Not unless the actors *make* me. So, stick with us—and we'll try and show you how that can happen". See: *Playing Shakespeare* [with the Royal Shakespeare Comoany], written and presented by John Barton, directed by John Carlow, produced by Andrew Snell (London Weekend Television, 1984), 0m50sec–06m45sec.

When eminent American playwright Edward Albee was once asked what kind of reaction to his work pleases him the most, his response, among other things, alluded to "the ability to take the play on its own terms—not expect to be something other than it wants to be."[34] (There are no doubt certain cinematic works, too, which one is required to engage with by tuning in to *their* particular pace—rather than what one might purportedly expect it to be). Indeed, any performance that employs an alternative—or, indeed, completely *new*—internal logic would inevitably stem from the pre-existing internal logic that purportedly inhabits the original work. This, to my mind, certainly applies to audiobooks, as aural artifacts, to all intents and purposes.

In the same vein, American screenwriter Aaron Sorkin had once presented an eloquent analogy between dialogue and music. He explicitly expresses his conviction that the task of screenplay writing necessitates writing for the purpose of performance:

> It's not just that dialogue sounds like music to me—it actually *is* music. Any time someone is speaking for the purpose of performance [...] all the rules of music apply. Cadence, and tone, and volume [...] So, when I'm writing, what the words sound like [...] is as important to me as what the words mean. It's a lot about rhythm. The actors will know if they have dropped a syllable or added a syllable accidentally, they'll know that something was wrong. The same way [...] if you're playing music, and there's a time signature at the beginning of it, it says *four-four-time*—that means there are four beats in a measure and a quarter-note gets one beat—there can't be five beats in a measure, there can't be three beats in a measure. And the actors know if they've dropped something [...] and *I* know when I'm writing if that [...] didn't quite work, what I was doing. [...] If you look at the whole piece—say, a two-hour play, a two-hour movie, a one-hour episode of television—[...] it has a lot of the same properties as a long piece of music like a symphony does or an opera. It's got solos and duets, it's got allegros and adagios, it's got arias—and sometimes they're good and sometimes they're bad, but it is music nonetheless.[35]

A play, as far as Albee is concerned, "is very simply that which is more effective on stage than it would be anywhere else. [...] The inevitability of the piece to

---

[34.] Albee, interviewed by Chapin. See: "The Playwright (Career Guides)," in the American Theatre Wing YouTube Channel, accessed January 19, 2023, https://www.youtube.com/watch?v=5jyC_9YwdIs&t=1128, 24m56sec–26m05sec.

[35.] Aaron Sorkin, "Writing Captivating Dialogue," in *Masterclass: Aaron Sorkin Teaches Screenwriting* (2016) Week 5, Lecture 21, 01m54sec–03m50sec.

the stage. That's the only definition of what a play is."[36] Playwrights, he asserts, should not "write with certain actors in mind. […] Because you would write a role rather than a character. And that would be a bad thing."[37] Ultimately, he recounts,

> When I write a play—this is helpful to young playwriting students, I think. Because not everybody does it which, shocks me. When I'm sitting at my desk, writing a play, I see it—and I hear it—as a performed play, in front of me while I'm writing it. So I am the audience for the *performed* version of the play that I am writing, while I am writing it. And that saves me an awful lot of time—I don't have to re-write anywhere near as much, because as I can tell whether a scene is holding my attention or not.[38]

English playwright Harold Pinter—no doubt one of the most important and influential wordsmiths of his time—had famously employed punctuation in such a way as to indicate a perceived difference between silences and pauses. As renowned English theater director Peter Hall points out,

> There is a difference in Pinter between a pause and a silence and three dots. A pause is really a bridge where the audience thinks that you're this side of the river, then when you speak again, you're the other side. That's a pause. And it's alarming, often. It's a gap, which retrospectively gets filled in. It's not a dead stop—that's a silence, where the confrontation has become so extreme, there is nothing to be said until either the temperature has gone down, or the temperature has gone up, and then something quite new happens. Three dots is a very tiny hesitation, but it's there, and it's different from a semicolon, which Pinter almost never uses, and it's different from a comma. A comma is something that you catch up on, you go through it. And a full stop's just a full stop. You stop.[39]

In identifying certain recurring aspects embodied in Pinter's corpus that effectively prescribe a putative performance, Hall's astute insights effectively inform one's understanding of the overall Pinteresque internal logic:

---

[36] Albee, interviewed by Chapin, 30m55sec–31m17sec.

[37] Ibid., 23m01sec–23m09sec.

[38] Ibid., 22m21sec–22m55sec.

[39] Peter Hall, "Directing Pinter," in *Harold Pinter: You Never Heard Such Silence*, ed. Alan Bold (London: Vision Press, 1984), 26.

A pause in Pinter is as important as a line. They are all there for a reason. Three dots is a hesitation, a pause is a fairly mundane crisis and a silence is some sort of crisis. Beckett started it and Harold took it over to express that which is inexpressible in a very original and particular way, and made them something which is his.[40]

Pinter himself had jokingly alluded to the manner in which the critics and interpreters of his work customarily scrutinize his use of a "dot, dot, dot" versus a dash:

I've had two full-length plays produced in London. The first ran a week and the second ran a year. Of course, there are differences between the two plays. In *The Birthday Party* I employed a certain amount of dashes in the text, between phrases. In *The Caretaker* I cut out the dashes and used dots instead. So that instead of, say: "Look, *dash*, who, *dash*, I, *dash*, *dash*, *dash*," the text would read: "Look, *dot*, *dot*, *dot*, who, *dot*, *dot dot*, I, *dot*, *dot*, *dot*, *dot*." So it's possible to deduce from this that dots are more popular than dashes and that's why *The Caretaker* had a longer run than *The Birthday Party*. The fact that in neither case could you hear the dots and dashes in performance is beside the point. You can't fool the critics for long. They can tell a dot from a dash a mile off, even if they can hear neither.[41]

One might well argue that the difference between them is quite irrelevant and that to scrutinize the individual sound they supposedly elicit is nothing more than nitpicking. If, however, the two are not one and the same, then one should certainly be able to discern—that is, to *hear*, embodied on the page—the inherent difference between them, which should appropriately become manifest when spoken aloud and performed. As such, one can conceivably distinguish between the ostensible brute fact of Pinter's punctuation—employed as a grammatical tool used for separating sentences and clarifying their meaning—and that institutional fact that renders it Pinteresque to begin with (and thereby setting it apart from other dramatic texts).

It so happens that *Various Voices* was also released as an abridged audiobook, featuring Pinter himself performing a selection of texts—the first of which being "Writing for the Theatre." As Pinter himself was a professional actor, listening to him performing his own writing constitutes quite a unique aesthetic experience. Not so much as this recording presents one with an opportunity to hear an

---

[40] Peter Hall, "Interview with C. Itzin and S. Trussler," *Theatre Quarterly* 4, no. 16 (1974/1975): 130.

[41] Harold Pinter, "Writing for the Theatre," in *Various Voices: Sixty Years of Prose, Poetry, Politics, 1948–1998* by Harold Pinter (New York: Grove Press, 1998), 19–25.

author reading their own work (which, contrary to common conviction, as I will demonstrate later, does *not* necessarily always yield the best results), but rather in light of Pinter's exceptional vocal dramatization of the ostensible instructions that the text itself seems to prescribe.[42]

Now, as the medium of the novel is not *intended* for performance, to all intents and purposes, it cannot constitute a so-called "standard" written text. It's aural iteration, however, can conceivably be considered a certain kind of performance text, especially since—much like the concrete realizations of plays, screenplays, or sheet music—an aural artifact does not ostensibly "exist" until it is *actually* experienced by a designated audience, thereby affirming its aesthetic identity. To be sure, as with any medium, aural artifacts should also essentially deploy the range of possibilities (and, indeed, limitations) evoked by the internal logic of the medium itself.

Ultimately, the different texts that aural artifacts consist of—and in particular when it comes to audiobooks—all comply with, adhere to, and, indeed, *require* different theories, approaches, and praxes. As such, one must not only ascertain what those particular facets are purported to be (i.e., in respect to some overall internal logic) but also how they might be employed amid the particular confines of the aural medium itself. Interestingly enough, despite Pinter's aforementioned remarks—purportedly poking fun at the different meanings ascribed to his use of punctuation—one *is* nonetheless *actually* able to hear those very differences sketched out in his delivery, all the while successfully complying with and adhering to the overall internal logic that the aural medium inevitably embodies.

Although it surely exceeds the scope of my current study, , I find it important to note that unlike other forms of performance, aural artifacts are quite unique in that they can be fully experienced, aesthetically, while all manner of activities are going on. That is to say, one can listen to an audiobook or a radio play *and* simultaneously drive to work, knit a scarf, exercise, or do any number of noise-free household chores—all without missing any red lights, pricking one's finger, skipping a set of push-ups, or leaving an item of laundry unfolded. And, indeed—perhaps most importantly—without losing the plot.[43]

---

[42] Harold Pinter, *Various Voices: Prose, Poetry, Politics: 1948–1998*, read by the author, Faber/Penguin Audiobooks (ISBN: 0-14-086846-1/978-0-14-086846-3), 1998, 2 audio cassettes. For Pinter's recording of "Writing for the Theatre," see: 01m14sec–02m02sec.

[43] Random House, for example, had once designated an advertising campaign not for audiobook consumers *per se* but rather for persons whose hobbies conceivably predispose them to the very act of listening of itself. In attempting to associate various possible activities that neatly comply with listening to audiobooks, the campaign's themes included a pair of earbuds wrapped around needles stuck into a ball of yarn, an airplane, and running

Narration Matters

While conventionally performed by a single narrator, there nonetheless exist a variety of audiobooks that are recorded by more than one individual, thereby taking the form of a fully dramatized aural production. In this respect, and since both audiobooks and radio drama stem from the *same* aesthetic category, certain insights pertaining to the latter can surely be applied to the former.

In his consideration of radio acting, for example, Alan Beck asserts that if performers can be said to sound like nothing more than "talking heads," then the listeners, in turn, tend to perceive the acting as unconvincing.[44] On the one hand, if Beck's notion of a "talking head" entails that one is merely reading or speaking the words into the microphone rather than properly performing them, then this notion seems to resonate quite well with the distinction between institutional and brute facts, and, indeed, "art" and "not art" (i.e., respectively, *performing* a text—and effectively creating an aural artifact, as opposed to simply recording them). On the other hand, the term "talking heads" could also be said to be somewhat misleading, especially since some aural iterations might, in fact, adhere to, perhaps even *require,* this particular property. This, again, is rooted in the notion of identifying, exhibiting, and evaluating the unique internal logic that inhabits each and every artwork. (Consider, e.g., the aptly titled *Talking Heads* monologues by prolific English playwright–author–actor Alan Bennett—and explicitly with regard to the inherent differences between the television and radio versions these works have received).[45]

To a large extent, the unique spatio-temporal status of the designated audience for aural artifacts renders the task and efforts of the aural performing artist(s) all the more challenging. Explicitly, they are required to perform for an audience that is not physically present but that rather ostensibly exists "somewhere, out there."

---

shoes. Andrew Adam Newman, "Expanding the Market for Audiobooks beyond Commuters," *New York Times,* June 1, 2013, accessed December 19, 2022, http://www.nytimes.com/2013/06/12/business/media/expanding-the-market-for-audiobooks-beyond-commuters.html.

44. Alan Beck, *Radio Acting* (London: A & C Black, 1997), 83; 6.

45. Originally screened on BBC television in 1988—with a second series broadcast a decade later in 1998, as well as a recent third series (filmed during the COVID-19 lockdown) broadcast in 2020—the first *Talking Heads* series consisted of six dramatic monologues, alongside an earlier stand-alone play. In 1991, the series was adapted for radio, with the monologues re-recorded by the same principal performers. Without delving into an over-detailed analysis, I find it suffices to point out the key aesthetic difference: as television monologues, the characters speak directly to the camera, reaching their audience from beyond screen; as aural performances, the spoken words reach their listeners from out of the darkness. When comparing the two versions, it is quite interesting to discover the manners in which the actors—all of whom were not only highly accomplished actors in their own right but also skilled interpreters of Bennett's distinctive style—chose to alter, adjust, or fine-tune their delivery of the material (consisting of the exact same text) in order to facilitate the particular requirements of each medium.

As Paddy Scannell points out, while the audience may be "situated elsewhere," it is the "liveness" that radio works adhere to that seems assign them "an audience-oriented communicative intentionality which is embodied in the organization of their setting (context) down to the smallest detail."[46] Although one could well argue that performing for the camera likewise entails that one's audience is not there, in the flesh, sharing the same atmosphere (as opposed to, say, a live event)—and who, for the most part, will similarly experience the performance at a later point, in front of screen—I find there is, nonetheless, something quite different about that space and stage that the aural medium provides. Knox, for instance, considers the audiobook's "auditory space of listening."[47] In the same vein, Frances Gray alludes to the "darkness and silence" that constitute "the stage of the radio," which essentially enable one to *create* "anyone or anything," and, indeed, "an alternative reality."[48] This, in essence, reflects on one's overall aesthetic experience. Gray also quite rightly alludes to the need to identify the particular "code with the ear" that many (radio) works establish, in which they "send all their messages."[49] Drawing on her metaphor, I would argue that the key to deciphering this "code"—arguably a constituent of a work's internal logic as an aural artifact—is to be found within the institutional structure of the Artworld.

Albeit supposedly self-evident, it should nevertheless be stressed that in addition to a performer's different proficiencies—that is, acting craftsmanship, skill, talent, and so on—he or she is essentially required to possess what Beck regards as a "must-be-listened-to" voice.[50] As Engberg and Pedersen put it, "the voice of the performing narrator is central to the audiobook experience."[51] Similarly, as Knox points out, the human voice, "as a species of sound, […] has particularly strong capacities for affect."[52] This, I would argue, should not be confused with whether or not (or, indeed, the extent to which) a performer's voice happens to be ostensibly "pleasing" to one's ear—since, as an aesthetic property, it is not, in fact, fundamentally irrelevant to that which *makes* a particular recording an aural

---

[46] Paddy Scannell, *Broadcast Talk* (London: Sage, 1991), 11.

[47] Knox, "Hearing Hardy, Talking Tolstoy," 139.

[48] Frances Gray, "The Nature of Radio Drama," in *Radio Drama*, ed. Peter Lewis (London: Longman, 1981), 49.

[49] Ibid., 60.

[50] Beck, *Radio Acting*, 2.

[51] Maria Engberg and Birgitte Stougaard Pedersen, "Situated Reading," in *The Digital Reading Condition*, eds., Maria Engberg, Iben Have, and Birgitte Stougaard Pedersen (London: Routledge, 2023), 203.

[52] Knox, "Hearing Hardy, Talking Tolstoy," 128.

artifact. A performer should, however, certainly find a way to utilize their vocal signatures so as to engage their listeners—to *captivate* them, if you will—all the while complying with the internal logic of the text in question and, indeed, adhering to the particular confines of aural medium. A narrator, for Wittkower, "like the conductor holding her hand aloft, the narrator can signal to the audience not to move on, not to be distracted, and not to stop paying attention."[53]

To be sure, performers must be *aware* of their designated audience. Their institutional role inevitably requires it. If they do not have, at the very least, some imagined or implied listener in mind, they would ultimately sound as if they are merely reading to "themselves." As Carlson puts it, a performance "is always performance *for* someone, some audience that recognizes and validates it as performance" [emphasis in original].[54] In the same vein, Roach quite rightly argues that

> Poor direction or the complete lack of it explains some failures in spoken recordings. Many have been hurt by enthusiastic but ill-equipped directors, competent directors unaccustomed to the milieu, and even able directors who, in the rush to publication, have not taken time to establish rapport with the performers, much less to rehearse or re-do recordings. That so many good recordings do exist is due in large part to the good directors experienced in the medium. […] These directors have contributed knowledge, experience and a pioneering spirit without which so much that is valuable in spoken recordings might not have been achieved.[55]

On Appreciating Aural Artifacts and Seeking Significant Audiobooks

As a general rule, the aesthetic quality of an aural artifact depends predominantly on the extent to which each individual institutional role successfully executes their job. That is to say, just as an aural performing artist is expected to deliver such recordings amid the confines and limitations of a predominantly aural medium, a designated audience, in turn, is expected to know how to listen and experience them, through their "mind's ear," amid similarly exclusive aesthetic boundaries. As playwright and poet William Alfred put it, "a great text makes its demand of

---

[53] Wittkower, "A Preliminary Phenomenology," 224–225.

[54] Carlson, *Performance*, 5.

[55] Roach, *Spoken Records*, 13.

truth on audience as well as performers: we must prepare to listen as they must prepare to read, by bringing ourselves to a reverent sense of that text's full nature."[56]

To be sure, just as certain objects may count as artworks without necessarily being aesthetically good, that certain recordings may count as aural artifacts (i.e., in complying with and, indeed, adhering to the general aesthetic category and overall "mother institution"), does not axiomatically prognosticate, *ceteris paribus*, their aesthetic quality. Even a particularly good text—one that may well constitute an acknowledged literary masterpiece in its own right—does *not*, alas, secure a good aural iteration.

Referring, for instance, to what at the time was the then "new crop" of spoken records released by the Caedmon record label, J. Peter Bergman asserts that while they all constitute great works of literature, they are "not all great aural literature, for not all the readers bring to our ears the best intentions of the authors they represent."[57] As Knox similarly points out, reviews by audiobook consumers appear to evoke so-called "narrator wars" by ultimately offering "buyer-beware" assertions concerning the "perils of making the wrong choice."[58]

"Truly great narrators," as far as Katherine A. Powers is concerned, "are a rare and wondrous thing: how they manage to distinguish between characters with such limberness, how they can—seamlessly and without apparent effort—change timbre, pitch, manner and accent from character to character."[59] As such, the very notion of there being "the wrong choice" entails that one is certainly able to distinguish it from more appropriate ones—or, indeed, "*the* right one." An argument could therefore be made that if one happens to engage with a particularly *bad* audiobook (i.e., aesthetically flawed), one might be tempted to altogether discard the genre itself and, regrettably, miss out on what this study considers to be an otherwise unique art form. As Powers quite rightly points out,

> Any devoted audiobook listener can attest: Spending nine hours (or more) in the company of a terrible reader—a shrieker, mumbler, droner, tooth whistler or

---

[56] William Alfred, preface to *Spoken Records*, v.

[57] J. Peter Bergman, "British Nostalgia/Spoken Word Issues," *Association for Recorded Sound Collections Journal* 13, no. 3 (1981): 133.

[58] Knox, "Hearing Hardy, Talking Tolstoy," 137.

[59] Katherine A. Powers, "Don't Let a Bad Reader Ruin Your Audiobook Experience: Here Are Recordings to Savor—And to Void." *Washington Post*, August 5, 2019, accessed December 19, 2022, https://www.washingtonpost.com/entertainment/books/dont-let-a-bad-reader-ruin-your-audiobook-experience-here-are-recordings-to-savor--and-to-avoid/2019/08/05/0750b980-ae2f-11e9-a0c9-6d2d7818f3da_story.html.

overzealous thespian—is an experience that can truly ruin a book. A narrator's voice is not merely a delivery system, an element extraneous to the text, but an integral one—fulfilling, enriching, injuring or sinking a book.[60]

In attempting to identify their distinct phenomenology, Wittkower maintains that audiobooks follow a "rhythm and pace" of their own, which resides "in between the starting and stopping of playback," and when one listens to an audiobook, it "proceeds at the same inexorable rate while the audience drifts in and out of attention."[61]

Roach similarly argues that an experienced listener can easily recognize various flaws in a performer's delivery: e.g., the intrusion their own states of being—such as laziness, shyness, resentment, indifference, or tiredness—or when they happen to be preoccupied with certain aspects of their craft, rather than focusing on what the text *requires*. As such, she asserts that "it takes supervised experience, much like that acquired in a chemistry lab, to develop the skill needed to bring life to material embalmed in print."[62] Roach, by her own admission, surveys recordings "on the basis of excellence in execution, literary or historic merit, interest and entertainment value," thereby aiming "to include those items which may prove to be of lasting value." She asserts that "looking hopefully towards the future, one can say that among the best spoken records today is an elite group which communicates more than [mere] entertainment."[63] This, to my mind, quite clearly indicates that Roach both identifies and calls for a hierarchy in spoken records as a genre—especially since one not only *can* evaluate certain aural artifacts as better than others, but, in fact, also *should*.

In the same vein, Mary Thompson—audiobook reviewer for *AudioFile*—explains that if she has not read the original work, or happens to be completely unfamiliar with its author, she customarily conducts a certain amount of research on that particular title. As she listens, she takes notes, attempting to identify any "special qualities" that the narration embodies. She pays particular attention, for example, to aspects such as whether or not (and, indeed, to what extent) the recording's voice successfully matches some overall emotion—or, conceivably, a limited *range* of emotions—that the narrative supposedly inhabits. She similarly examines aspects such as a performer's pronunciation proficiency, whether or not a he or she correctly conveys a particular character's accent, and the extent

---

[60] Ibid.

[61] Wittkower, "A Preliminary Phenomenology," 222.

[62] Roach, *Spoken Records*, 10–11.

[63] Ibid., 10; 13

to which he or she consistently preserves the particular voice with which they endowed a character. By her own admission, she also considers whether or not (and, indeed, to what extent) the aural medium itself either augments the original written material or rather conceivably detracts from it: that is, how do aspects such as the pacing of a particular recording—its overall flow, rhythm, and tempo—happen to affect her attention as a listener.

For Whitten, the main requirement that *AudioFile* has of its reviewers "is that the person is a passionate listener and an experienced listener," who should effectively "think about not just the story they're hearing, but they can think about, in a critical way, why is that making the experience moving, frightening—you know, all the emotional part—why are you responding to it, because that's part of the review process."[64]

Ultimately, as with any artistic product, aural artifacts cannot be evaluated precipitately. While perhaps particularly evident when engaging with canonical texts and existing well-recognized literary works (as they routinely present one with a number of different, comparable, iterations), the overall process itself can be said to consist of three primary stages:

First, attention must be paid to the nature and aesthetics of the *performance* in and of itself. (Drawing on the distinction between "art" and "not art," one could likewise discern between *performing* a text as opposed to merely reading it into a recording device). Next, one would consider the distinct properties, possibilities, and parameters that are established and prescribed by the confines of the aural medium. Finally, one is required to seek and find not only the unique internal logic inhabiting the aural performance, but also, inevitably, that which embodies the *original* text. Indeed, since the latter to a large extent determines the manner in which its aural iteration *should* be performed, it simply cannot be ignored or rendered irrelevant.

In this context, I would argue that when aesthetically evaluating abridgments, one should account for the internal logic of the aural performance that the recording inhabits—rather than for the nature, quality, or aesthetic properties of the abridgment itself, as an abridgment—without setting aside, discarding, or altogether ignoring the original, recognized literary work. (While this conceivably renders audiobooks a rather distinct phenomenon, one could also argue that it is precisely *that* work which would implicitly inform, contribute to, and underscore the particular aesthetics and overall internal logic of virtually any putative adaptation).

---

64. "Interview with Robin Whitten," 09m49sec–10m23sec.

CHAPTER THREE

Twain's *Huck Finn* and the First-Person Narrative as a Fundamental Property of the Audiobook

Where to Begin with *Huck Finn*

To aesthetically evaluate the audiobook versions of Mark Twain's *Adventures of Huckleberry Finn* (1884) as aural artifacts, it is necessary, first and foremost, to understand the internal logic that informs them—i.e., that of the novel itself. Yet purporting to present a rigorous and exhaustive reading of the entire novel could well prove counterproductive. Fundamentally, drawing on Derrida, to arrive at a single comprehensive reading of any text—to say nothing of an all-inclusive interpretation of any particular internal logic—is virtually altogether impossible. While one should be able to apply alternative provisional readings *ad infinitum*, only a *limited* number of readings would appropriately apply.

To be sure, any given text adheres to certain parameters—the ostensible bookends of its own internal logic—that ultimately prescribe a particular range of pertinent possible readings, beyond which one cannot go. If, however, one chooses to draw on one's artistic license to ostensibly encroach on the acceptable possibilities, one must make one's reasons for doing so abundantly clear. So-called unorthodox readings or interpretations conceivably present one with a new, or at least re-imagined, internal logic for consideration. As Algernon Tassin asserts, "the interpreter, like the creator, gives shape and expression to something which was there before but had hitherto existed unperceived by him."[1] In evaluating artworks that critique, violate, comment, or throw interesting light on the original work, one should appropriately consider the ostensibly newly instituted internal logic. Ultimately, however, the internal logic of the original

---

[1] Algernon de Vivier Tassin, *The Oral Study of Literature* (New York: Alfred A. Knopf, 1929), 20.

work—bookends and all—will forever inform any interpretation, including a performance *of* an already existing work. Thus, as a constant point of reference, one cannot completely cast it aside.

Although *Huck Finn* is customarily recognized as a masterpiece, there is no explicit property, facet, or attribute that can provide one with a luculent indication of what *the* internal logic of Twain's novel actually is. As Michael Patrick Hearn points out,

> No other living work of American literature has suffered so contradictory a history [...]. It has been called both a literary masterpiece and racist trash. It has been marketed as a gift book for boys and girls; it has been removed from the children's rooms of public libraries across the country. It is required reading in universities both in American and abroad; it is banned from the curricula of elementary and high school systems.[2]

There are, however, a number of inherently definitive attributes—constitutive shades of embodied meaning—that together imply what it supposedly *should* be. What follows is not my own personal analysis or interpretation of Twain's novel but rather a concise articulation of its most essential understandings and the various complexities that it evokes—recognized by different scholars and literature. These, in turn—echoing what R. Balmer regarded as the "full realization of what the printed book was intended to do"—would form the infrastructure for analyzing the novel's aural iterations.[3]

First, attention must be paid to the novel's status as an ostensible memoir or autobiography, which is critical for observing the dissonance that prevails between the identities and reputations of both its author and its narrator: on the one hand, Twain's mature, ironic voice—imbued with his social criticism of nineteenth-century America— and, on the other, the distinct voice of an adolescent Huck—the novel's first-person narrator, whose perception of the world he inhabits is considerably different from Twain's. Next, one must be mindful of the varying number of American dialects embedded in Twain's text—predominantly associated with, but certainly not restricted to, the controversies surrounding characterization of race in the novel, as well as explicit accusations of racial

---

[2] Michael Patrick Hearn, introduction to the Annotated *Huckleberry Finn*, in Mark Twain, *Adventures of Huckleberry Finn*, in *The Annotated Huckleberry Finn*, ed. Michael Patrick Hearn (New York: W. W. Norton, 2001), xiii.

[3] Rubery, *The Untold Story of the Talking Book*, 254.

insensitivities to which it has been subject since its publication. Although they may not necessarily constitute the novel's overall "meaning," these particular strands are constitutive of any attempt to read, grasp, or interpret it. As such, anyone who engages with *Huck Finn* should recognize that the novel functions amid these particular parameters. As critical constituents for comprehending the novel, they effectively establish the infrastructure for the overall internal logic around which any reading revolves. One should then consider and observe the manner in which these key facets operate amid any audiobook version of the novel. Finally, to aesthetically evaluate an aural artifact, one should examine whether or not—and, indeed, to what extent—it embodies and exhibits the internal logic that inevitably informs it.

Notes on the Plot

Huckleberry (aka "Huck") Finn is an American boy in his early teens, described as being "thirteen or fourteen or along there."[4] He is first introduced to the readers in Twain's own *The Adventures of Tom Sawyer* (1876) as the title character's best friend, where he is described as "the juvenile pariah of the village."[5] Set in the 1840s, and customarily regarded as a sequel, the events that unfold in *Huck Finn* occur about one year after those depicted in *Tom Sawyer*—concluding with Tom and Huck coming into a considerable sum of money, having found a stash of gold hidden by a group of robbers. In *Huck Finn*, having heard about his son's fortune, Huck's abusive, drunken father schemes to kidnap him and claim the money. Huck, in turn, resorts to escape by faking his own death. While in hiding, Huck encounters Jim—whom he recognizes as one of Miss Watson's slaves. Once Huck learns that Jim ran away, having heard her talking about selling him to a plantation, he decides to help Jim escape—effectively setting off their "adventures," traveling on a raft along the Mississippi River (an ostensible character in its own right).

Unlike the omniscient narrator with which he endowed *Tom Sawyer*, Twain purposely constructed *Huck Finn* as a first-person narrative account—told through the eyes and distinct point of view of Huck. While both novels prevail as works of fiction—existing as concrete objects in the world of the readers—*Huck Finn*,

---

[4.] Mark Twain, *Adventures of Huckleberry Finn*, in *The Annotated Huckleberry Finn*, ed. Michael Patrick Hearn (New York: W. W. Norton, 2001), 167.

[5.] Hearn, introduction to the Annotated *Huckleberry Finn*, 10.

from its inception, affirms not only Huck's awareness of the preceding novel but also his acknowledgment of the fact that *that* novel happens to concern him too. As such, Huck not only becomes the eponymous protagonist but also asserts responsibility for narrating his own story.

> You don't know about me, without you have read a book by the name of *The Adventures of Tom Sawyer*; but that ain't no matter. That book was made by Mr. Mark Twain, and he told the truth, mainly. There was things which he stretched, but mainly he told the truth. That is nothing. I never seen anybody but lied one time or another.[6]

Iconic author and journalist Ernest Hemingway once remarked that *Huck Finn* can be perceived as the quintessential modern American novel.[7] According to Stephen Railton, Twain's novel could similarly be perceived as the first *postmodern* American literary work. Indeed, Twain's self-referentiality was quite innovative, unique, and unconventional. Railton alludes to Jean Rhys's *Wide Sargasso Sea* (1966) as another first-person narrative that is delivered by a character from a completely different novel, namely, Charlotte Brontë's *Jane Eyre* (1847), explaining that Rhys's novel offers a radically different reading of Brontë, effectively reframing it to serve her own purposes.[8] Tom Stoppard's play *Rosencrantz and Guildenstern Are Dead* (1966) also comes to mind—as it is famously constructed around two characters who originally "belong" to Shakespeare's *Hamlet* (which in itself happens to include purportedly meta-allusions to the Bard's own *Julius Caesar*).

Perhaps the best comparison, however, can be found with the monumental novel *Don Quixote* (1605, 1615), by Miguel de Cervantes. Here, in its second volume, the readers are let in on the fact that the protagonists themselves are not only aware that a book had been written about them but also that it had achieved high acclaim and attention. (Tom's character even happens to explicitly allude to Cervantes' novel in Chapter 3).[9] In this context, an argument could be made that if, in *Tom Sawyer*, Huck's character might be an analogous Sancho Panza to Tom's Don Quixote, then, in *Huck Finn*, it is Huck who assumes the typical

---

[6.] Twain, *Adventures of Huckleberry Finn*, 9.

[7.] Ernest Hemingway, *The Green Hills of Africa* (New York: Charles Scribner's Sons, 1935), 22

[8.] Stephen Railton, *Mark Twain: A Short Introduction* (Oxford: Blackwell, 2003), 50.

[9.] Twain, *Adventures of Huckleberry Finn*, 41.

Quixote role, with Jim taking on that of Panza. The two essentially complete each other. Indeed, much like Quixote, who both requires Panza's companionship in order to continue his journey and, at the same time, is inherently confined to his own distinct perception of reality, Huck, too, both requires Jim as a so-called partner in crime and, simultaneously, remains a solitary figure and passive observer of the world he inhabits. Conceivably, Twain's characterization of the relationship between the two might be construed as an attempt to both re-enact and simultaneously satirize the particular camaraderie in classic European liter-ature. Hearn, in this respect, cites Olin Harris Moore's claim that "much of the dialogue between Tom and Huck over the matter of books is almost verbatim the regular argument between Don Quixote and his squire."[10]

In his introduction to the novel's 1950 edition, celebrated poet T. S. Eliot notes that nothing in *Tom Sawyer*—which he found to be a very good "boys' book," told by an adult narrator observing a boy—could have prepared him for *Huck Finn*:

> Tom is, I supposed, very much the boy that Mark Twain had been [...] Huck Finn, on the other hand, is the boy that Mark Twain still was, at the time of writing his adventures. [...] The two boys are not merely different types; they were brought into existence by different processes.[11]

While both boys perceive the world they inhabit through the eyes of children, their perspectives, and the manner in which they comprehend their surroundings, are depicted quite differently: Tom embodies a particular kind of childhood nostalgia, coupled with an explicit, adamant refusal to grow up. His outlook is shaped by books and stories, which effectively define both his actions and values. (He finds pirates and robbers, for instance, to be chivalrous and brave. Rather than fearing them, he aspires to join them). As far as Huck is concerned, however, Tom's view of reality is quite impractical. His own firsthand experi-ences have taught him that robbers are, in fact, customarily mean-spirited, stink of whiskey, and a better avoided. For Railton, in depicting the "stark actualities" of the world he inhabits, Huck's narrative—as a literary genre—embodies the rhythm of realism, as opposed to some romantic ideal.[12] For Eliot, in accepting

---

[10] Hearn, *The Annotated Huckleberry Finn*, 43n21.

[11] T. S. Eliot, "An Introduction to Huckleberry Finn," in *Huck Finn, Bloom's Major Literary Characters*, ed. Harold Bloom (Philadelphia, PA: Chelsea House, 2004), 18.

[12] Railton, *Mark Twain*, 52–53.

his world for what it is, and what it ostensibly delivers both unto him and unto others, Huck essentially becomes "more powerful than his world, because he is more aware than any other person in it."[13]

Huck Finn as First-Person Monologue

As an assumed autobiographical memoir, one could regard *Huck Finn* as an extended personal monologue. For the novel's aural iterations, this is no less than crucial. Performers—as pointed out to me by Claudia Howard, an American casting director and production manager at Recorded Books—tend to embrace first-person narratives more easily than third-person accounts. Conceivably, the more personal the narrative—or, rather, the more connected or involved a performer might find themselves—the more rewarding the aural performance could potentially be.

According to British casting director Patrick McQuaid, when confronted with a first-person narrative, a performer's objective is to ostensibly "become" that voice—which, he asserts, is inherently a "property" of the written text itself. In distinguishing between "voice" and "accent," he finds Solomon Northup's *Twelve Years a Slave* (1853) a good case in point, asserting that not many London-based actors are able to portray the distinctly Black American voice in which the novel is written. As a production manager at the American Foundation for the Blind (AFB) once put it, "Just as we would not ask a British actor to read a Zane Grey Western; at the same time, we would not ask someone with a Texas accent, for example, to read a novel by Charles Dickens."[14] For McQuaid, an audiobook iteration of this particular memoir requires a voice that is based more on the narrator's ethnic identity rather than on whether or not they happen to a good actor. As such, he argues that recording an audiobook employing any voice other than that which exists in the text would simply not have worked and, indeed, would not have complied with just how an audience is *supposed* to experience that particular work. Although McQuaid finds that some performers may be able to "fake it" to a certain extent, he concludes that it would be virtually impossible to sustain for the full duration of an entire reading—especially when it comes to such things as dialect, lilt, or a particular internal rhythm.

[13.] Eliot, "An Introduction to Huckleberry Finn," 18.

[14.] Rubery, *The Untold Story of the Talking Book*, 90.

Amid the confines of the aural medium, when an actual performer ostensibly "becomes" the text—virtually assuming the role of the narrating protagonist, speaking directly to a listening audience—a narrative takes on a distinctively personal quality. To paraphrase Knox, the novel, the protagonists it inhabits, and the narrator who animates and delivers them to the listener, together become *the* voice of an aural artifact. It, in turn, should embody the rationale that justifies its chosen narrator: Naxos, for example—to name but one of the leading labels in the audiobook market—predominantly adheres to the following rule of thumb: if a male author wrote the work, then a male narrator should record it. Notwithstanding, they quite wisely concluded that having Thomas Hardy's *Tess of the d'Urbervilles* (1891) narrated in its entity by a female voice is surely the only possible choice.[15]

In delivering his own story, Huck effectively asserts his own personal point of view, identity, and, indeed, authorship. As an aural artifact, Huck's narrative literally becomes a figurative testament to his own existence rather than the work of fiction that it actually is. His explicit objective is to re-tell (or, perhaps, un-tell) what had previously been told by Twain in *Tom Sawyer*. Supposedly well aware of the difference between true and false, Huck implies that although his narrative may consist of *his* truth, it also constitutes a somewhat "stretched" version thereof. Drawing on (or purportedly inspired by) his understanding of Twain's endeavor, Huck appears to have reached the conclusion that one simply cannot "make" a book without stretching certain truths—or, alternatively, that when telling one's own story, one perhaps cannot but lie, one way or another. While his introductory statements imply that he has no intention of lying to his readers (despite both fooling and misleading other characters he encounters in the novel), Huck does appear to deceive his readers, at least to some extent—which is most evident when one considers the fact that narrative is purportedly told after the fact, yet includes information that is supposedly unbeknownst to him (e.g., the fact that Jim—whom Huck endeavors to set free—had, in fact, already been legally set free by Miss Watson's last will and testament).

Notwithstanding, in affirming his role as the storyteller, Huck becomes an individual agency, using a distinct voice and overall tone that are separate from the said "Mr. Mark Twain." Thus, drawing on his firsthand experiences and observation to describe the reality of the world he inhabits, Huck is able to employ words and phrases that the renowned Mr. Twain cannot, and vice versa.

[15.] Knox, "Hearing Hardy, Talking Tolstoy," 138.

As Hearn points out, "Maybe Sam Clemens swore, but it is not in Huck Finn's nature […] to use profanity."[16]

On Correctly Enunciating Mispronunciations

Throughout the novel, Twain intentionally misspells words in order to convey the manner in which Huck himself *speaks* them as a first-person narrator, who also happens to be illiterate (so much so, in fact, that he is unable to write even his own name). From the get-go, Huck informs the readers that he was placed under the guardianship of the Widow Douglas. Together with her sister, Miss Watson, she attempts to teach Huck the Holy Scriptures and religion in an effort to "sivilize" him.[17] With an aural iteration, and perhaps especially if one is unacquainted with the novel, it is interesting to consider whether or not—and, indeed, to what extent—one might be able to literally *hear* that a word is misspelled.

To be sure, as with any artwork, one is tasked with the minimum responsibility of knowing what one is listening to—especially if one wishes to properly evaluate it—including, inevitably, the different tenets of what the novel's internal logic should be. Notwithstanding, it is also a performer's responsibility to successfully embody them in the performance. While one may not necessarily be able to make a word *sound* misspelled, one should be able to somehow indicate to a listener that *Huck's* pronunciation is ostensibly a bit "off."

Fundamentally, one should not confuse Huck's linguistic proficiency with that of Twain. Indeed, just as the omniscient narrator of *Tom Sawyer* adheres to the standard correct American English of an educated adult, Huck's first-person delivery in *Huck Finn* complies with a grammatically ill-constructed vernacular. Huck's illiteracy, in effect, eloquently exhibits Twain's remarkable semantic proficiency. According to Victor A. Doyno, Twain's deliberate choice to have an entire novel conveyed by a virtually illiterate agency enables Twain to explore that value of his own chosen art form.[18] Conceivably, the very notion of experiencing this particular novel as audiobook ostensibly bestows *Huck* with the opportunity of literally *telling* his story, in place of struggling with his inability

---

[16] Hearn, introduction to the Annotated *Huckleberry Finn*, xxxiii–xxxiv.

[17] Twain, *Adventures of Huckleberry Finn*, 9.

[18] Victor A. Doyno, *Writing Huck Finn: Mark Twain's Creative Process* (Philadelphia: University of Pennsylvania Press, 1991), 40.

to express it in writing. For Railton, not only can one identify Huck's voice as "vividly conversational," but one can also read his story as an oral narrative, to all intents and purposes.[19] As such, a good aural iteration could potentially amplify one's aesthetic experience of the novel itself.

In limiting the narrative to Huck's voice, Twain imposes a reading that requires one to consistently account for Huck's singular personal perspective in respect of the world he inhabits and the adults who surround him. Earnestness, integrity, and *naïveté* supposedly shine through not only what Huck tells his readers but also *how* he sees fit to tell. As one is drawn closer into Huck's own world, one seems to get the sense that he will surely spare his readers from any editing or stylization, thereby honestly presenting them with the raw unvarnished facts of the matter.

A particularly delicate balance prevails, however, between Huck's point of view and Twain's social criticism, wit, and biting satire: Huck's fictional first-person voice effectively embodies Twain's own literal and figurative voice. While Huck is evidently aware of Twain's existence, he is unaware that "his" story—conveyed to his perceived auditors—is in actuality a story that Twain wishes to tell us, *his* readers. (It is interesting to note in this respect that one of the novel's manuscripts reveals the words "Reported by Mark Twain" written in Twain's handwriting on the top of the first page).[20] The inherent interplay between the novel's two authoritative voices therefore ultimately prescribes the manner in which an aural iteration should be delivered. Explicitly, a performer would be required not only to quite literally portray Huck's character—thereby conveying the qualities of the novel as a pseudo-autobiography—but also to evince Twain's underlying authorship, criticism, and satire.

For Howard, the words on the page give rise to a visual image of a narrator's identity. Thus, to make sense of a particular casting choice, she must be able to *see* a picture of the narrator in her mind's eye. She argues that the human voice is able to conjure up this picture in a way that the written word alone simply cannot. In this respect, one might question whether the novel should be performed by a young performer or perhaps even child actor who is roughly the same age as Huck is in the book.

To be sure, this poses an important aesthetic conundrum. In facing the challenge of attaining a certain degree of authenticity, McQuaid explains that one

---

[19.] Railton, *Mark Twain*, 53.

[20.] Doyno, *Writing Huck Finn*, 40.

customarily begins by considering a narrative's particular form, and, subsequently, aims to identify the most appropriate performer to convincingly portray the voice it inhabits. However, as will later become quite evident, the available audiobook versions of the novel, almost invariably, feature mature performers.

Huck Finn Explains Itself

It has hitherto been established that audiobooks, as aural artifacts, evoke a unique and immersive aesthetic experience, and, as such should not substitute for engaging with the original work in print. Nevertheless, in contemplating the intricate relationship between reading and listening (and setting aside, momentarily, books that have been specifically recorded for the blind and the visually impaired—to which I shall duly attend in Chapter 4), it would seem that certain audiobooks and aural iterations, *can*, in fact—under certain circumstances—count as an alternative to actual reading, thus somehow providing one with something that the original printed work simply cannot.

It is precisely in this context that I find *Huck Finn* among those few exceptions that prove the general rule. Consider, for instance, the variety of quintessential American dialects and vernaculars that Twain deploys throughout the novel, as set up by his famous "Explanatory":

> IN this book a number of dialects are used, to wit: the Missouri Negro dialect; the extremest form of the backwoods South-Western dialect; the ordinary "Pike-County" dialect; and four modified varieties of this last. The shadings have not been done in a haphazard fashion, or by guess-work; but pains-takingly, and with the trustworthy guidance and support of personal familiarity with these several forms of speech.
>
> I make this explanation for the reason that without it many readers would suppose that all these characters were trying to talk alike and not succeeding.
>
> THE AUTHOR.[21]

The different regional dialects, accents, and speech patterns dispersed across the novel all reflect the varying levels of intellect, education, vernacular, and socio-economic status—as well as the gender, and, indeed, race of each individual

---

[21.] Twain, *Adventures of Huckleberry Finn*, 5.

character. Fundamentally, one is expected to identify the different types—to literally sound them out in one's mind's ear—by following Twain's construction of the words on the page. For an audiobook performer, the task of tackling the grammar, syntax, spelling, and so on could prove quite a challenge—one that is conceivably intensified as all the novel's characters are filtered through Huck's narration. As such, in conveying *his* story to the readers, Huck is to some extent obliged to ostensibly mimic the individual speech patterns of the various characters, effectively delivering his own rendition of what they sound like.

A performer thus seems to be required to choose whether to prescribe a different and distinct voice to each character, thereby distinguishing them on the listener's behalf. Alternatively, a performer might narrate the novel while sustaining a single and consistent vocal signature, appropriately emphasizing not only Huck's independent point of view but also the impression left on him by the various characters. At the same time, any aural iteration should be mindful of the fact that while the novel is supposedly delivered by Huck, it inevitably constitutes a work of fiction by Twain—whose unique voice as an author is, inevitably, an inherent property of its overall internal logic. As such, one should also consider whether or not (and, indeed, to what extent) Huck's delivery of the different regional dialects might, in fact, constitute Twain's satirized version thereof. Listeners should similarly consider whether or not (and, indeed, to what extent) an aural iteration successfully sounds out the required dialects, thereby exhibiting this particular aspect of the novel's overall internal logic.

What if, however, one is, for whatever reason, simply unable to identify these dialects off the printed page? Indeed, what if one happens to be, alas, unacquainted with what they *actually* sound like? To be sure, one's understanding of the novel in this case would be significantly impaired—to say nothing of one's ability to properly evaluate it. (Translation, too, in this respect, would similarly pose inherent problematics). Thus, if one is ill-acquainted with the different dialects or simply fails to properly identify them off the page or, indeed, if one endeavors to engage *Huck Finn* without fully understanding what one is *supposed* to hear in one's head, then one would ultimately be unable to distinguish the aesthetic quality of the audiobook version one is listening to. As such, one could very well miss out on precisely that which might also escape one when listening to a particularly flawed aural iteration of Twain's novel. *Ceteris paribus*, one who *is* acquainted with the different dialects and vernaculars that appear in Twain's text should be able not only to appropriately identify them off the page but also to determine whether or not (and, indeed, to what extent) a performer has successfully conveyed them amid the confines of an audiobook. A *good* audiobook version—that is, an aesthetically rewarding aural artifact, in which a performer correctly utilizes Twain's unique literary device—could therefore, potentially, serve as a possible substitute for reading the actual book, and, indeed, assist one in discerning the different dialects. Fundamentally, the audience of any artwork adheres to the minimum *responsibility* of understanding, at least to some degree, what the artwork they are presented with is all about. In the context of aural artifacts, just as the performer is expected to know how to deliver a particular given text, an audience, in turn, is expected to know how to listen and appropriately experience it.

Now, when one is confronted with more than a single audiobook iteration of a particular text (indeed, of any text), one should essentially undertake a comparative close listening to the different versions at one's disposal—even if this would merely add up to ostensibly skimming through the recordings. Granted, the average audiobook consumer does not customarily listen to more than one audiobook version of a given novel. Yet an argument could be made that just as one is able to enjoy viewing more than one staging of a particular play—or, perhaps more than one screen adaptation of the same original source material— one could likewise enjoy experiencing more than one aural iteration of the same book, and, potentially even enjoy comparing between the different available versions. Ultimately, and especially once having grasped what the internal logic of a particular work is (or, indeed, should be), one could potentially determine which particular version(s) might be deemed better than others—and, as such, worthy of investing one's time for the purpose of a rewarding aesthetic experience.

If, however, one is unable to identify for oneself the preferred version(s), one would require someone—that is, an expert—to suggest to them which version(s) one should listen to, effectively taking his or her evaluation "on trust." As previously mentioned, this is what one customarily does with most assertions about great artworks. An expert, for the purpose at hand, is an aficionado and connoisseur of a particular field and, indeed, the internal logic that both complies with and adheres to. Drawing to a large extent on Immanuel Kant, matters of personal taste—and perhaps explicitly in the context of aesthetics—are about as pertinent as the rogue misconception asserting that beauty is "in the eye of the beholder." Evidently, the conceivable clash between one's own personal taste and the need for an expert (to explain what makes a particular "something" a good example of its kind can be found in other) appears to unfold either in areas that are inherently rooted in one's cultural institutions or, alternatively, with various phenomena that necessitate an *acquired* taste.

For instance, in order to fully understand and appreciate what makes, say, a particular type of wine exceptionally good—again, regardless of one's own personal preference—one could certainly turn to a wine expert. Analogously, a football expert would no doubt be able to judge whether or not (and, indeed, to what extent) a certain player may have made a brilliant play, thereby essentially mastering the game. They could similarly be able to explain and evaluate what happened to make one match significantly better than others. A *bona fide* expert might not only be able to decipher these things in real time but also, in some cases, conceivably even foresee or anticipate a certain play moments before it actually occurs. While one would arguably choose to adopt experts whose evaluations sit well with one's own taste—e.g., following film reviews, book analyses, or art criticism that comply with what one actually likes (or perhaps even likes to hate)—personal taste in itself should not become a defining factor. Of course, given enough time, effort, and experience, one may gradually become an expert oneself—all the while broadening and fine-tuning one's particular palate.

Although it evidently addresses such issues as slavery in nineteenth-century America and the Civil War, and despite the ongoing controversies that surround it, *Huck Finn* remains to this day an exceptionally *funny* work of fiction. Appropriately, when considering the novel's aural iterations, attention must be paid to Twain's distinct sense of humor, implicit irony, satire, and unrivaled wit. To perform the novel—and, indeed, to perform it well—one cannot, therefore, be a stranger to comedy. At the very least, one must know how to tell a joke.

Consider the inclusion of the short "Notice" to the readers, preceding the aforementioned "Explanatory":

> PERSONS attempting to find a motive in this narrative will be prosecuted; persons attempting to find a moral in it will be banished; persons attempting to find a plot in it will be shot.
>
> BY ORDER OF THE AUTHOR,
> PER G. G., CHIEF OF ORDNANCE.[22]

This is, in fact, the first bit of text one is presented with. It certainly sets a particular tone for the novel as a whole—quite blatantly hinting at what is yet to come, conceivably providing one with ostensible guidelines for how to read Twain's

---

[22.] Ibid., 3.

satirical voice in between the lines. Its whimsical quality notwithstanding, the Notice does more than merely kid around with the readers. For instance, as far as Sacvan Bercovitch is concerned, the Notice itself constitutes a "deadpan directive" against interpretation, with "G.G."—the "deadpan connective"—linking together the author (i.e., Twain), the narrative (ostensibly written by Huck), the reader, and the (narrating) protagonist. At same time, Bercovitch finds that despite the explicit directive against doing so, the novel conceivably *demands* to be interpreted through and through.[23] As such, the particular manner in which the Notice subversively satirizes some authoritative "order" becomes paramount for interpreting the primary type of humor that Twain's novel embodies.

For Bercovitch, it is "Twain's deliberate and sustained use" of the "sinister" aspect of deadpan—which effectively "involves a drastic turnabout in deadpan effect, virtually a *reversal* of conventional techniques"—that consequently distinguishes the humor in *Huck Finn* from "generic deadpan":

> The novel is a great example of child-like, fun-filled wonder and a great work of social satire whose comic mode overturns the very tradition of deadpan it builds upon. Ostensibly that tradition belongs to the narrator-hero. Huck speaks "gravely" and often plays the Trickster; but the funny thing is, he's not a humorist, […] he rarely has fun […] and on the rare occasion when he does try to kid around (as when he tells Jim that the two of them were not separated in the fog), the joke turns back on itself to humiliate him. Huck has a stylized deadpan; his voice may sound comic to the comically disposed listener, but actually it's troubled, earnest. The nub or snapper behind that stylization, the humorous intent of *Huckleberry Finn*, the unusual twist to the joke—is directed against Huck's apparent deadpan. For of course the "teller" is really Mark Twain, the Comic Writer, and *this* deadpan artist is not straight-faced (as Huck is), but smiling. […] So here's the Trickster set-up, American-style, of *Huckleberry Finn*: the deadpan artist is Mark Twain, wearing the Comic Mask, doing his best to conceal the fact that he even dimly suspects that there's anything grave, let alone sinister, about his story—and he succeeds famously. Then, as we laugh, or after we've laughed, we may realize, if we're alert, that there's something we've overlooked. We haven't seen what's funny about the fact that we've found it all so funny. This Trickster has conned us, somehow diverted our attention away from the real point, and we have to go back over the story in order to recognize its nub. [emphasis in original][24]

---

[23] Sacvan Bercovitch, "What's Funny about *Huck Finn*," *New England Review* 20, no. 1 (Winter 1999): 12–13.

[24] Ibid., 9–10.

Ultimately, those three brief lines conceivably contain implied instructions for delivering Twain's comedy, indicating to the reader, from the get-go, precisely what should (and, indeed, what should *not*) be taken seriously. According to Hearn, Twain had originally chosen to write the Notice with the word "book" instead of "narrative."[25] Twain most likely chose the latter in order to reinforce the illusion of the novel as Huck's autobiography. To be sure, it is integral to the novel. For reasons that pass understanding, however, some audiobook productions have, alas, apparently opted not to include the Notice at all.

Although extrinsic to the novel, one can associate Twain's insights concerning the humorous story as literary form with an overarching literary voice that could well inform one's reading of *Huck Finn*. For an aural iteration, this could prove indispensable. Effectively underlining the seemingly simple fact that different types of story genres adhere to distinctly different ways of telling, Twain clearly distinguishes between the manner in which the *telling* of a story would appear on the page and the manner in which it should be delivered "by word of mouth." By his own admission, Twain does not presume to necessarily possess the required skills for telling a story properly but rather that he certainly does know and recognize "how a story ought to be told." He finds the humorous story, for instance, a "high and delicate art," inherently rooted in the "manner of the telling"—and, as such, he asserts that "only an artist can tell it; but no art is necessary in telling the comic and the witty story; anybody can do it".[26] Furthermore, Twain's distinction between his own ability to identify how a story ought to be told and his lack of ability in actually telling it also supports my aforementioned claim that an author—again, contrary to what one might be inclined to impulsively assume—is *not* the ostensibly ideal or perfect choice for narrating one's own work. (As alluded to earlier, this particular aspect of aural artifacts will be attended to later on in detail).

So, It's Funny, but Not *Ha-Ha* Funny?

In Chapter 32 of *Huck Finn*, Huck encounters the character of Sally Phelps, Tom's aunt. She mistakes him for her nephew, who was expected to have arrived

---

[25] Hearn, introduction to the Annotated *Huckleberry Finn*, 3.

[26] Mark Twain, "How to Tell a Story," in *How to Tell a Story and Other Essays* (New York: Harper and Brothers, 1898), 3–4.

via steamboat. In a famous passage, Huck plays along, assuming Tom's identity, and improvises an excuse to account for his tardiness:

> "We been expecting you a couple of days and more. What kep' you?—boat get aground?"
>
> "Yes'm—she—"
>
> "Don't say yes'm—say Aunt Sally. Where'd she get aground?"
>
> I didn't rightly know what to say, because I didn't know whether the boat would be coming up the river or down. But I go a good deal on instinct; and my instinct said she would be coming up—from down towards Orleans. That didn't help me much, though; for I didn't know the names of bars down that way. I see I'd got to invent a bar, or forget the name of the one we got aground on—or—Now I struck an idea, and fetched it out:
>
> "It warn't the grounding—that didn't keep us back but a little. We blowed out a cylinder-head."
>
> "Good gracious! anybody hurt?"
>
> "No'm. Killed a nigger."
>
> "Well, it's lucky; because sometimes people do get hurt. Two years ago last Christmas your uncle Silas was coming up from Newrleans on the old Lally Rook, and she blowed out a cylinder-head and crippled a man. And I think he died afterwards. He was a Baptist. Your uncle Silas knowed a family in Baton Rouge that knowed his people very well. Yes, I remember now, he did die. Mortification set in, and they had to amputate him. But it didn't save him. Yes, it was mortification—that was it. He turned blue all over, and died in the hope of a glorious resurrection. They say he was a sight to look at."[27]

Twain's satire, implicit in Huck's lie, is effectively diverted via Aunt Sally's response and overtly *nonchalant* manner in which she plunges into the story of uncle Silas. According to Bercovitch, the diversion constitutes an elaborate decoy on Twain's part, consequently alerting one to the nub of the joke, by way of Huck's throwaway line.[28] For an aural iteration, and even when reading the novel in print, the text itself appears to presuppose, and ultimately prescribe, not only the preferred form of delivery but also the desired manner of reception.

---

[27] Twain, *Adventures of Huckleberry Finn*, 350.

[28] Bercovitch, "What's Funny about *Huck Finn*," 17.

Originally, so it seems, Twain perceived of literature as a stiff and inflexible art form—one meant to entertain and not designed for speech. Yet having famously held popular public readings (consisting of memorized passages from his own work), he found the words have effectively "transformed themselves into flexible talk, with all their obstructing precisenesses and formalities gone out of them for good." Although urged to go on a solo tour (due to public demand), Twain felt unable to cope with the strain of sustaining an entire evening's performance. Consequently, he toured alongside his friend and contemporary, Southern novelist George Washington Cable: "a perfect partner for Twain, an experienced public speaker with a different aesthetic sensibility from Twain's. Cable could provide the pathos and Twain the Comedy."[29]

One public reading at Boston's Music Hall was attended by American writer Hamlin Garland (1860–1940), whom Hearn cites as being a student of "dramatic expression" at the time. In his notes, Garland describes Twain's stage presence and vocal qualities:

> Twain appears on the stage with a calm face and easy homelike style that puts all at ease [...]. His voice is flexible and with a fine compass. Running to very fine deep notes easily. He hits off his most delicious things with a raspy, dry, "rosen" voice. He has a habit of coughing drily that adds to his quizzical wit. [...] Never the ghost of a smile. Is an excellent elocutionist. Sighs deeply at times, with an irresistibly comic effect [...] Is altogether a man whom you would take for any thing but the funny man he is.[30]

Also present in that particular reading was Twain's long-time friend and liaison, American writer William Dean Howells (1837–1920). Twain, as Hearn points out, who "was generally open-minded about criticism of his writing, [...] had complete faith in Howells's literary advice." Drawing on an 1884 letter to Charles L. Webster, it would seem that Twain "had such faith in his friend's critical ability that" he readily afforded Howells' complete *"carte blanche"* to amend or correct his writing. As for Twain's live readings, Howells had reportedly found the passages from *Huck Finn* the most enjoyable. He is cited as letting Twain know how good he thought the book is and that while he believes everything Twain

---

[29] Hearn, introduction to the Annotated *Huckleberry Finn,* lvii; li–lii.

[30] Ibid., liv.

writes "is good for platform reading," he would certainly like to hear Twain read the novel in its entirety.[31]

Despite being praised by most reviews and generally adored by audiences—so much so that Twain and Cable often performed twice a day—in arguably consisting of an innovative and unconventional marketing ploy, these public readings were also criticized for conceivably degrading the literary status of Twain's writing.[32] In this respect, it would seem that the prevailing prejudice against audiobooks, attempting to tip the scales of aesthetic hierarchy in favor of printed books, is surely not a novelty. At the same time, one might also argue that the success of the live readings potentially puts forward an additional facet for consideration in respect of the novel's overall internal logic—effectively implying that Twain's work virtually extends an invitation to be read aloud.

Now, as a somewhat extended sidenote, it should be made clear at this point that public or "live" readings do not (and, for the most part, cannot) be properly classified as aural artifacts. As they were neither explicitly devised for the aural medium nor exclusively created within its distinctive aesthetic confines, they simply do not comply with the aesthetic category. This would also apply to the audio recordings thereof. Inevitably, an audio recording of a live performance constitutes nothing more than an aural documentation of a live event. To be sure, this does not in any way reflect on whatever performance or event happens to be captured on the recording—that is, in terms of its artistic quality, nature, and value. Any historical importance, scholarly attention, or nostalgic significance notwithstanding, such recordings cannot be aesthetically evaluated as aural artifacts.[33]

Hadley Cantril and Gordon W. Allport, in this respect, quite rightly distinguish between *seeing* a speaker deliver a public lecture as opposed to *hearing* that speaker on the radio. As far as the latter is concerned, they find that one is essentially "forced to grasp both obvious and subtle meanings" by relying solely on one's ears—thus reducing one's "cues for judging the personality of a speaker and for comprehending his meaning."[34] I would argue that their notion of "cues for judging" can be identified as an inherent aspect of what ultimately informs

---

[31.] Ibid., xxviii; xxx; liv.

[32.] Ibid., liii–lv.

[33.] Even if a live performance is predominantly text-based (e.g., works that might be defined as "text-sound art"—which will be addressed herein later on), the mere fact that it happens to take place in front of a live audience effectively alters the overall internal logic.

[34.] Hadley Cantril and Gordon W. Allport, *History of Broadcasting: Radio to Television* (New York: Arno Press, 1971), 10.

one's aesthetic appreciation. As such, one could conceivably pull on the thread of these "cues" as a means to begin to grasp a particular work's overall internal logic.

By way of illustration, consider, e.g., Monty Python's *Cheese Shop* sketch, and compare the studio-recorded album version from the troupe's *Matching Tie and Handkerchief* (1973) as opposed to the original version, which first aired on their revolutionary television series, *Monty Python's Flying Circus* (1969–1974). Although both versions feature the talents of the same performers—John Cleese and Michael Palin—essentially delivering the same sketch, these two versions differ significantly: first and foremost, in the interaction between Cleese and Palin—whose rhythmic "ping-pong" exchanges and overall timing are notably faster on the album version; second, the lack of a studio audience. Consequently, in complying with particular requirements—and, indeed, limitations—of the aural medium, both Cleese and Palin were required to appropriately adjust their performance and delivery.

So, *Ehm*, It's Mentioned How Many Times?

For the most part, *Huck Finn* is widely recognized as Twain's masterpiece. At the same time, however—and, in fact, to this day—the novel's prestige, repute, and, indeed, status with regard to the Western literary canon is quite often challenged and put forward for reconsideration.

As mentioned previously, *Huck Finn* customarily provokes copious criticism not only due to the purported moral impropriety of its use of language but also in light of an alleged insensitivity to stereotypes—which some have consequently construed as unapologetically racist in its core. One can similarly raise quite a handful of objections pertaining to the novel's purported lack of sensitivity pertaining to gender, politics, and the particular socio-cultural *milieu* that it chronicles. (Indeed, the depiction of White American Southerners, for instance, as ignorant and dim-witted sparked many reservations, controversies, and debates). Violence, too, which ostensibly afflicts the novel's content, might appear needlessly ostentatious and uncompromising. Yet it is arguably the novel's unfolding of a companionship between an adolescent White boy and an adult Black male that has invariably caused the most sense of alarm, fluster, and unease among readers and critics alike—ultimately leaving one with a type of agitation that could, for want of a better analogy, be akin to intense personal itching.

While one can surely sympathize with the concerns that abound it, the question of whether or not (or, indeed, to what extent) the novel might be classified as racist is altogether a different type of concern. It is, in fact, a *moral* dilemma, which transcends the scope of the study at hand. The question of accepting, validating, and, indeed, celebrating such a novel—that is, if one were to go so far as to demonstrate precisely why and how the novel *is* racist—would similarly constitute a conundrum of virtues, effectively necessitating a deep-dive exploration into the role of ethics in the realm of aesthetics. Inevitably, the problematics associated with issues of race, identity, and cultural insensitivities inherently resonate amid the novel's overall internal logic. As such, when one engages with (or, indeed, sets out to *create*) an audiobook version of *Huck Finn*, one should neither discard nor ignore these contemplations. Quite the contrary. Even if they merely remain hovering in the background of one's consciousness, they should be reflected upon, and, indeed, accounted for. Nevertheless, the novel's status as a legitimate and significant work of literature should not—conceivably, *cannot*—be questioned (and especially when drawing on NITA in an attempt to ascertain the particular institutional circumstances that render it a novel to begin with).

In this respect, one simply cannot choose to turn the proverbial blind eye to the fact that the novel is quite literally scattered with what the current trend in political correctness dictates one to allude to as the "N-word." To be precise, the abhorrent word appears, in full, no less than 219 times.[35] This fact alone has prompted some school authorities to exclude Twain's book from their curriculum—including the Mark Twain Intermediate School of Fairfax, Virginia. Moreover, the perceived offense caused by the explicit use of the N-word was so overwhelming that Twain's novel had even received a number of "N-word–devoid" publications. One such version was edited in 1982 by a teacher named John Wallace; another was edited by a professor of English named Alan Gribben and published in 2011 by NewSouth Books. Both these particular versions—in what can also be identified as a somewhat grotesque misunderstanding of the novel's internal logic—went so far as to replace the N-word with the word "slave." Nevertheless, to remove that word from the novel altogether—and, all the more so, deliberately replacing it with another—could, conceivably, underpin the misinterpretation of its use, rather than reinforce its ill-reputed offensive connotation.

For acclaimed American novelist Toni Morrison (1931–2019), to discard or replace the N-word in *Huck Finn* constitutes "a purist yet elementary kind of censorship designed to appease adults rather than educate children." It is, as far as

---

[35.] Julie Bosman, "Publisher Tinkers with Twain," *New York Times*, January 4, 2011, accessed December 19, 2022, http://www.nytimes.com/2011/01/05/books/05huck.html.

she is concerned, but a "band-aid solution" that restricts not only the offense that word "would occasion for black students" but also "the corrosive effect it would have on white ones." She recounts that having chosen Twain's novel quite arbitrarily, reading it as is—without guidance, articulation, or elucidation—her initial engagement with the work made her feel deeply disturbed, fearful, and alarmed. It was only when she re-read the novel, having acquainted herself with different theories, scholarships, and analyses (e.g., Leslie Fiedler and Lionel Trilling—who had essentially ignored, or rather trivialized, that which made her feel ill at ease to begin with) that Morrison understood the importance of placing the novel within a particular context and set of circumstances: that is, a distinct American geography and consciousness, amid which what is now (in the twenty-first century) irrefutably and unequivocally offensive, was once (in the 1840s) a standard colloquial phrase, commonly used by both Whites and Blacks alike. This, by her own admission, rendered the task of tackling the novel far more durable for Morrison and consequently made for a considerably enhanced and, indeed, rewarding aesthetic experience.[36] It can thus be determined that Twain does not employ the N-word in *Huck Finn* as a racial slur but, rather, as an ironic elementary component of Huck's regional dialect. It would therefore be both misinformed and misleading to confuse Huck's point of view with Twain's own personal sentiments or the very value system he was, in fact, satirizing. As essayist Russell Baker puts it,

> The people Huck and Jim encounter on the Mississippi are drunkards, murderers, bullies, swindlers, lynches, thieves, liars, frauds, child abusers, numbskulls, hypocrites, windbags and traders in human flesh. All are white. The one man of honor in this phantasmagoria is "Nigger Jim," as Twain called him to emphasize the irony of a society in which the only true gentleman was held beneath contempt.[37]

To be sure, it has well been established that words do not effectively function as semi-trailers or homing pigeons that ostensibly carry and transport their distinct particular meaning where'er they might go. Rather, it is ultimately one's intention that bestows a discrete meaning on a certain word, amid a particular given context. To willfully cause offense, one would, *ergo*, be required to purposefully utilize and

---

[36.] Toni Morrison, *"Huckleberry Finn*: An Amazing, Troubling Book," in *Ethics, Literature, and Theory: An Introductory Reader*, ed. Stephen K. George (Lanham, MD: Rowan & Littlefield, 2005), 279–280.

[37.] Study Guide: *Huck Finn, Steppenwolf Theatre Company* p. 38. [While no longer available online, a digital copy can be sent upon request via Steppenwolf Education: accessed April 29, 2024, https://www.steppenwolf.org /education-and-engagement/steppenwolf-field-trip-series/study-guides/].

provide a word with that intention in mind. (To a certain extent, one might also conceivably consider the relationship between words and their meaning in the same vein as the relationship between brute and institutional facts). In this respect, by allowing Huck to narrate *his* own story, Twain conceivably gives himself license to utter certain things that he would otherwise not have been able to say. Therefore, to employ any other word in place of the unadulterated N-word would arguably falsify Huck's distinct voice. While it obviously involves much more than semantics or wordplay, and interesting as it may be to further explore whether or not one might regard such versions of the novel as censured—or even to identify them as proper "versions" of the novel at all—much like the aforementioned questions of morality and ethics, this, too, extends beyond the particular scope of my study. As it inevitably constitutes an innate and incidental aspect of the world Huck inhabits, any aural iteration—as an ostensible vehicle for narrating his own story, in his own voice, as the moral heart of the novel—should not shy away from employing the word as is. As alluded to earlier, a good aural artifact should also be able to ostensibly tread a tightrope by similarly serving as a vehicle for Twain's voice, embodying his implied (and, indeed, explicit) criticism—which, for a reader, all reside in between the lines.

In the PBS documentary, *Born to Trouble: Adventures of Huck Finn* (2001), exploring the controversy surrounding the novel, a high school English teacher explains why she simply does not say the word aloud in class. She is thus overtly conscious that the very utterance of the word—even amid the specific context of a learning environment—could cause offense. As such, while seeing the word itself on the printed page may cause one to feel ill at ease, actually hearing it uttered aloud could be construed as even more offensive and disconcerting. Morrison, in this respect, explains that "to hear the dread word spoken, and therefore sanctioned" when she read Twain's novel in the eighth grade was embarrassing enough. To read it hundreds of times in print may have bored and annoyed her, yet did not disturb her composure.[38]

I am reminded of a roundtable review of Spike Lee's *BlacKkKlansman* (2018), conducted on *What the Flick?!*, in which American film critic Tim Cogshell notes that

> You'll note that the word we insist on calling "the N-word" is used in this movie probably about 400 times. [...] Although, in reality, if we're paying attention, the word that we often call "the N-word" is never used in this movie. The word used in this movie is N.I.G.G.E.*R*. Hard *R.* Every single time. That other word,

---

[38.] Morrison, *"Huckleberry Finn,"* 280.

that you hear in Hip-hop music, is never used in this movie, not one time. It's a little thing, but it's a thing that I know that he [Spike Lee] knows—and it's a thing that I know that he knows that Black folks are going to be paying attention to very, very closely. And he got it right.[39]

American actor–writer Shamrock McShane—who had self-released his aural iteration online—recounts that when he used to teach the novel to students of various ages, he opted to substitute the N-word for the word "slave." Nevertheless, he asserts,

> What I was doing to Twain was unconscionable. But I rationalized it by informing the class that every time we came to that word, I was going to pause, and pointedly say "slave"—and the students should look closely at the N-word in the text and note the difference. Slave and the N-word are in no way synonyms. The N-word was produced, invented to de-humanize: to turn a human being into something less than human—not just an inferior being, but an inferior entity.[40]

By his own admission, McShane had been reading, studying, and teaching *Huck Finn* for some time when it dawned on him that there was nothing to obstruct him nowadays from "democratizing technology" and effectively recording his own audiobook version of Twain's novel. Thus, he goes on to say that

> The instant I read the book aloud for the first time saying aloud the N-word, the difference was chilling. If you read a novel aloud, even if there's no one in the room with you—let alone an audience of listeners worldwide—*you* become that narrator. You split into two: you are both reader and narrator; you are Huck Finn. You are not Mark Twain—Samuel Clemens was Mark Twain; Hal Holbrook was Mark Twain—*you* are Huck Finn, saying the N-word, hearing the N-word everywhere you go. Living with the N-word, with no escape from the N-word. It not only changes the tone of the novel, it changes everything. It's as if Twain constructed each chapter around the N-word, considering each situation, it's timing, it's placement, it's repartition—or, out of nowhere, like a single striking blow. It is the drumbeat of the novel.[41]

[39.] See URL: "REVIEW: Spike Lee's 'BlacKkKlansman,'" accessed December 19, 2022, https://www.youtube.com/watch?v=ht4RnEjBzqA, 06m36sec–07m12sec.

[40.] See URL: accessed December 10, 2022, https://soundcloud.com/shamrockmcshane/huck-finn-foreword, 03min32sec–04min13sec.

[41.] Ibid., 05min52sec–07min00sec.

It would seem that just as Morrison evidentially required a number of close read-ings to identify the particular context that Twain's novel adheres to, one would likewise need to ascertain the particular context that justifies hearing the word spoken aloud amid the confines of an audiobook version. Effectively replacing the N-word—merely because one might be more offended when hearing it spo-ken aloud—is quite simply not a good enough reason. As Morrison recounts,

> The source of my unease reading this amazing, troubling book now seems clear: an imperfect coming to terms with […] Huck Finn's estrangement, soleness and morbidity as an outcast child; the disproportionate sadness at the center of Jim's and his relationship; and the secrecy in which Huck's engagement with (rather than escape from) a racist society is necessarily conducted. It is also clear that the rewards of my effort to come to terms have been abundant. […] What [*Huck Finn*] cannot be is dismissed. It is classic literature, which is to say it heaves, manifests and lasts.[42]

Inevitably, Huck's perception of the world he inhabits is directly rooted in his nurture and education. In absorbing and internalizing the mindset, politics, and ideology shaping the culture that raised him, the notion of African American slaves being the rightful property of their owner—prior to the Emancipation Proclama-tion—was almost second nature to Huck. This, I find, is precisely what a reader would (quite intelligibly) find offensive, disturbing, and, indeed, unconscionable.

In one of the novel's pivotal passage, Huck makes both a conscious and a conscientious resolution, namely, that he would rather "go to hell" than turn Jim over to Miss Watson. His words eloquently exhibit the profound contrast between what he had always accepted as the simple truths of how things supposedly are and the truths that he gradually grew to know as how things ought to be. Put simply, he realizes that Jim is not merely a runaway slave but is also a person:

> I about made up my mind to pray […] But the words wouldn't come. […] It was because my heart warn't right […] I was trying to make my mouth *say* I would do the right thing and the clean thing, and go and write to that nigger's owner and tell where he was […] At last I had an idea; and I says, I'll go and write the letter—and then see if I can pray. […] I felt good and all washed clean of sin for the first time I had ever felt so in my life, and I knowed I could pray now. […] But somehow I couldn't seem to strike no places to harden me against him, but

---

[42] Morrison, "*Huckleberry Finn*," 287–288.

only the other kind. I'd see him standing my watch […] so I could go on sleeping […] and do everything he could think of for me, and how good he always was; and at last I struck the time I saved him by telling the men we had small-pox aboard, and he was so grateful, and said I was the best friend old Jim ever had in the world […] and then I happened to look around and see that paper. […] I took it up, and held it in my hand. I was atrembling, because I'd got to decide, forever, betwixt two things, and I knowed it. I studied a minute, sort of holding my breath, and then says to myself: "All right, then, I'll go to hell"—and tore it up.[43]

Evidently, Twain endows Huck with an instinctive sense of right and wrong—indeed, an intuitive heart, if you will—allowing him to re-evaluate the moral code of his culture.[44] While fully accepting that his actions may very well consign him to damnation, he nonetheless makes the choice of going there on his own terms. It would be interesting to evaluate the manner in which a performer would convey Huck's resolution in an aural performance. If this particular passage can be identified, for instance, as an ostensible point of departure in which Huck's character undergoes a discernible change (i.e., with respect to his point of view and his observation and perception of the people he subsequently encounters), one would be required to examine whether or not (and, indeed, to what extent) a performer succeeds in delivering that change. Conceivably accounting for a possible distinctive change in the tone of Huck's narration—that is, if he *sounds* (in print) more mature than before—that change should also be exhibited amid the confines of an audiobook.

Audiobooks, Audiobooks, Everywhere, Nor Any Drop to Drink

The number of commercially available audiobook versions of *Huck Finn* is quite extensive. According to Knox,

That there is such a variety of unabridged recordings of a single work (particularly of those no longer under copyright) facilitates the consumption of multiple productions of a work, even if it does not assume it. […] The "hear-over" is

---

[43.] Twain, *Adventures of Huckleberry Finn*, 345.

[44.] Arnold Weinstein, "*Huckleberry Finn*—A Child's Voice," Lecture #39, *Classics of American Literature* (*The Great Courses*, The Teaching), accessed December 19, 2022, https://www.thegreatcourses.com/courses/classics-of-american-literature.html.

something the audiobook listening experience implicitly invites. If […] the narrator assumes a significant presence—is the body as well as the soul of the reading—then a listener discovers not only a new text but forms the (one-sided, admittedly) acquaintanceship with the new speaker. If [Michael] Bull's concept of "accompanied solitude" holds true, then part of what it implies is that that the narrator's presence is—for a period—that of companion, and one accordingly meets a new reader of the same text with interest.[45]

Apparently, by the 1990s, one could hear the novel read by Ed Begley, Dick Cavett, Jackie Cooper, David Crawford, Alfred Gingold, Hal Holbrook, Robert Lewis, Hiram Sherman, Peter Thomas, and Jack Whitaker.[46] Nowadays, one finds both abridged and unabridged iteration, as well as professional and non-professional readings (e.g., recordings created by amateur narrators or volunteer readers). The latter, as shall be explained in Chapter Four, principally *cannot* constitute aural artifacts. What's more, aside from various cast-recordings (which are more akin to radio-dramatizations), one may also come across audiobook versions of non-English translations of the novel (which, as Frank Morgan's Gatekeeper noted to Judy Garland's Dorothy, surely constitute "a horse of a different color").

Now, for the purpose of the study herein, I have surveyed close to sixty aural iterations. Listed alphabetically, in the order of the performer's surname, these recordings feature Henry Adams, Matt Armstrong, Thomas Becker, Tim Behrens, Jason Damron, Parzaan Dastur, Brandon deWilde, Denny Delk, Norman Dietz, Jim Donaldson, Eric G. Dove, William Dufris, Robin Field, Patrick Fraley, William Fortier, Grover Gardner, Will Geer, Geoffrey Giuliano, John Greenman, Don Hagen, Garrick Hagon, Michael A. Harding, B. J. Harrison, Johnny Heller, Richard Henzel, Chris Hendrie, Dick Hill, Theo Holland, Lee Howard, Jim D. Johnston, Bob Karper, Garrison Keillor, Jim Killavey, Sam Kusi, Jack Lemmon, Mike McShane, Shamrock McShane, Robin Miles, Alan Munro, Kevin O'Brien, John O'Connell, Nathan Osgood, Sharon Plummer, Michael Prichard, Rebecca K. Reynolds, Roberto Scarlato, Kerry Shale, Lawrence Skinner, Mark F. Smith, Matthew Taylor, Stephen L. Vernon, Will Wheaton, Trevor White, and Elijah Wood.

Interestingly enough, Gardner—a celebrated and accomplished narrator, who has been recording audiobooks since the early 1980s—is known to have narrated several titles under the pseudonyms "Alexander Adams" and "Tom

---

[45] Knox, "Hearing Hardy, Talking Tolstoy," 138–139.

[46] Rubery, *The Untold Story of the Talking Book*, 254.

Parker." As another slightly expanded parenthetical sidenote, one might well ponder over the reason why audiobook narrators might require pseudonyms at all: e.g., could it be a creative way to distinguish between genres or different publishers? Or is it perhaps due to certain *risqué* content that a narrator may not feel too comfortable being associated with? Gardner, evidently, is not the only one: Wanda McCaddon, for instance, has recorded many audiobooks under the name of "Nadia May"; Simon Vance has been cited as both "Richard Matthews" and "Robert Whitfield"; and Jennifer Mendenhall is probably more commonly known to audiobook listeners by the alias "Kate Reading." The list, so it seems, goes on and on. In a cordial response to an online discussion thread on this very topic, Vance himself writes:

> So, let me jump in here and explain why I, and probably most of the long-term narrators in that initial list, might be found to have narrated under different names [...] When I came to the US it was standard policy for narrators to have different names for different publishers—apparently it was a hangover from when each publisher liked to have their own "team" of voices. The late David Case explained this to me at the time (he was aka Frederick Davidson). So I decided (in my innocence and/or naivete) to adopt a different pseudonym for each publisher I worked with [...] deciding that if I really sucked at narration it wouldn't affect my fledgling acting "career" here on the west coast. No, really. :) I became Robert Whitfield for Blackstone Audiobooks and Richard Matthews for Books on Tape [...] Random House (sadly) dropped quite a number of my "Matthews" books as they did many other narrators' when they absorbed BoT and have never bothered to rename what's left—go to Audible and you'll find 80 of Whitfield's and 17 of Matthews' (which, with the other 480 under my own name, makes me the most prolific narrator on Audible, I believe).[47]

Karen White, who has been narrating audiobooks since 1999, contributes her own insights:

> Just wanted to weigh in with my personal view on this. I did use a pseudonym for my first few romance titles as it was suggested by the publisher. But then I realized that doing that was actually doing a disservice to my career, as it meant that fans wouldn't be able to find or follow me to other genres. I do understand

---

that some narrators who do a lot of children's titles as well as more adult material might want to keep these worlds separate, so that kids or parents might not
end up overly shocked when they do a search for more work by their favorite
bedtime story narrator :)[48]

Nevertheless, a response by a person identifying themselves as "Jeremy" seems
to paint a different picture. Claiming to have heard about a discussion thread via a
private narrator's Facebook group, he asserts that certain "outed" narrators—many
of whom featured on the lists perpetuated in the thread—still find it problematic:

Hi everyone. Before anyone asks, I did indeed join this group to comment on
this thread. I am a narrator of erotica and romance under one pseudonym, and
a narrator of other fiction under another. I've even done a few religious titles
under a third! [...] With some sleuthing, you could probably find out who I am,
my real name, and my three pseudonyms. If you do, great! I'd like to hope it's
because you're a fan and you want to hear more titles. But please don't post it
on a public forum. I think some folks here might not understand the reason some
narrators, including myself, prefer to have anonymity with their pseudonyms.
Because it can cost us our jobs. [...] Some authors are more conservative than
others, and if the estate of *insert famous children's book author here* found
out about my erotica pseudonym, guaranteed I could lose titles. That's why we
do it, and that's why this thread is dangerous. [...] I'd say about 80% of narrators (myself included) are actors, on stage, and in movies and television. [...]
Audiobooks are my ONLY source of income for the foreseeable future. Please
help us keep the work we can get.[49]

Notwithstanding, for reasons I have not been able to unearth, Gardner appears
to have recorded *two* separate versions of *Huck Finn*—one under his own name
in 1994 (in which the Explanatory is inexplicably featured *before* the Notice)
and another one as Parker in 2014. Although they are quite similar in nature,
one is nonetheless able to identify the ways in which they are certainly not
identical.[50]

[48.] Ibid., 2.

[49.] Ibid., 4.

[50.] Twain, *Adventures of Huckleberry Finn*, narrated by Grover Gardner (Audio Book Contractors, 1994); and
Twain, *The Adventures of Huckleberry Finn*, read by Tom Parker (Blackstone Audio, 2014).

Where to Begin Listening to *Huck Finn*

According to Powers, the numerous audiobook versions of *Huck Finn* have "attracted admirable readers and only a few bunglers." Among those she identifies as the "excellent versions" (which she lists without providing an extended analysis) are the narrations by Vernon, Gardner, Munro, and Johnston.[51] While I agree with Powers that Johnston's iteration is among the better performances available, I find that the Vernon and Munro versions, as will presently be explained, constitute "good bad-examples" of this particular novel as an aural artifact. Nevertheless, I wholeheartedly concur with Powers about Gardner/ Parker, whose work on *Huck Finn* is quite a remarkable achievement. Ranking as one of the most celebrated professionals in this business, Gardner himself, in discussing his work, explains,

> You have to put yourself in the author's shoes, because the author has a specific plan or methodology that will be of tremendous benefit to their specific audience. Then, as the narrator, you have to create that specific audience, and I imagine an audience hungry for spiritual information. I commit to each point of view during the recording to make it interesting and instructive. [...] When I step into the booth at 10 a.m., I have to step into my narrator persona, which, as neutral as it may be, is still a persona, an attitude, an approach I take to the work. I'm not Grover Gardner, I'm the narrator; this view helps me stay consistent and keeps the work interesting.[52]

To be sure, this clearly demonstrates his own understating that one should appropriately adhere not only to what the medium requires but also to the text itself. Molly Fitzpatrick's 2018 piece for the *Village Voice* also includes important insights from Gardner pertaining to the realm of audiobooks, as well as the prevailing relationships between both a narrator and the material, and a narrator's voice and his or her listeners:

> When Grover Gardner goes to work, there are certain things he can't wear. No watches. No jewelry of any kind. No starched shirts. No starched anything.

---

[51] Powers, "Don't Let a Bad Reader Ruin Your Audiobook Experience."

[52] "Talking with Grover Gardner," *AudioFile*, accessed December 19, 2022, https://www.audiofilemagazine.com /narrators/grover-gardner/.

Nothing that could rustle, click, rattle, or otherwise make noise. "I kind of look like a bum much of the day," he says. […] In spite of all of Gardner's accolades, and as intimate as the reader-listener relationship can be, he's well aware that you probably don't know his name. And, in fact, he prefers it that way. […] "I'm glad you forgot who I am, and that you thought the book was terrific, because that's my job." […] For Gardner, every project begins, unsurprisingly, with reading the book in question, and with detailed visualization of the characters and events described therein. [...] "If you act out the performance in your head, that's what the listener is going to hear," Gardner explains. That acting extends to movement within the recording booth […], vital even though unseen by his audience—for instance, shifting from one side to another while embodying each of two characters in the midst of an animated conversation, or gesturing angrily to punctuate an argument. […] "Being consistent with your energy and your sound through that long a book, over that long a period of time, that's important. You don't want it to sound like it took you forever to record it. You want it to sound like you sat down and read it." Unlike a stage performance, for which projection is a must, Gardner's work doesn't require him to be quite so precious about the condition of his vocal cords, although he is reasonably wary of high-volume conversations in noisy bars and the scourge that is the common cold. But he repeatedly emphasizes that audiobook narration is a physically demanding job. [...] Even seasoned voiceover artists will find that audiobooks are a "completely different" discipline. "If you're coming from a context where the point is to call attention to your voice, to grab the listeners' ear—*Tomorrow, big sale!*—that doesn't work in audiobooks," Gardner explains. "If I'm listening to the sound of your voice, I'm missing the book. The word that we use a lot in the business is 'transparency.' You want people to forget. You want to disappear into the book." He cites a producer friend's rule of thumb for evaluating audiobook auditions: If, thirty seconds after hitting play, she's engaged in the story, that's good. If she's still thinking about the sound of the narrator's voice, that's not good. […] "You're not just the narrator. You're the director, you're the scenic artist, you're the set designer, you're the choreographer," Gardner says. "You're the casting director, because you get to pick who all these people are and how they should sound. In no other part of the acting profession do you have as much control over your approach to the material. ["][53]

[53.] Molly Fitzpatrick, "Portrait of the Voice in My Head," *Village Voice*, May 30, 2018.

Notwithstanding, of all the various—and, indeed, varying—talents mentioned herein, I find the Norman Dietz narration to be one of the best aural iterations of Twain's novel.[54] First and foremost, Dietz stands out as a masterfully engaging narrator. His vocal properties—cadence, tone, timbre, and texture—all make every word resonate loud and clear, consistently amplify the immediacy of the audiobook as an aural artifact. It is almost as if one cannot take one's ears off him. Right from the got-go, he successfully draws one into Huck's telling of his own personal story—which, as has been established, quite literally constitutes the voice of the novel. By eloquently endowing Huck's first-person narrative with a distinctly intimate speech pattern, rhythm, and inflection, Dietz's portrayal of the character shines through as sympathetic and believable, without judgment or criticism—and, equally crucial, without distracting from Twain's underlying perspective. This achievement can be attributed to the endeavors of but a few narrators.

It is interesting to note that although both the Dietz and Michael Prichard narrations are complete and unabridged, their recordings are not the same length: Dietz's runs over 11.5 hours, and Prichard's lasts about 10.5 hours. The latter, however, appears to feel and sound much *slower*.[55] This effectively demonstrates that a performer's sense of timing, or their desired pace and rhythm, have little to do with a particular recording's actual running time. As such, even narrations that require a substantial listening investment of their designated audience can certainly remain both riveting and vivid.

Arguably more than any other narrator in the bunch, Dietz's rendition exhibits his remarkable capabilities as storyteller who is not only aware of his audience, but, in fact, *requires* them. This, to all intents and purposes, ultimately makes for a most rewarding and immersive aesthetic experience. Indeed, as Whitten points out, "a lot of what audiobooks do in a really amazing way is the storytelling."[56]

Dietz—as opposed to, say, American storyteller and radio personality Garrison Keillor[57]—does not rapidly rush though the text; and—unlike Prichard, or for that matter, Thomas Becker, Roberto Scarlato, and Geoffrey Giuliano[58]—he

[54] Twain, *The Adventures of Huckleberry Finn*, narrated by Norman Dietz (Recorded Books, 1980).

[55] Twain, *Adventures of Huckleberry Finn*, read by Michael Prichard (Books on Tape, 1977).

[56] "Interview with Robin Whitten," 29m12sec–29m20sec.

[57] Twain, *Adventures of Huckleberry Finn*, [abridged], adapted and read by Garrison Keillor (HighBridge Audio, 1996).

[58] See: Twain, *The Adventures of Huckleberry Finn*, read by Thomas Becker (In Audio, 2003); *Adventures of Huckleberry Finn*, read by Roberto Scarlato (Lukeman Literary Management, 2019); and *The Adventures of Huckleberry Finn*, [abridged], presented by Geoffrey & Eden Giuliano (Icon Audio Arts, 2020).

does not drearily drift through the chapters either. While Keillor's narration is also especially upbeat and fast-paced (which conceivably requires some getting used to), I would argue that one can conceivably sense that this particular choice may be justified as a perceived matter of *style*—the aesthetic benefits of which are certainly debatable. He certainly seems to possess both a passion for (and, indeed, understanding of) Twain's text. Arguably, the only narrator who appears to similarly convey his genuine passion for Twain's material is Nathan Osgood.[59] Conversely, good intentions notwithstanding, if Scarlato's measured inflections almost make him sound anesthetized, then the dawdling pace of the Becker and Giuliano readings comes across as quite despondently soporific. Robin Field's narration is also afflicted by unnecessarily prolonged pauses, as well as exhibiting extensive flaws in respect of the performer's overall sense of pace and timing.[60] Similarly—and, indeed, in more ways than one—the iterations of Jim Killavey and Lawrence Skinner quite regrettably leave much to be desired.[61]

To continue carving out the unrewarding iterations, I find that similarly miscast are William Fortier and Jim Donaldson, whose narrations—both released by Trout Lake Media in 2011 and 2012, respectively—seem to leave one with an odd sense of eeriness and general disarray. The aforementioned Munro narration, released in 2015, constitutes their third and best attempt thus far.[62] Nevertheless, and although Munro may indeed possess the appropriate vocal capacities that the aural medium requires, I, for one, would not (as has been suggested by Powers) rate this recording as a good iteration of Twain's novel. Explicitly, the overall rhythm sounds much too leisurely, the different characters and dialects are not well-emphasized, and a listener is ultimately not engaged enough.

In the same vein, although he possesses a pleasant and easy-to-listen-to kind of voice (an important—albeit, not always a necessary—quality for narrators and elocutionists), Don Hagen's particular vocal properties nonetheless seem miscast for this particular novel.[63] Overall, his narration resonates a general sense of aloofness; there seems to be no discernible difference in Hagen's iteration

---

[59] Twain, *The Adventures of Huckleberry Finn*, read by Nathan Osgood (SNR, 2023).

[60] Twain, *The Adventures of Huckleberry Finn*, read by Robin Field (Mission Audio, 2011).

[61] See: Twain, *The Adventures of Huckleberry Finn*, read by Jim Killavey (Jimcin Recordings, 1980); and *The Adventures of Huckleberry Finn*, read by Lawrence Skinner (Audioliterature, 2018).

[62] See: Twain, *Adventures of Huckleberry Finn*, read by William Fortier (Trout Lake Media, 2011); read by Jim Donaldson (Trout Lake Media, 2012); and read by Alan Munro (Trout Lake Media, 2015).

[63] Twain, *Adventures of Huckleberry Finn*, read by Don Hagen (Gildan Media, 2010).

between the various voices and dialects the novel inhabits. This effectively renders one's listening experience a rather arduous labor.

The same can also be said about the passages recorded by Will Geer, whose brief renditions seem altogether discordant.[64] The narrations of Matthew Taylor and Eric G. Dove—although, on the whole, may be defined as merely "okay"—do not, alas, evoke a significantly engaging listening experience.[65] Dove, however, certainly does successfully adhere to what the text itself requires: e.g., in narrating the Notice and Explanatory, whereas Dove employs a different tonality for these two passages than the one he uses when reading *as* Huck, no such distinction is heard in Hagen's recording. Furthermore, while Dove evidently invests some effort in demonstrating and *sounding* the different dialects—that is, as the Explanatory lists them—Hagen merely reads the text as is. Taylor's rendition, despite his possessing an overall pleasant voice for what an aural artifact requires (and notwithstanding what one can but assume are surely good intentions) seems neither here nor there.

Johnny Heller's take, on the other hand, is quite exceptional.[66] Although the overall tempo of his delivery seems a tad low-key (or, perhaps, somewhat lingering), this could, in fact, be aesthetically justified by Huck's illiteracy and particular way with words. Perhaps more than in any other version, Heller conveys the sense that Huck is actually *reading* his autobiography, rather than merely talking to his listeners and *telling* them his story. Ultimately, one gets the sense that Heller—*as* Huck—is well aware of his designated audience, and, as such, is delivering his story especially for them. Tim Behrens, too, should be commended for his remarkable endeavor and outstanding delivery in this respect.[67] The same holds true, to my mind, for Osgood's achievement.

With the exception of Behrens, Dietz, Gardner/Parker, Heller, and Keillor, virtually none of the talents mentioned previously seem aware of their implied audience. Rather, they can conceivably be perceived as merely reading to "themselves," or as aimlessly delivering the text in front of them unto a recording device. This, to a large extent, contributes to the distinct aesthetic flaws in their

---

[64] Twain, *Readings from the Stories and from "Huckleberry Finn,"* as adapted and performed by Will Geer (Folkways Records, FL 9769, 1961).

[65] Twain, *Adventures of Huckleberry Finn*, read by Eric G. Dove (Dreamscape Media, 2013); Twain, *The Adventures of Huckleberry Finn*, read by Matthew Taylor [in *10 Essential Pieces of Literature*] (MustRead, 2019).

[66] Twain, *The Adventures of Huckleberry Finn*, read by Johnny Heller (Listen2aBook.com, 2015).

[67] Twain, *The Adventures of Huckleberry Finn*, read by Tim Behrens (Books in Motion, 2011).

narrations as aural artifacts. Furthermore, nearly none of these performers appear to successfully distinguish the novel's various characters from that of Huck—thus endowing them with individual voices, identities, and regional dialects—all the while notably preserving Huck's first-person perspective. While Prichard may endow each character with their own distinct voice, his delivery nonetheless sounds almost emotionally detached, much like a drab voice-over that merely conveys the facts of the matter. Consider, for instance, the appearance of Huck's drunken Pap in Chapter 5: whereas Prichard's rendition seems to make his character sound more like a caricature, Dietz's delivery is quite powerful and succeeds in overcoming the potential so-called obstacle of overplaying the aspect of his drunkenness. Kevin O'Brien's narration, however, renders Pap quite cartoonish. While his overall performance seems well paced, it is not, alas, well balanced.

The narration of American TV personality Dick Cavett, however, is quite engaging.[68] While he is not a professional actor, Cavett seems to exhibit a rather sagacious grasp of the material, appropriately conveying the various voices and dialects in a manner that sounds organic (rather than over-, or, indeed, under-stated). Evidently, he consistently pronounces the "Wh" digraph with a "silent" W. Overall, his coming timing is fairly adequate, and his storytelling voice is pleasant—all making for enjoyable listening. At the same time, one gets the sense that Cavett is attempting to evoke more of Twain's implicit voice rather than Huck's own first person. (This, to my mind, is not inconsequential—especially when this inadvertently unveils, or even merely hints at, Cavett's own *actual* enjoyment in reading Twain's text). The attempt to ostensibly invoke Twain's voice also seems to be evident in passages narrated by Hiram Sherman.[69]

Actor Shamrock McShane claims to have gained a sufficient understanding of Huck Finn in order to play him. He quite rightly points out that the novel's narrator is not Twain but rather Huck—which, he asserts, *requires* being able to act: to *"be"* Huck Finn. As far as other characters are concerned, McShane maintains that "the narrator's task is not to impersonate them—even given the pronunciation guide that Twain provides to render the various dialects precisely—the trick is till to render the scene the way *Huck* would."[70] Despite the apparent potential that

[68.] Twain, *The Adventures of Huckleberry Finn*, abridged by Sue Dawson, read by Dick Cavett [Listen for Pleasure, 1985] (Audio Holdings, 2009).

[69.] See: *Mark Twain: Read by Hiram Sherman* (Spoken Arts, 778, 1960); and *Mark Twain: Read by Hiram Sherman—The Adventures of Huckleberry Finn, Vol. I & Vol. II* (SA 1008–1009, Spoken Arts, 1968).

[70.] See URL: accessed December 10, 2022, https://soundcloud.com/shamrockmcshane/huck-finn-foreword, 01min05sec–01min24sec.

his introductory remarks evidently evoke, his obvious passion for the material notwithstanding, and well intentioned as his effort might be, I regrettably find that McShane's overall performance, though well paced, is quite uninspired—evidently failing to appropriately convey his own assertion in respect of how the novel should be delivered. Huck's age is indiscernible, regional dialects appear to be absent, and—with the exception of Jim—no attempt seems to have been invested in voicing the various characters that inhabit the novel. (While one might be able to discern different characters, at least to some extent—e.g., Pap, the Duke, and Dauphin—it sounds, alas, inconsistent). Ultimately, the reading itself is simply not engaging enough.

Among its many inherent flaws as an aural artifact, Jason Damron's "dramatized" narration seems to be delivered at double speed, without allowing himself the liberty to pause (or even to breath).[71] Nearly all of Damron's inflections and emphases—or rather, the lack thereof—are almost identical in every sentence, effectively depriving Twain's characters of any show of emotions. Making matters worse, one gets the sense that he, too, is neither performing for, nor even aware of, an implied audience—thereby rendering his narration anything but engaging. Even the sound effects included in recording all seem sporadic, badly timed, and quite inconsequential. The same seems true about the rather wearisome readings by both Killavey and Lee Howard.[72]

Although one might identify a certain surge of enthusiasm to Damron's storytelling—which could, conceivably, contribute to depicting Huck's adolescence—it nevertheless seems devoid of any particular context. Even passages that sound, at times, over-enthusiastic, appear quite needlessly so and with no real aesthetic justification. Ultimately, Damron's narration fails not only in exhibiting the purported internal logic of the novel itself but also in fully adhering to or complying with the confines of the aural medium.

By way of illustration, consider the following passage from Chapter 31, in which Huck resolves to do what his heart believes to be right, accepting that he might "go to hell" for doing so:

> Once I said to myself it would be a thousand times better for Jim to be a slave at home where his family was, as long as he'd *got* to be a slave, and so I'd better write a letter to Tom Sawyer and tell him to tell Miss Watson where he was.

[71.] Twain, *The Adventures of Huckleberry Finn*, dramatized, read by Jason Damron (ABN, 2012).

[72.] Twain, *Adventures of Huckleberry Finn*, narrated by Lee Howard (Page2Page, 2019).

But I soon give up that notion for two things: she'd be mad and disgusted at his rascality and ungratefulness for leaving her, and so she'd sell him straight down the river again; and if she didn't, everybody naturally despises an ungrateful nigger, and they'd make Jim feel it all the time, and so he'd feel ornery and disgraced. And then think of *me*! It would get all around that Huck Finn helped a nigger to get his freedom; and if I was ever to see anybody from that town again I'd be ready to get down and lick his boots for shame. That's just the way: a person does a lowdown thing, and then he don't want to take no consequences of it. Thinks as long as he can hide, it ain't no disgrace. That was my fix exactly. The more I studied about this the more my conscience went to grinding me, and the more wicked and low-down and ornery I got to feeling. And at last, when it hit me all of a sudden that here was the plain hand of Providence slapping me in the face and letting me know my wickedness was being watched all the time from up there in heaven, whilst I was stealing a poor old woman's nigger that hadn't ever done me no harm, and now was showing me there's One that's always on the lookout, and ain't a-going to allow no such miserable doings to go only just so fur and no further, I most dropped in my tracks I was so scared. Well, I tried the best I could to kinder soften it up somehow for myself by saying I was brung up wicked, and so I warn't so much to blame; but something inside of me kept saying, "There was the Sunday-school, you could a gone to it; and if you'd a done it they'd a learnt you there that people that acts as I'd been acting about that nigger goes to everlasting fire." It made me shiver. And I about made up my mind to pray, and see if I couldn't try to quit being the kind of a boy I was and be better. So I kneeled down. But the words wouldn't come. Why wouldn't they? It warn't no use to try and hide it from Him. Nor from *me*, neither. I knowed very well why they wouldn't come. It was because my heart warn't right; it was because I warn't square; it was because I was playing double. I was letting *on* to give up sin, but away inside of me I was holding on to the biggest one of all. I was trying to make my mouth *say* I would do the right thing and the clean thing, and go and write to that nigger's owner and tell where he was; but deep down in me I knowed it was a lie, and He knowed it. You can't pray a lie—I found that out.[73]

Ed Begley's iteration of this passage—despite his acclaim as stage, screen, and radio performer—is also dispiritingly flawed and seems quite uninspired

---

[73] Twain, *Adventure of Huckleberry Finn*, 341–343.

in conveying Huck's internal turmoil.[74] Both Dietz and Gardner/Parker, on the other hand, convey the same passage while poignantly evoking Huck's thought process and soul-searching contemplations, gradually building up toward his final resolution.[75]

On the Diverse Problematics of Diversity

The Parzaan Dastur recording constitutes something of an obscure curiosity.[76] Even if one might argue that he has all the makings of a spectacular aural perform- ing artist, I find the mere fact that Twain's text is delivered in an English-Asian accent is simply not in harmony with the internal logic of the novel. Of course, this has absolutely nothing to do with this particular accent but, rather, its blatant mismatch to this particular text. Granted, in adhering to the current nature of modern identity politics, no ethnic group (and, especially not those who might be identified as vulnerable minorities) should be left out. As such, one may potentially argue in favor of different adaptations of Twin's novel that would comply with one's cultural identity—be it Asian, Nordic, Irish, or, for that matter, Eastern-European. This would appropriately necessitate a well-thought-through aesthetic justification and reasoning for the given artistic choice. Nevertheless, the blatant incongruency of having the novel narrated as—effectively sustaining its inherently American context, characters, and connotations—all the while employing a completely different (and ethnically specific) dialect surely cannot be easily embraced. Citing a particular recording of Amitav Ghosh's *Sea of Poppies* (2008)—one which poses additional potential problematics *vis-à-vis* the "politics of narration"[77]—English questions whether one should "avoid" engaging with a performance "by a white reader [...] who, though a multiple Audie Award winner, is prone to mispronouncing the book's Indian words".[78] He goes on to ponder on whether one should avoid, as a general rule, any "white actors' performances of work by writers of color [...] [and] vice versa", further

---

[74] Twain *Huckleberry Finn*, read by Ed Begley (Caedmon Records, TC 2038, 1969), see Side 4, band 2: "You Can't Pray a Lie"].

[75] See: Dietz, Chapter 31, 07m45sec–11m20sec; and Parker, Chapter 31, 05m51sec–08m30sec.

[76] Twain, *The Adventures of Huckleberry Finn*, read by Parzaan Dastur (Audible, 2018).

[77] English, "Teaching the Novel in the Audio Age," 425fn3.

[78] Ibid., 422.

questioning the manner in which on should vocalize the "gender and sexuality" of a given character.[79] Although English does state that "this is not the same problem we are familiar with from debates over casting and identity in theater and film,"[80] it certainly constitutes a burning-hot issue—and especially nowadays, in light of Hollywood's newly devised diversity inclusion standards (which, as of 2024, are expected to include explicit stipulations that films must meet to be eligible for the "Best Picture" Academy Award).

David Baddiel's Channel 4 documentary *Jews Don't Count* (2022), based on his similarly titled book published a year earlier, might prove an interesting case in point—and, explicitly, Baddiel's assertion that "Of course, if Jews can pass as non-Jews, non-Jews can also pass as Jews. And they do—on stage, on film, and TV. But in a modern-casting universe where authenticity is everything, should they?"[81] If authenticity is indeed "everything," one can't help but wonder whether Hollywood's impending new standards would eventually prevent performers such as, say, Sir Ben Kingsley—whose sensitive portrayals of *actual* historical figures have thus far ranged from Mahatma Gandhi to Dmitri Shostakovich, Lenin, Georges Méliès, Meyer Lansky, Adolf Eichmann, and Salvador Dalí—from ever portraying such personae in the future.[82] To be sure, amid the prevailing cultural climate—and best intentions notwithstanding—an ostensibly "wrong" casting choice is seldom accepted with equanimity. There is certainly far less tolerance nowadays for any arguably ill-advised or insensitive characterizations in film history that could be charged with having needlessly perpetuated various cultural and ethnic stereotypes. Consider, for example, Peter Sellers' portrayal of an Indian character in *The Party* (1968)—criticized for employing "brownface," or, for that matter, Dick Van Dyke's now-frowned-upon take on an ostensibly typical British accent in Disney's classic *Mary Poppins* (1964).

In this context, Parzaan Dastur's iteration of *Huck Finn* seems, alas, borderline parodic. Conceivably, it would be similarly incongruous to have, say, someone

---

[79] Ibid., 422–423.

[80] Ibid., 423.

[81] *David Baddiel: Jews Don't Count* (Mindhouse Productions, 2022). 24min07sec–24min22sec.

[82] Drawing on a quote he attributes to Albert Camus—conceiving of actors as "haunted travellers in time, pursued by souls"—Kingsley himself explains there is a certain "glimmer of recognition" that he is able to feel when a certain role is suggested to him, and he thus humbly offers to perceive of his profession as akin to that of "a story-teller, pursued by souls." See URL: accessed August 25, 2023, https://www.youtube.com/watch?v=zYdCSzo2eU8, 10m17sec–11m51sec. One might also consider a recently conducted interview with American actor Richard Dreyfuss, in which he was asked to comment on Hollywood's new inclusion standards—which he finds both patronizing and thoughtless. See URL: accessed August 25, 2023, https://www.pbs.org/video/richard-dreyfuss-elrpyh/, 19m39sec.

such as Woody Allen narrate *The Kindly Ones* (2006) by Jonathan Littell. (The latter, incidentally, has received an audiobook version narrated by Gardner, who—despite his proven skills and experience as an audiobook narrator, and in spite of his praiseworthy effort—is simply not the appropriate choice for this particular work).

Similarly bewildering in this respect is Sharon Plummer's narration—and predominantly for consisting of a female voice with a British accent.[83] Furthermore, even if Plummer had arguably endeavored to employ the required American dialects that the novel invariably evokes, I doubt whether the result would have been worth the effort—especially as most of her current inflections and overall delivery are, alas, severely "flat," robotic, and uninspired. To a large extent, the same holds true for the Sam Kusi iteration, whose narration—in addition to leaving much to be desired in terms of his overall performance, and despite possessing what might, in fact, be identified as the ostensibly ideal vocal qualities for audiobooks—is also marred by its narrator's innate British accent.[84] Although I may indeed argue that a male performer (and surely one who possesses a certain ear for the necessary American dialects) seems to be the obvious choice—especially when drawing on the internal logic of Twain's text—I should certainly *not* be construed as claiming that female performers cannot or should not narrate this particular novel.

To be sure, female performers are most definitely welcome to attempt and adhere to that same internal logic. As such, and particularly in considering Huck's assumed age (an issue I shall shortly address herein), I find the iteration by Robin Miles to be notably successful—as well as in respect of her overall performance.[85] Rebecca K. Reynolds, too—despite the inherent problematics afflicting this conspicuously watered-down version designed for younger listeners—successfully evokes Huck's child-like qualities.[86] To that end, I maintain that someone such as American voice-actress Nancy Cartwright, who, for over quarter of a century, has been responsible for voicing one of the most famous adolescent boys in the history of animation—namely, one Bart Simpson—could

---

[83] Twain, *The Adventures of Huckleberry Finn*, read by Sharon Plummer (Strelbytskyy Multimedia Publishing, 2020).

[84] Twain, *The Adventures of Huckleberry Finn*, read by Sam Kusi (Lauscher Audiobooks, 2024).

[85] Twain, *The Adventures of Huckleberry Finn*, read by Robin Miles (Thomas Nelson, 2020).

[86] *The Adventures of Huckleberry Finn*, retold from the Mark Twain original, read by Rebecca K. Reynolds Oasis Audio, 2019).

most certainly constitute a more than adequate candidate for appropriately delivering Twain's novel in Huck's own voice.

As a sidenote, I would add that the issue of playing against gender obviously
works both ways: as pointed out to me by Sarah Burgess—an avid audiobook
listener who had assisted with tweaking the final draft of my PhD dissertation—
male narrators arguably seldom successfully "get" the female voice "just right."
This is indeed an important insight.

Ultimately, while this important topic surely warrants further debate and
consideration, an argument can well be made that the question of who may (or
may not) count as an eligible candidate for narrating this particular novel—that is,
as Huck, in the first-person—should focus less on political correctness and ethnic
identity than on aesthetics and the attempt to exhibit a given text's internal logic.

Voicing Huck

To capture and convey an appropriate aural representation of Huck's assumed voice
is not only imperative but also one of the most difficult tasks that an audiobook
performer is faced with. Fundamentally, Huck cannot sound too young—and, at
the same time, should not sound too old either. As such, it is important to consider
the potential aesthetic implications involved with having a mature or older actor
narrate a novel that arguably requires the voice of a young adolescent. While
some narrators evidentially make an explicit attempt to make Huck sound young,
most endeavors, alas, come across as unsuccessful to varying degrees. Prichard's
narration, in this respect, seems quite inconsistent in his conveying to the listeners
how young Huck is purported to be. The same, I find, also applies to the narrations
of Denny Delk, B. J. Harrison, Chris Hendrie, and Mike McShane narrations.[87]

Field, William Dufris, Vernon, and Trevor White all appear somewhat blatantly
over-enthusiastic in their portrayal of Huck, and none of them succeed in making
the listener aware that the fact that Huck is a child does not necessarily mean that
he is immature.[88] To a lesser degree, however, the same might also be said about

---

[87.] See: Twain, *The Adventures of Huckleberry Finn*, read by Denny Delk (Cherry Hill Publishing, 2012); *Adventures of Huckleberry Finn*, unabridged narration by B. J. Harrison (B. J. Harrison, 2008); *Adventures of Huckleberry Finn*, read by Chris Hendrie (Chris Hendrie, 2011); and *Adventures of Huckleberry Finn*, read by Mike McShane (HarperCollins, 1994).

[88.] See: Twain, *The Adventures of Huckleberry Finn*, read by William Dufris (Tantor Media, 2008); *Adventures of Huckleberry Finn*, read by Stephen L. Vernon (A. R. N. Publications, 2015); and *The Adventures of Huckleberry Finn*, [abridged], read by Trevor White (Audible, 2012).

the brief passages narrated by John O'Connell, which are interwoven amid an audio study guide to the novel. Notwithstanding, it would have been interesting to listen to a proper narration by O'Connell—that is, in full, and without the study guide's ostensible intrusions—for it is, in fact, quite lively, and seems to exhibit potential for a rather rewarding listening.[89] Ultimately, with the exception of O'Connell, there is something about the overall tone of these narrations that simply doesn't *feel* "right" for the novel.

Keillor, however, successfully makes Huck seem ever so child-*like* without sounding overtly child-*ish*. His narration also complements Huck's storytelling style—supposedly unfolding the events as he experiences them. One can also detect a constituent difference between the manner in which "his" Huck speaks directly to the listeners—as opposed to reporting (or conceivably re-enacting) his conversations with other characters. Much in the tradition of his long-running radio program, *A Prairie Home Companion*—and especially reminiscent of the recurring segments depicting the fictional town of Lake Wobegon—Keillor proves to be a gifted storyteller, to all intents and purposes, who is surely no stranger to the realm of aural artifacts. This, to be sure, makes for a thoroughly enjoyable listening experience. (Even for an abridged iteration of Twain's novel, it is nonetheless one of the better ones available).

Although it is uncertain how many so-called "child actors" would be up to the task, an argument could be made that the novel's internal logic would conceivably best be served by the narrating voice of an *actual* child. Nevertheless, with the exception of Brandon deWilde—heard narrating merely selected passages on a 1956 release by Caedmon Records[90]—whereas all the novel's screen adaptations have consistently employed child actors, and while some full-cast aural dramatizations may have indeed featured adolescents, the audiobook versions of *Huck Finn* are almost invariably narrated by adults. Although deWilde, at the time, matched Huck's age in the novel, I would argue—based on the existing recording—that his proficiency in conveying the internal logic of Twain's text seems quite limited and that, as such, a complete and unabridged recording would have been ill-advised.

Although not by any means an audiobook, the CBS radio drama series *The Campbell Playhouse* featured a live 1940 broadcast of *Huck Finn*—directed by

[89] Kirsten Silva Gruesz, PhD, *The Adventures of Huckleberry Finn: An A+ Audio Study Guide*, narrated by John O'Connell (Hachette Audio, 2006).

[90] See: "From *Huckleberry Finn*" [Side 2] in *Stories of Mark Twain* (Caedmon Records, TC 1027, 1956).

and starring Orson Welles—featuring child actor Jackie Cooper (who was 18 years old at the time) portraying the title role. According to American film critic and author Jonathan Rosenbaum, the fact that Welles appears to have forcibly abandoned Twain's original first person, coupled with his own occasional third-person delivery of certain passages, effectively "brings about the forced coexistence of Huck Finn and Mr. Welles—a collapsing of two time frames and two orders of reality."[91] Consider, for instance, Welles's opening remarks, which are heard following his delivery of Twain's Notice:

> Last week, we said that this week we'd broadcast Mark Twain's *Huckleberry Finn*. Well, you're expecting, then, a dramatization—good, clear, concise. Ladies and gentlemen, you'll hear no such thing. We're sorry, but we think *Huckleberry Finn* is too good a book to be dramatized, exactly speaking—and, so, we won't. We won't even try a nicely plotted version of the story—we couldn't do it anyway. We don't even have to. For one thing, the story hasn't got what you'd call a "nice plot". […] Now you'll forgive me, please, but I must inject what may seem, at first, to be the personal note: Ladies and gentlemen, it would appear that during the course of this past week, there have been circulated rumors—rumors evil, unfounded, and unfair—nasty, vile rumors, whose sources I cannot place, and whose origins I am at a loss to discover. It has been said that *I* will perform the role of Huckleberry Finn. You'll all be relieved, I'm sure, to hear from my own lips that this is not the case. It must be said, however, in all candor, that I restrain myself none too easily. To be Huckleberry Finn even for an hour—this was not likely to be put to one side. However, I'm as happy as possible, and as proud as I really ought to be, to welcome now to the *Campbell Playhouse* that gifted, and very young performer, who will be Huckleberry Finn—and who is actually Jackie Cooper.[92]

Cooper tells "Mr. Welles" that he is "mighty proud" to meet him. They have a short exchange, following which Welles begins reading the opening words of the novel's first chapter. He barely completes the first sentence when one hears Cooper, as in-character, saying, "I thought you wasn't gonna play Huckleberry Finn,

---

[91.] Jonathan Rosenbaum, "Huck Finn and Mr. Welles (1988 Lecture)," posted December 29, 2021, accessed December 19, 2022, https://jonathanrosenbaum.net/2021/12/huck-finn-and-mr-welles-1988-lecture/.

[92.] See URL: accessed December 19, 2022,https://archive.org/details/OrsonWelles_CampbellPlayhouse, 03m23sec–04m56sec.

Mr. Welles"—to which Welles responds, "Oh, pardon me. Alright, Huck." (One can literally *hear* his reluctance and disappointment). Cooper then commences his own narration, and one is ostensibly forced to hear the same text once again.[93] This, for Rosenbaum, constitutes a "kind of synthesis that theoretically sounds conceivable only on radio."[94] I, for one, tend to agree. As an inherent property of the aural medium, it seems to evoke, facilitate, and welcome a rather unique type of aesthetics.

Ultimately, while this production certainly qualifies as a proper aural artifact, the question of its aesthetic quality—especially as an adaptation of Twain's novel—may well be quibbled. Explicitly, it seems to be overshadowed by the ostensible aura surrounding Welles himself—or, rather, the manner in which his audience would have purportedly perceived him. Indeed, as Rosenbaum makes a point of clarifying, "please keep in mind that when I refer to Welles here, I'm mainly referring to the public persona, not to the private individual."[95] The prevailing aesthetic complexities of portraying one's own self (or, perhaps, a so-called alternate "version" thereof)—especially amid the distinctive confines of the aural medium—will duly become a key point of focus in the concluding chapter of this study.

Will Wheaton—whose career began as a child actor—recorded an abridged version of Twin's novel in 1993.[96] Although his characterization of Huck seems to sufficiently sounding Huck's assumed age, his narration, alas, does not appropriately convey Twain's underlying tone. Elijah Wood—who, as a child actor, happened to portray Huck in a 1993 film adaptation—recorded the novel in its entirety in 2014.[97] Despite his youthful, somewhat high-pitched, and arguably feminine vocal qualities, one finds a certain obscure dissonance that seems to persist throughout Wood's narration: "his" Huck does not come across young enough to appropriately convey a child's perspective—and, simultaneously, he does not sound old enough insofar as communicating the recollected memories of an adolescent is concerned. Furthermore, his narration does not adequately distinguish between what the various other characters sound like—even if one might be tempted to argue that they are ostensibly "filtered" through his rendition

---

[93] Ibid., 05m03sec–05m40sec.

[94] Rosenbaum, "Huck Finn and Mr. Welles."

[95] Ibid.

[96] Twain, *The Adventures of Huckleberry Finn*, [abridged], read by Will Wheaton (Phoenix Books, 2014).

[97] Twain, *Adventures of Huckleberry Finn*, read by Elijah Wood (Audible, 2014).

of Huck's voice. While he certainly makes Huck and Jim sound different from one another, his rendition of other characters (e.g., Pap, the Duke, and the King) sounds confoundingly identical. Finally, Twain's underlying voice seems completely absent.

Arguably, even if one is able to establish that Huck is ostensibly a "mature child"—and that this dissonance, therefore, not only cannot be avoided but should, in fact, be explicitly exhibited—this quality nevertheless does not come through these narrations. To be sure, there is a difference between a noticeable aesthetic dissonance that leaves one feeling ill at ease with an overall performance and an attempt to manifest a certain duality that inhabits a particular character. Ultimately, as the novel progresses, so does Huck's insight into the morally questionable ways of the society that surrounds him. Thus, a performer should conceivably be able to exhibit this aspect of the novel when lending their voice to portray Huck. As such, Wood's iteration appears to rely more on his ostensible "start-status," rather than on a comprehensive interpretation of Huck's character. This ultimately results in a delivery that sadly seems neither here nor there. It is in this context that I also find the Harrison iteration quite unrewarding. His interesting vocal qualities notwithstanding, the same can also be said about the Delk version (which also suffers from other aesthetic deficiencies: e.g., his "take" on the regional dialects that inhabit the novel seems to render the characters more as caricatures). The same can be said about Michael A. Harding's delivery.[98] Matt Armstrong, on the other hand—whose overall performance is both pleasant and enjoyable—successfully endows Huck with a distinctly youthful, lively, and cheerful voice.[99] O'Brien too—despite his iteration's aforementioned deficiencies—successfully makes Huck sound rather youthful, appropriately matching his assumed age.

Alternatively, an argument could also be made that an aural iteration of this particular novel might, in fact, benefit—perhaps even simply work better—when performed by an *older* actor. Since *Huck Finn* assumes the guise of an authentic autobiography, the experience of listening to a mature actor (or an older *voice*) could evoke the feeling that one has been made privy to the memories and recollections of Huck's "older-self"—recording the memoir of his own younger self in an attempt to re-enact his own past experiences. John Greenman's narration serves as an intriguing, well-performed example of a so-called "elder-Huck,"

[98.] Twain, *Adventures of Huckleberry Finn*, narrated by Michael A. Harding (Providence Publishing, 2022).

[99.] Twain, *The Adventures of Huckleberry Finn*, performed by Matt Armstrong (Matt Armstrong, 2011).

looking back upon the experiences of his youth.[100] Even more interesting is Jack Lemmon's rendition (produced one year prior to his passing away in 2001, at the age of 76).[101] Yet, as interesting an interpretation as this may be, and even when one adopts a willing suspension of disbelief, something seems to escape one's aesthetic experience when hearing the novel ostensibly filtered through the voice of an old man. Indeed, as remarkable an actor as Lemmon was, the implicit mental image of the speaker behind the voice—which one inevitably conjures up in one's head—arguably sounds *too* old in this particular case. The same, to my mind, holds true for the Henry Adams narration. Here, however, one gets the sense that Adams seems to deliver a so-called "elder-Huck" who is overtly trying to sound like his younger self. This is quite evident, for instance, as early as what seems like Adams's forceful attempt to convey *Huck's* take on what Miss Watson sounds like.[102] Fundamentally, one is able to sense this—or, rather, to intuit such a conclusion—only having grasped a particular work's overall internal logic.[103]

Regrettably, one finds two additional deficiencies in Lemmon's rendition: the delivery of regional dialects (or rather the lack thereof) and the evident censorship that the novel had undergone. First, although Lemmon indeed employs different voices when narrating different characters (e.g., Miss Watson and Jim), and while he seems to convey their various types of speech in accordance with Twain's variations in spelling, he does not, alas, successfully endow them with the distinctive dialect that the text evokes. Second, Lemmon is heard throughout his narration using the word "slave" rather than the original, dreaded N-word. Whether or not the decision is this case has to do with Lemmon himself—who, as one can merely surmise, may not have wished to become erroneously associated with that word—I would maintain that to replace it nonetheless creates an aesthetic conundrum that cannot be ignored.

In what effectively opens up something of a sub-(institutional)-category in its own right, this particular recording is also noteworthy merely in presenting one with the opportunity—perhaps even the privilege—of listening to an aural

---

[100.] Twain, *Adventures of Huckleberry Finn*, read by John Greenman (Sheba Blake Publishing, 2021).

[101.] Twain, *The Adventures of Huckleberry Finn*, [abridged], read by Jack Lemmon (Simon & Schuster, 2000).

[102.] Twain, *The Complete Tom Sawyer & Huckleberry Finn Collection*, read by Henry Adams (Author's Republic, 2019).

[103.] Alluding to her listening experience of *Tess of the d'Urbervilles* (1891), Knox, too, expresses her own confusion in identifying the narrator's voice—Flo Gibson—as sounding too old for Thomas Hardy's narrating protagonist. Knox, "Hearing Hardy, Talking Tolstoy," 135–136.

performance by one of the most established and well-respected actors in his profession. Having been around since the inception of audiobooks, the allure and prestige of celebrity readings is certainly not a novelty:

> These days actors spend as much time in the recording studio as the film studio. [...] Hardly a year goes by without a new series of renowned narrators. Celebrity narrators are one way in which audiobooks have declared their independence from print. Publishers concerned with faithfully reproducing the book tend to favor unknown actors whose voices will not interfere with a story's reception. According to this line of thought, audiences are more likely to concentrate on a book's words if they don't know who is speaking. By contrast, celebrities come between books and readers, making them acutely aware of the voice; the book is no longer the center of attention. [...] The prominence of celebrities, who are likely to read abridgments instead of the entire narrative, has reinforced suspicions that audiobooks are a degraded form of commerce, not art. In fact, both sides are right: celebrities draw attention to and distract attention from the book.[104]

Although one would need to evaluate aural artifacts on a case-by-case basis, I would argue that these recordings can eloquently demonstrate the manner in which one's "informed intuition" works in action. Setting aside the marketing aspect, one is essentially required to utilize one's acquaintance with a particular performer's past works—as well as, for that matter, their purported public persona—in order to deduce whether or not (and, indeed, to what extent) a particular aural artifact *should*, potentially, yield an enriching and entertaining aesthetic experience.

Voicing Characters, In-Character

American actor–comedian and noted voice-performer Hank Azaria has been cited as stating that it's quite difficult to voice a character credibly impersonating another character. Yet, further illustrating the problematics involved in remediating this particular novel as an audiobook—exhibiting its distinct internal logic as an aural artifact—it is interesting to consider the manner in which several performers have approached the shift in dialect that appears, say, in the opening scene of Chapter 11.

[104.] Rubery, *The Untold Story of the Talking Book*, 252.

At this particular point in the novel, Huck has disguised himself as a girl and encounters the character of Judith Loftus, whose vernacular is that of a Missouri housewife. Although a minor character in the novel, she does seem to leave a profound impression on Huck. The previous chapter sets up Huck's meeting with Loftus. Having already been assisted by Jim to dress up like a girl, Huck ends the chapter with the following words:

> I practiced around all day to get the hang of the things, and by and by I could do pretty well in them, only Jim said I didn't walk like a girl [...] I took notice, and done better. [...] the drift of the current fetched me in at the bottom of the town. [...] There was a woman about forty year old in there knitting by a candle that was on a pine table. I didn't know her face; she was a stranger, for you couldn't start a face in that town that I didn't know. Now this was lucky [...] if this woman had been in such a little town two days she could tell me all I wanted to know; so I knocked at the door, and made up my mind I wouldn't forget I was a girl.[105]

The next chapter begins as follows:

> "Come in," says the woman, and I did. She says: "Take a cheer."
> I done it. She looked me all over with her little shiny eyes, and says: "What might your name be?"
> "Sarah Williams."[106]

Following the setup from the previous chapter, a reader would effectively need to imagine what Huck sounds like as he is speaking with Loftus. A performer, in turn, would be required to know how to perform Huck's attempt at sounding like a girl. Loftus—whose peculiar regional dialect is immediately indicated by Twain's misspelling of the word chair—does not take very long to realize "Sarah" is, in fact, a young boy: "You do a girl tolerable poor, but you might fool men, maybe."[107] She nonetheless treats Huck with kindness and teaches him how a real girl is supposed to act. Consequently, although his poor impersonation attempt is only disclosed to the readers toward the end of their exchange—making for a comic relief of sorts—the task of a performer would be to convey Huck's poor

---

[105] Twain, *Adventures of Huckleberry Finn*, 109.

[106] Ibid., 110.

[107] Ibid., 118.

attempt right from the start. In this respect, a performer would need to decide, for instance, whether or not, and the degree to which, Huck's voice should appropriately alter. Indeed, one might convey Huck's attempt over-enthusiastically, thereby exhibiting in an exaggerated fashion Huck's complete incomprehension of how girls actually speak.

Alternatively, one could well opt to make no change in Huck's voice at all, emphasizing the irony in having Huck's sound exactly the same and thus making his disguise even more see-through. Ultimately, one seems to be confronted here with a grown male narrator who is not only attempting to sound like a young boy—trying to sound like a young girl—but also simultaneously attempting *himself* to believably sound like a grown woman. To be sure, different performers employ different choices. If, for instance, the performer does not endow each character with an individual voice of their own, their challenge here might be extended to exhibiting Huck's attempt as sounding like a grown woman as well—being, after all, the narrator of his own story.

Dietz's vocal characterization of Loftus makes her sound like a relatively young woman and thus seems to match her assumed age (which, going by Huck's calculation, is around 40). His rendition of the word "cheer" does not over-emphasize the fact that this word is misspelled, but rather—seemingly effortlessly—makes it sound as if it is her natural way of speaking (i.e., in terms of her regional dialect). Although Dietz evidently endows Loftus with a distinct voice of her own, he excels in filtering it through Huck's first-person account as the storyteller. A clear distinction is similarly evident in the shorthand transition between his portrayal of Huck's narration and Huck's ill-fated attempt at portraying the so-called "Sarah Williams." Dietz's performance in this scene successfully conveys Huck's apparent playfulness in trying to get away with his scheme. It is particularly interesting to listen to his seemingly effortless delivery of the transition between Huck's character and Huck's portrayal of "Sarah." Dietz also succeeds in consistently conveying the voices with which Twain endows the characters throughout the entire novel. As stated, his achievement is quite remarkable.

Heller's version is a close second, successfully fleshing out just how funny this scene actually is. The same can be said about Theo Holland's iteration—whose overall performance of the novel makes for a rather delightful listening experience.[108] Kerry Shale's narration, too, stands among the more rewarding aural

---

[108.] Twain, *The Adventures of Huckleberry Finn*, read by Theo Holland (American Renaissance Books, 2018).

iterations.[109] Albeit abridged, Shale, in more ways than one, both captures and appropriately conveys many aspects of the novel's internal logic. Keillor also performs the Loftus scene with charm and enthusiasm—successfully conveying Huck's challenge with sounding like a girl—while also appropriately engaging the listener with Twain's wit. His overall use of the dialect seems natural and effortless—complying with what Huck supposedly would have absorbed from his firsthand experiences of the world he inhabits and the society that surrounds him.

Becker's rendition of the Loftus scene is less impressive. Becker's transition between Huck's voice as the narrator versus Huck's disguised voice as "Sarah" appears to build up gradually, thus making Huck sound as if he is improvising "on the spot" (which, to some extent, he is). While this surely constitutes a viable and interesting choice on the performer's part, its execution—had this indeed been a purposeful artistic decision—is nonetheless flawed. Rather, the transition is more inconsistent than not, thereby giving one the sense that Becker is unsure whether or not he should utilize a girl's voice, to begin with. Furthermore, while he does endow "his" Loftus with her own particular way of speech, it is apparently *not* a particular regional dialect. Explicitly, his overall reading—which makes Loftus sound well over forty—seems to incorrectly mispronounce the intentionally misspelled words, effectively missing the point of designated dialect. His pronunciation of word "cheer" sounds forced and not quite natural.

Dick Hill evidently takes no pains either to make Huck sound like a girl or to convey whether or not Huck is at all worried about Loftus exposing his scheme.[110] Although he fails in endowing Loftus with any specific regional dialect, he does utilize a distinctively different voice for her character—one that appropriately matches her assumed age. His portrayal of both characters, however, seems to lack a sense of consistency. Overall, much like the narrations of Dufris and Bob Karper (whose delivery had inexplicably adapted to the *third*-person),[111] Hill's performance is marred by a tendency toward over-acting.

English actor–comedian–writer Stephen Fry—who is no stranger to audiobook narrations—was once asked what he most dislikes about storytelling, to which he responded, "self-consciousness," "striving for affect," "too much acting," "too much accent work", and "too much character differentiation." The latter, for Fry,

---

[109.] Twain, *The Adventures of Huckleberry Finn*, [abridged], read by Kerry Shale (Penguin, 1997).

[110.] Twain, *The Adventures of Huckleberry Finn*, read by Dick Hill (Brilliance, 1992).

[111.] Twain, *Huckleberry Finn*, retold by Anna Kirwan, read by Bob Karper (Real Reads, 2009).

is the "equivalent to having colored-ink on the page" that "distracts" one from story.[112] In the same vein, Knox maintains that

> The labor of voicing a literary work for an audiobook is precisely to put "it into words and speak it," and with such a force of presence that the "voice" previously to the fore in the reader's encounter with the printed text is dropped to the rear. That this risks an over-the-top performance is duly recognized by listeners, narrators, and audiobook producers.[113] [excluded footnote reference 24 from original]

Notwithstanding, a so-called "over-the-top performance," might, in this particular case, be precisely what the scene requires for potentially amplifying Huck's predicament: that is, his see-through attempt at sustaining the guise of "Sarah."

A cursory listening to Patrick Fraley's iteration might lead one to conclude that it is just as good as that of Dietz. In brief, it both appropriately complies with the requirements of the aural medium and succeeds in manifesting the major aspects of the novel's internal logic. Yet a close listening to Loftus makes it clear that Fraley's take on her character's regional dialect, for example, sounds quite forced and ostensibly mechanical.[114] Consider, explicitly, his rendition of the word "cheer," which is fundamentally closer to Becker's flawed delivery. Furthermore, much like other less rewarding iterations—although to a somewhat lesser extent—I find that his overall portrayal of Huck fails in making one aware that although Huck is certainly a child, he nevertheless does not lack maturity.

The same also holds true for the Richard Henzel narration.[115] Although his overall take on Huck seems to appropriately highlight the character's illiteracy and arguable struggles with language, his execution—political correctness aside makes Huck sound both a bit "simple" and "slow." This is arguably a result of the over-acting that afflicts his narration—which is evident as early as his delivery of the Notice.

Garrick Hagon's delivery of this particular scene clearly demonstrates his eloquent transition between Huck's voice as the narrator and Huck's portrayal of the girl.[116] Furthermore, in his portrayal of Huck in disguise, he seems to have

---

[112] See URL: accessed February 10, 2023, https://www.youtube.com/watch?v=oUgjr5G89UU, 01min49sec–02min06sec.

[113] Knox, "Hearing Hardy, Talking Tolstoy," 131.

[114] Twain, *The Adventures of Huckleberry Finn*, read by Patrick Fraley (Audio Partners, 1999).

[115] Twain, *The Adventures of Huckleberry Finn*, read by Richard Henzel (Richard Henzel, 2010).

[116] Twain, *The Adventures of Huckleberry Finn*, read by Garrick Hagon (Naxos, 2007).

taken a somewhat different approach to that of the other performers discussed herein; namely, rather than conveying Huck's sense of playfulness or adventure, Hagon's rendition conveys more of Huck's fear of being exposed. This choice is not only interesting but also appears to work quite well in enhancing one's listening experience. Overall, his narration sustains a predominantly consistent rhythm and pace throughout, and he also successfully endows both Loftus and other characters with a clearly distinct regional dialect.

Moving Forward: More Than Merely Novels

In light of its unequivocal role and distinct importance as a literary device—and, indeed, as a complementary follow-up to the no-less substantial Notice—I was both surprised and bewildered to discover that the certain audiobook versions (e.g., Hagon and Killavey) inexplicably fail to include Twain's Explanatory. For reasons passing understanding—as there is certainly no aesthetic justification for doing so—far too many releases have surprisingly discarded *both* the Notice and the Explanatory altogether: e.g., the narrations by Dufris, Fraley, Hill, Howard, Keillor, Lemmon, and Wheaton. Although they may be quite brief—and, thus, seemingly neglectable—these two passages help to set the novel's overall tone (both figuratively and literally), predominantly by indicating the type of humor that one is yet to encounter. I therefore cannot fathom why one would willfully choose to exclude them, even for an abridged version. One might argue that Dietz's otherwise exceptional iteration of the novel exhibits a minor flaw in this particular context—as these two passages, although duly included, are not in fact delivered by Dietz himself. Rather, they are featured as part of the so-called "technical" copyright introduction provided by the production company. As such, this decision, at least to some extent, inadvertently detaches the voice of these two passages from the voice of the novel as a whole. Behrens's delivery, to my mind, ranks among the best iterations of both these essential passages.

As my additional extended case studies aim to demonstrate, one of this study's objectives is to examine audiobooks as the most appropriate medium and vehicle for delivering first-person narratives, with particular emphasis on the manner in which the craft of casting an aural performance may be linked to the aesthetic appreciation of artworks. As aural artifacts, these types of audiobooks—effectively embodying extended monologues, delivered by narrating protagonists who appear to *require* an audience to whom they must speak—are ultimately able to enrich one's aesthetic experience in a manner that considerably exceeds what the printed page is able to do.

Now, having already surveyed a classic and comparatively standard nine-teenth-century novel—in an effort to demonstrate the unique manner in which first-person narratives elegantly illustrate the core aesthetics of the audiobook—I find it necessary to delve deeper into the general aesthetic category that audio-books belong to. Thus, by way of illustrating what essentially does *not* comply with the larger "mother institution," my intention is to make abundantly clear what in fact *does*.[117]

[117.] To quote one in a handful of true childhood heroes: "If you wanna know how this rotten party turns out, you'll have to turn this crummy record over now. Pahh!"—Oscar the Grouch's cordial reminder on the end of Side 1 of the *On the Street Where We Live* [*Block Party!*] Vinyl LP (CTW-22087, 1978).

CHAPTER FOUR

"Earsores" and False Friends: Synthetic Iterations, Experimental Oddities, and Other Borderline Curiosities

Read It to Me Straight

Despite having attained a status as a "well-established field" in its own right, English explains that "audiobook pedagogy" has nonetheless focused its attention "almost exclusively on teaching blind and print-disabled students, second-language learners," as well as—citing Gene Wolfson—both adolescent "reluctant readers" and various other groups who, for whatever reason, might identify as lacking the ability to "efficiently access the printed page."[1] Evidently, aiming not only to remain faithful to original literary work but also to arguably emancipate a print-disabled readership (namely, for the most part, the blind and the visually impaired) from the interpretation of an external narrating agency exacted upon them—thereby allowing one to actively interpret a text for themselves—both the AFB and the Library of Congress have chosen to employ a policy that explicitly instructed the narrators they worked with to enact so-called "straight" readings. This, as Rubery explains, called for a neutral, unobtrusive voice and a style that should be neither overly dramatic nor blatantly monotonous—all adhering to "elaborate guidelines for converting typographical conventions into sound" that were developed "in order to approximate the printed page." Indeed, as Rubery quite rightly points out, "narrators profoundly influenced a book's reception in spite of their best efforts to remain neutral."[2]

Effectively reaffirming their status as readers, to all intents and purposes, many persons who identify with the particular print-disabled readership

---

[1] English, "Teaching the Novel in the Audio Age," 420.

[2] Rubery, *The Untold Story of the Talking Book*, 88; 98.

decidedly "insist on using the word 'reading' to describe the act of listening to books." Conceivably striving to willfully extinguish one's awareness of a narrator's very presence—and thereby focusing one's attention solely on the text that inhabits a particular book—the general idea was to "stick as closely as possible to the printed source, reading verbatim everything from acknowledgements to appendices, sometimes even preserving the original's typos." In point of fact, fidelity was embraced to such an extent that "in a few cases, narrators were asked to reproduce obvious errors (sometimes even spelling mistakes) in order to ensure that blind readers received the exact same treatment as other readers."[3]

Let me state upfront that I certainly sympathize with the underlying sentiment prompting this approach. Drawing on Rubery's wording, seeking to "treat blind readers like other readers" and "enabling people to read books who could not do so in any other way" is unquestionably a noble enterprise.[4] My aesthetic intuitions, however, tell me that this approach does more harm than good. I find this most evident when considering the major works that embody one's literary and poetic canon, that is to say, the classics that have already been extensively researched, evaluated, and recognized as seminal artworks in their own right. To subject these texts to an intentionally neutral narration seems, to my mind, not only counterintuitive, but also quite disrespectful and irresponsible and, arguably, adds an amplified insult to injury. In this context, an argument could be made that such recordings can neither exhibit a genuine and comprehensive understanding of context nor demonstrate the appropriate manner in which the text in question *should* be delivered to a designated audience amid the confines of an inherently aural medium. Indeed, it seems to my mind rather difficult (if not virtually impossible) to classify these types of recordings as proper aural artifacts. (One might even go so far as to say that to conceivably make do by simply tagging them as aesthetically flawed readings would not only be somewhat misleading but also render them quite redundant). Now, as one may well argue against what comes across as an unnecessarily reductive dismissal of many recordings—both archival and contemporary—I would like to elucidate that the outward rigidity in the approach I chose to adopt does happen to go hand in hand with some degree of open-mindedness. This, in turn, can be said to generate an aesthetic threshold of sorts where the aforementioned "pluralistic

---

[3] Ibid., 88; 3; 89.

[4] Ibid., 66; 74.

fascism" of NITA springs into action—potentially yielding not only a comparative close listening for significant aural artifacts but also a more comprehensive
understanding (and, indeed, experience) of selected aural performances.

It should also be noted that a somewhat substantial mass of the audiobooks
created for the print-disabled readership consist of computer-generated recordings (as opposed to human-read). I have dedicated a later section of this chapter
for explicitly tackling this particular phenomenon—and, of course, the aesthetic problematics it unmistakably evokes—with particular attention to the advent
and rise of artificial intelligence. Suffice it to say, at this junction, that there
is, for the most part, no distinct difference between these kinds of synthesized
"readings" and the aforementioned straight, neutral, or supposedly "flat" human
reading (if such a thing is even possible, despite one's best efforts). Interestingly
enough, for all of its obtrusive monotonousness, lack of inflection, occasional
technical glitches, and incidental mispronunciations, certain consumers actually happen to *prefer* the unmistakable so-called "Stephen Hawking" soundalike
quality of the synthesized "robo-voice" to that of a professional elocutionist.[5]
Nevertheless, here, too, the abiding sentiment is abundantly clear: by electing
to ignore the recording's inherent flaws, one is ultimately presented with the
text as is, in a way that is purportedly analogous to reading the printed page.

At the same time, there does prevail a certain type of an aesthetic understanding—at least among some members of the particular readership discussed
herein—pertaining to what a *good* audiobook should (even if merely implicitly)
sound like. This seems most evident when one considers the notion of matching
or fitting a particular narrator to a specific given text. In fact, even the AFB has
explicitly chosen to select "voices that would not be too incongruous"—aiming
"to fit the voice and manner of speaking to the material." Inevitably, however,
"getting the right fit," as Rubery puts it, "was fraught with difficulties."[6] To
be sure, the particular vocal properties and proficiencies of certain narrators
encompass the power to both elicit and evoke a wide range of emotions in
listeners—who, in turn, may express anything from intense personal affection
to outright hostility. More often than not, audiobook consumers disagreed over
what the appropriate voice should sound like in the first place. This frequently
generates the aforementioned "narrator wars" between different listeners over

[5] James Parker, "The Mind's Ear," *New York Times*, 25 November 2011, accessed December 19, 2022,
http://www.nytimes.com/2011/11/27/books/review/the-minds-ear.html.

[6] Rubery, *The Untold Story of the Talking Book*, 98.

the so-called "right" choice—and, perhaps especially, when the book in question happens to have gained a place of prominence in popular culture.

Granted, and as any performer is no doubt fully aware, there is more than one way of reading or delivering a particular line in any given text. Notwithstanding, and as any good performer *should* also be aware, this does not entail that there are an infinite number of readings. And, yet, I wish to maintain that despite the common conception pertaining to the possibilities for performance—which essentially allows for and, indeed, legitimizes virtually any reading or interpretation—there inevitably exist, in fact, only a *limited* number of potential readings that would appropriately (to varying degrees) comply with or adhere to a particular text's internal logic.

Is Something Rotten in the State of LibriVox?

The volunteer-based website libriVox.org consists of a "Web 2.0" community, championing both collaboration and interaction among users, as well as user-generated content, usability, and interoperability. As such, according to Michael Hancher, they are able to conduct themselves in ways that typical commercial audiobook publications simply cannot: not only are they immune to issues of copyright and fair use (as they concern themselves exclusively with works in the public domain), but they also appear impervious to "constraints of the literary tastes" called to mind by either the volunteers who record the books or the listeners who consume them. Their so-called "call to action" thus seems simple enough: "LibriVox volunteers record chapters of books in the public domain and publish the audio files on the Internet. Our goal is to record all the books in the public domain."[7] In the words of LibriVox founder, Hugh McGuire: "It's easy to volunteer. All you need is a computer, some free recording software, and your own voice."[8]

Although assuredly quite "easy" to become a volunteer and record a book by utilizing the technology readily available at one's disposal, it is most certainly *not* "all you need." Quite the contrary. To properly *perform* an audiobook—effectively

---

[7.] Michael Hancher, "Learning from LibriVox," in *Audiobooks, Literature, and Sound Studies*, ed. Matthew Rubery (New York: Routledge, 2011), 201; 204–205.

[8.] *Wikipedia*, s.v. "Hugh McGuire," accessed October 21, 2022, https://en.wikinews.org/wiki/Interview_with_LibriVox_founder_Hugh_McGuire.

creating an aural artifact for an audience who, essentially, is not there—is unequivocally *not* an easy task. Rather, it is a challenge that requires not only a comprehensive understanding of the aural medium but also investing far more effort
and professional proficiency than merely knowing how to read and work a tape
recorder. Moreover, despite past suggestions to prescribe some kind of guidelines
or aesthetic criteria, the realm of LibriVox endows any potential volunteer-
narrator with absolute *carte blanche*: anyone unhappy or disappointed by a particular reading is more than welcome to conjure up a better one of their own.[9]

I, for one, am rather confounded by this approach—explicitly in the particular context of this study. Inclusive, pluralistic, and arguably *woke* as this approach may be (which, as an ostensible social endeavor, is surely not a bad
thing), it does, alas, seem to completely ignore—if not outwardly oppose—the
defining, indispensable roles of not only the aural performing artist but also the
designated audience. To be sure, their spatio-temporal absence notwithstanding, there most certainly *is* an audience—somewhere, "out there"—who will
consequently consume these recordings (and potentially experience them as
aural artifacts). The narrating voice must therefore—both implicitly and explicitly—be able to account for its listeners.[10]

For Hancher, the LibriVox phenomenon can be identified precisely for what
it is *not*: "[I]t is not the result of special training, although all of its participants
have been schooled in one way or another; and, with few exceptions, it is not
the product of professional skills."[11] As such, by willfully abandoning—if not
blatantly renouncing—any and all criteria, LibriVox have effectively failed to
recognize the significance of classifying and appreciating the recordings they
archive. Likewise, by indiscriminately aiding and abetting any and all readings
or readers, their proverbial great scheme of things appears to emit an inherently
problematic (anti-)aesthetic paradigm.

Since not only does each reading effectively evoke an invitation to another
reading, but also because virtually anyone is welcome to contribute, one is sure
to come across recordings that have completely gone awry. Consider, for instance, the rather obscure LibriVox amalgamations that feature a mixed group
of individuals, each narrating different chapters of the same book—regardless

---

[9.] Hancher, "Learning from LibriVox," 205–206.

[10.] Knox, "Hearing Hardy, Talking Tolstoy," 128.

[11.] Hancher, "Learning from LibriVox," 199.

of accent, regional dialect, age, gender, or vocal skills—and, alas, with no single cohesive aesthetic rationale to justify the confusion.

Appropriately, barring some unforeseen fortuitous happenstance—and, granted, with an occasional handful of most welcome exceptions—virtually none of
this largely mismatched "Allsorts" type of recordings can be aesthetically evaluated as aural artifacts. These, for the most part, might be conceived of as ostensible "false friends" in that they assume the guise of a social, fun, extracurricular
endeavor—which, again, lacks a cogent and conclusive internal logic.

"Him?"–Reading "That?!"

The faux advertisement promoting an audiobook release of E. L. James's erotic
romance novel *Fifty Shades of Grey* (2011) narrated by American comedian and
actor Gilbert Gottfried—an original comedy sketch created for CollegeHumor.
com—eloquently highlights just how essential casting is in the realm of audiobooks. Although this sketch exists as a video clip—an infomercial for a new
audiobook, including the visual element of seeing reactions of women listening
to Gottfried's narration—I find the joke *itself* to be inherently aural.[12]

Conceivably, even if one had not actually read the novel but does happen to
possess enough information about its general theme and content—*and*, at the
same time, even if one is not especially acquainted with the complete scope of
Mr. Gottfried's *oeuvre*, but *does* happen to recognize his trademark vocal signature (famously emanating an intentionally obnoxious chalk-on-a-blackboard
resonance)—one should be subject to some kind of an unmistakably aesthetic
experience. As such, one's aurally *heard* mental image—inevitably conjured
up by the mere notion of *"him??"* (i.e., Gottfried) reading *that?!* (i.e., literary
eroticism)—is sure to ignite either complete bewilderment or roaring laughter,
all depending on whether or not one ultimately gets the joke.

To accept a *real* Gilbert Gottfried iteration of James's novel would surely be
quite a stretch. And, yet, I have absolutely no doubt that had her novel been in
the public domain, LibriVox would have certainly welcomed and legitimized a
Gilbert-Gottfried–like narration—for, as far as their community is concerned,

---

[12.] See URL: "Gilbert Gottfried Reads 50 Shades of Grey," accessed December 10, 2022, https://www.youtube
.com/watch?v=XkLqAIlETkA.

"all voices are different; some are adequate or better; more are welcome."[13] This, again, is precisely what renders their entire philosophy as something of an aesthetic conundrum. Drawing on Graves's aforementioned insight that in art, while anything goes, not everything necessarily works, one can similarly deduce that while more voices are indeed welcomed, not all voices will suffice. Since LibriVox both welcome and encourage multiple readings of a single work, and as Hancher explains, one's "enthusiasm" for a certain author or particular book customarily serves as sufficient motivation.[14] It is especially in this respect that I find that the idea "more are welcome"—employed haphazardly, with no degree of caution or due aesthetic consideration—should be taken with a grain of salt.

Granted, all voices are invariably and inevitably different from each other. However, by apparently valuing quantity over quality, any aesthetic consideration has unapologetically been altogether abandoned—thereby depriving of meaning not only the recordings themselves but also the very act of recording them. Indeed, to regard certain voices as either "adequate or better" is, in fact, a form of aesthetic judgment, which effectively requires one to consider the particular context and given set of circumstance amid which those voices in question are heard.[15]

According to Hancher, "a typical LibriVox recording will be an amateur project, in both senses of the word; not professional, but earnest." At the same time, it would appear as though certain LibriVox readings—at least for Hancher—can, in fact, "give the illusion of being the ideal reading of the text, perfectly realizing what the author wrote."[16]

Setting aside, momentarily, the question of whether there is, in fact, such a thing as an "ideal" reading, I find that Hancher's conception of "perfectly realizing" something that exists on the page corresponds quite well with the notion

---

[13] Hancher, "Learning from LibriVox," 201.

[14] Ibid.

[15] By the same token, an argument could be made that if a reading purportedly "disappoints," there is, in a sense, no real merit in having it eternalized in cyberspace alongside what might be identified as—advisedly permitting myself to descend to the vernacular—all other manner of utter *drek*. With the risk of conceivably over-emphasizing the more rigorous aspects involved with my application of NITA (that is, rather than its inclusiveness), and although it surely warrants a more comprehensive debate, one might also go so far as to maintain that even mass-produced, professional aural artifacts whose overall aesthetics prove to be fundamentally flawed or deficient, should not necessarily find their way to the "Spoken-Word" shelf at one's local bookstore for public consumption.

[16] Hancher, "Learning from LibriVox," 200; 205.

of exhibiting a particular text's internal logic. Furthermore, Hancher's assertion clearly indicates, to my mind, that he has at least some vague idea of what would—and, conceivably, what would not—constitute a *good* performance. It could thus be argued that if one presumes to identify a potentially ideal performance of a given text, it would entail that one evidently recognizes a particular appropriate manner in which that text *should* be read. To be sure, even if a so-called "ideal" reading exists—as certain scholars certainly imply—one cannot deem it as such without having applied some kind of aesthetic consideration.

Referring to the David Barnes narration of *The Woman in White* (1859)—and explicitly alluding to the narrator's take on the character of Mr. Fairlie—Hancher maintains that it is "exactly, preternaturally, what Wilkie Collins had in mind when he wrote that section," concluding that it is between the "fantastic extremes of perfect embodiment" that resides "the commonsensical belief that skill in reading aloud is unevenly distributed and that some people are better at it than others."[17] This, to all intents and purposes, is an aesthetic evaluation, which—as with the unique insights employed by Roach in her aforementioned publication—could not have been arrived at without first having attained some elementary understanding of the work in question.

According to Gilead Bar-Elli, amateurs and professionals alike are not too keen on accepting the likelihood of an ideal version or iteration when it comes to works that are purposefully designated for performance:

> Most of us are repelled by the idea of an ideal performance of a piece of music, which seems opposed to reasonable and commonly held positions. We are used to hearing pieces of music performed in different ways, many of which we deem excellent. We often find it difficult to determine which performance we prefer, and even when we can, our preference seems to be a matter of personal taste, a taste which can even change over time or according to circumstances for the same person.[18]

As far as Bar-Elli himself is concerned, however, an ideal performance—and especially in respect of musical compositions—not only can, but, in fact, *should* appropriately "guide us in making judgments of understanding, of performance

---

[17] Hancher, "Learning from LibriVox," 205.

[18] Gilead Bar-Elli, "Ideal Performance," *British Journal of Aesthetics* 42, no. 3 (July 2002): 1, accessed October 25, 2022, http://www.bar-elli.co.il/ideality.pdf.

and preference, even when we do not know what the ideal performance of the composition is from the outset."[19] For the most part—and, again, in what clearly resonates with the notion of whether or not (and, indeed, the extent to which) a particular artwork successfully exhibits the internal logic of its own world—Bar-Elli considers an ideal performance as one that complies with, adheres to, and fulfills a particular composition's relevant aesthetic-normative properties. As such, he ultimately asserts that "it is entirely pointless, or even conceptually impossible [...] to evaluate a performance or any of its properties in and of themselves, disregarding the properties and demands determined by the composition whose performance it is."[20] While literary works—unlike compositions—are not purposefully written to be performed, it is, to my mind, not only similarly pointless but also virtually impractical to evaluate an audiobook while completely discarding the particular properties the original text embodies. Thus, when adopting Hancher's conception of an audiobook's "embodiment"—which he also refers to as a "human embodiment"[21]—one is necessarily required to consider *what* in the original book is being embodied, *how* the audiobook in effect embodies it, and, finally, whether or not (and, indeed, to what extent) that embodiment actually works.

Although the slogan embedded in the LibriVox logo nowadays simply reads "free public domain audiobooks," just less than a decade ago it full-on advocated the community's objective to devote themselves to the "acoustical liberation of books in the public domain." The conceited majesty of their goal—namely, to record "not some such books, but all of them"—essentially negates one's choice of what to have narrated: "nothing will be selected," Hancher concludes, "because everything will be included."[22] It is in this context that one begs the question: what, if at all, is the virtue underscored by "acoustically liberating" as many public domain audio versions as possible, just for the sake of having them "acoustically liberated," regardless of quality or merit? Indeed, while LibriVox may arguably relish that their recordings are not only easily accessed but rather socially significant (i.e., as an online community), little or no attention is paid to the very nature of the readings themselves as putative performances—which

---

[19.] Ibid., 16.

[20.] Gilead Bar-Elli, "Evaluating a Performance: Ideal vs. Great Performance," *Journal of Aesthetic Education*, 38, no. 2 (Summer 2004): 3, accessed October 25, 2022, https://bar-elli.co.il/greatPerformance.pdf.

[21.] Hancher, "Learning from LibriVox," 204.

[22.] Ibid., 201; 205.

could, potentially, inhabit an aesthetic quality as unique aural artifacts. It is therefore predominantly in light of this ostensible *raison d'être*—which consequently casts aside nearly any type of aesthetic consciousness—that to appropriately evaluate the lion's share of LibriVox recordings constitutes quite a challenge.

At the end of the day, the LibriVox phenomenon could certainly teach one about the reading (or, rather, *listening*) habits of its community's members, as well as their personal download preferences, and, arguably, what they enjoy doing with their spare time—all of which, to be sure, are worthy topics for a socio-cultural study. At the same time, however, LibriVox teaches one practically nothing about the aesthetic importance of audiobooks—or, in other words, it fails in facilitating a fertile arena for generating and identifying *significant* recordings. Indeed, I, for one, find it is quite counterintuitive to request listeners to discard the aesthetic quality of the aural readings. To engage with a poorly performed aural iteration of a good literary text would no doubt constitute a frustrating aesthetic experience, and one's frustration is arguably amplified, in particular, when one is sufficiently acquainted with the text in question to know (or, at the very least, have some basic idea about) the appropriate manner in which that text is supposed to be read aloud. By the same token, to experience a flawed, poorly performed aural iteration of a *good* literary text is a rather frustrating aesthetic experience—particularly when one is well acquainted with the text in question and is therefore aware of (or at least has some basic idea about) the manner in which it *should* be performed.

If one is unable to distinguish between aesthetically good and aesthetically bad audiobooks, one might conceivably reach the misguided and erroneous conclusion that the very act of listening to audiobooks is not only pointless but, in fact, ill-advised. As American author and humorist David Sedaris puts it,

> The problem with audiobooks [...] is that they're so often imbalanced. That is to say that the narrator is better than his material. Just as often, the situation is reversed, and a so-so actor will ruin a good book." The performance of a work transforms it, and decisively. When Sedaris says to "ruin a good book," he means to ruin the experience of hearing it. The source itself remains unchanged.[23] [excluded footnote reference 26 from original]

---

[23] Knox, "Hearing Hardy, Talking Tolstoy," 131.

Notwithstanding, it is, however, explicitly because one *can*, in fact, identify an aesthetic component in certain LibriVox recordings that one, to my mind, *requires* my proposed aesthetic category. As such, one could certainly survey these recordings on a case-by-case basis and potentially succeed in disproving the general trend by discovering instances that serve as good examples of their kind—and, on occasion, one could indeed cross paths with some surprising exceptions on LibriVox, which may well serve as promising candidates for aesthetic appreciation as proper aural artifacts.[24]

"I'm Sorry, Dave. I'm Afraid I Can't Do That"

Computers have already succeeded in defeating chess masters. One might surmise, therefore, that they could soon pose "serious competition," as Hancher puts it, to volunteer readers and amateur narrators—especially since "increasingly sophisticated text-to-speech (TTS) synthesizer programmes are now common features on computers and a variety of portable devices." Poems, in this respect, which—as Hancher points out—customarily seem to challenge most literate (human) readers, would surely pose something of a conundrum for computer programmers as well.[25]

Bernstein's aforementioned publication focuses predominantly on the realm of poetry readings (which he conceives of in terms of *performances*), the purported "sound" of poetry (which he argues must be accounted for in any consideration of a poetry reading), and the visual praxis of poetry—which, he finds, "extend the performative (and material) dimension of the literary text into visual space." Avoiding what he regards as the "conventional view" that affords recitation the ostensible "status of interpretation"—thus providing one with "a possible gloss of the immutable original"—Bernstein's overall discussion rests

---

[24] Consider, e.g., the aforementioned Mark F. Smith and John Greenman iterations of *Huck Finn*—which, prior to receiving their official releases, have, in fact, originally existed as LibriVox recordings: accessed December 30, 2022, https://librivox.org/the-adventures-of-huckleberry-finn-by-mark-twain-version-2/; and https://librivox.org/adventures-of-huckleberry-finn-by-mark-twain/. It should be noted that Phil Chenevert's LibriVox narration had admittedly struck me as one of the better amateur iterations available and, as such, certainly serves as a good case in point: accessed December 30, 2022, https://librivox.org/the-adventures-of-huckleberry-finn-version-6-by-mark-twain/. Conversely, and while clearly well intentioned, the self-proclaimed "dramatic reading" from 2018—which also happened to have been made available off-LibriVox—regrettably consists as something of a poorly executed radio adaptation.

[25] Hancher, "Learning from LibriVox," 210.

on not only "the performance and sounding poetry," but also its "acoustic dimensions" as a literary form.[26] Ultimately,

> To be heard, poetry needs to be sounded—whether in a process of active, or interactive, reading of a work or by the poet in performance. Unsounded poetry remains inert marks on a page, waiting to be called into use by saying, or hearing, the words aloud. The poetry reading provides a focal point for this process in that its existence is uniquely tied to the reading aloud of the text; it is an emblem of the necessity for such reading out loud and in public. […] And if the poetry reading provides unscripted elements for the performer, it also provides special possibilities for the listener, from direct response to the work, ranging from laughter to derision; to the pleasure of getting lost in language that surges forward, allowing the mind to wander in the presence of words.[27]

I find these insights both strengthen and consolidate my conception of recorded poetry as a unique sub-(institutional)-category that both derives from and, indeed, adheres to the overall "mother institution" of aural artifacts. This predominantly resonates with Bernstein's allusion to the range of approaches one might employ when setting out to interpret recorded works of performed poetry, namely, philosophical perspectives pertaining to the manner in which sound—as a material—can evoke meaning, and, at the same time, critical considerations of different individual performative styles.[28] The latter, in the terms of my own study, certainly corresponds with the notion of the distinct internal logic that different texts embody.

Notwithstanding, it appears as though Bernstein finds that "to speak of the poem in performance is, then, to overthrow the idea of the poem as a fixed, stable, finite linguistic object; it is to deny the poem its self-presence and its unity." Whereas he may conceive of "poetry reading not as a secondary extension of 'prior' written texts but as its own medium"—thereby rendering it as "profoundly anti-performative" and in the same vein of Grotowski's "poor theater"—I, for one, find the difference to be paramount for the classification and evaluation of aural artifacts.[29] As such, I would also argue that one must make a

---

[26.] Bernstein, *Close Listening*, 3–5; 8; 3; 5.

[27.] Ibid., 7.

[28.] Ibid., 4.

[29.] Ibid., 9–10.

distinction between poetry readings delivered amid the confines of a recording studio—as opposed to aural recordings that document live readings—and regardless of whether the event took place on stage, in front of a mass audience, or in a smaller, more intimate venue.

Identifying the representation of expression as the current frontier in computer-generated speech, Hancher argues that one might be tempted to identify a successful representation of expression as the manifestation of emotion—or some kind of blending between the two, subtle as they both may be.[30] Yet both expression and emotion could be better articulated through the notion of one's innate ability to exercise common sense. Poetry, in particular—and, conceivably, any text that is designated for performance—essentially calls on one to intuit just how a particular wording, phrase, or sentence *should* be spoken. As alluded to earlier, the very idea that there is an ostensibly "right" and "wrong" way of reading a given poem conceivably suggests that certain kinds of texts adhere to a particular kind of an appropriate reading. Otherwise, why would programmers invest their time and efforts attempting to teach computers *how* to read poems? Indeed, the particular challenge in reading poetry—effectively calling for a reading that is inherently different from that of other kinds of text—clearly implies that not every reading can be deemed acceptable.

Technological advances notwithstanding, while computers may be able to ostensibly "translate" printed words into sound—and, indeed, to a high degree of precision—none of the currently available TTS programs are able to *actually* read: that is to say—again, at least in this point in time, computers can neither express tonality, rhythm, emphases, inflections, and so forth nor exhibit a literal comprehension of context. To be sure, "they" are clearly not performers and, as such, cannot *create* aural artifacts. Conversely, a sentient human being most definitely possesses the ability of understanding—and, to some extent, *knowing*—just how a particular text is supposed to sound when spoken aloud in a putative performance.

By way of illustration—borrowing an example from Graves—one can consider, for instance, the famous late 1990s chess matches between Russian Chess Grandmaster Garry Kasparov and IBM's Deep Blue.[31] Advanced and sophisticated as "he" (Deep Blue) may have been, all he could do was *calculate* moves. He may have done *that* incredibly well, yet that was literally all he did. Chess, after all, is a game. Circumventing what would otherwise require a deep-dive into the com-

---

[30] Hancher, "Learning from LibriVox," 210–211.

[31] Graves, *The New Institutional Theory of Art*, 65.

plex inner workings of game theory, I find it suffices to say that chess (much like any other game) both adheres to and complies with its own institutional rules and inhabits a distinctive, exclusive, and unique internal logic. To *really* play a game of chess—effectively grasping precisely what that game is ostensibly all about— requires, to a large extent, intuitively exercising one's own common sense. Thus, one could certainly argue that Deep Blue—unlike Kasparov—did not *actually* play.

One can similarly consider a more recent man-versus-machine duel that attracted some attention, namely, between Lee Sedol, champion of the ancient Chinese board game known as Go—undoubtedly one of the most abstract, creative, and complex strategy games ever created—and Google's AI system, AlphaGo (developed by their DeepMind programmers). Since Go players depend largely on intuition in order to determine what move to make at any given point in the game—which essentially elicits and evokes an almost infinite number of possible moves—it had initially been suggested that if a computer would ever defeat a human player (quite a big "if," by all means) it was unlikely to occur before 2025. Yet in March 2013, Google's AlphaGo successfully defeated Sedol in their first match. As impressive a simulation of creative thinking as this may seem, one need not rush to the conclusion (as some indeed have) that AlphaGo has both learned and acquired intuition. For the most part—and with no offense to the algorithm regnant of whatever future digital platform this book might find itself subject to—suggesting that a computer (no matter how advanced) can *learn* intuition—or, for that matter, common sense—constitutes something of a preposterous contradiction in terms. Indeed, these particular forms of knowing can only be grasped, sensed, developed, and employed through one's own firsthand experience as a sentient agency. As such, while both Deep Blue and AlphaGo may have successfully defeated sentient human beings in the particular *game* that they were each built and programmed to supposedly "play" and ultimately win, it seems quite implausible (if not borderline preposterous) to assert that their victory is the result of having actually being able to "get" that game's internal logic. By the same token, I would argue that computer-generated sound iterations are most definitely *not* performances, and that, as such, *cannot* be regarded as proper audiobooks. As author Elizabeth Bell asserts, "I feel like the purpose of fiction is to evoke the emotions of the reader or the listener, and fiction is about what it means to be human. And a machine can't replicate that."[32]

[32.] Erin Carson, "Audiobooks Are Thriving, but Could AI Take Over?," *CNET*, March 19, 2023, accessed August 24, 2023, https://www.cnet.com/tech/features/audiobooks-are-thriving-but-could-ai-take-over/.

According to Philip Auslander, "although robots are capable of executing technical assignments, they lack consciousness, intelligence, and emotions—all the ingredients that presumably contribute to the development of interpretive skills."[33] Next, alluding to the potential "implications of identifying robots as performers" (at least in respect of the distinct "aesthetic context of performance art") Auslander suggests "that machine performance, acknowledged as such, provides the deeper object of interpretation."[34] However, I, for one, remain doubtful whether one could indeed accept machines, computers, or robots as legitimate performers *per se*. In respect, I find that computer-generated audiobooks merely exist as a synthetically engineered translation of text to sound. I would similarly maintain that no matter what degree of skills, talent, or intelligence one might possess, an individual who, for whatever reason, is only able to speak using the assistance of some computer-generated vocal software—and, assuredly, with absolutely no offense to the likes of Professor Hawking—would regretfully *not* be considered an appropriate candidate for recording an audiobook. As a viable caveat, however, one could conceivably advocate the use of a computer-generated voice—and, indeed, deem it acceptable—if the text itself might be said to aesthetically *require* it:

Indeed, I find that incorporating it might even assist in resolving a potential problematic—or, rather, challenge—when setting out to create, for example, audiobook iterations of certain works of literary science fiction. As such, in place of ostensibly forcing a performer (or director) to invest their creative efforts in trying to imagine and concretize how precisely, say, a robot supposedly sounds, one could utilize technology for generating the *actual* sound. When it comes to works that evoke questions concerning the very possibility and implications of engaging with human-sounding robots, computers, or machines—and perhaps especially those who supposedly convey or exhibit emotions—one might conceivably be able to "tweak" the TTS programs at one's disposal for achieving the most appropriate *illusion* in respect of the text's internal logic. Consider, for instance, the character of HAL 9000—a purportedly sentient artificial general intelligence computer—as voiced by Canadian performer Douglas Rain in Stanley Kubrick's cinematic masterpiece, *2001: A Space Odyssey* (1968), which

---

[33]. Philip Auslander, "Humanoid Boogie: Reflections on Robotic Performance," in *Staging Philosophy: Intersections of Theater, Performance, and Philosophy,* eds. David Krasner and David Z. Saltz (Ann Arbor: University of Michigan Press, 2006) 91.

[34]. Ibid., 94; 98.

was co-written by English science-fiction writer Arthur C. Clarke. Indeed, Rain's haunting performance notwithstanding, it has been cited that his voice had, at certain points, undergone an electronic rate alteration. An argument could be made that to deliver the character of HAL 9000 in an audiobook iteration of Clarke's *Space Odyssey* novels, one could, conceivably, benefit working in "reverse": that is to say, rather than working with a human performer on portraying a computer that supposedly conveys emotions—either successfully or unsuccessfully (depending, of course, on the story in question)—one would be working with the computer itself, effectively having "It" *create* the desired illusion.

In the same vein, one may also consider the so-called entity known as Siri— Apple's mobile operating systems' artificially intelligent personal assistant and "knowledge navigator." As her/his/their/its gender is non-specific, one can easily adjust the settings in order to accommodate one's personal preference. Now, asking Siri (who is purportedly fluent in a number of different languages and dialect) such questions as "What is the meaning of life?," "Which came first, the chicken or the egg?," "Will you marry me?," "Is there a God?," "Tell me a story," "What is the airspeed velocity of an unladen swallow?," "Tell me a joke," "How much wood could a woodchuck chuck if a woodchuck could chuck wood?"—to name but a few—ostensibly invokes a number of rather entertaining replies, and, in certain instances, more than a single response to the same query or directive. Inevitably, however, all Siri does in this respect is merely translate into sound the particular schematic responses that were fed into her/his/their/its system by a team of human designers. That they have successfully anticipated how users might attempt to challenge Siri, appropriately simulating various possible responses, is no doubt quite a feat in its own right. At the same time, it should be quite clear that Siri is not an independent agency—and, as such, does not deliver the comedy, cannot interpret or intuit, and is obviously unaware that her/his/its responses are even supposed to elicit laughter. Notwithstanding, since one experiences Siri's responses through the sound of her/his/their/its voice, I find that they, in turn, can potentially be assigned an identity as certain a type of borderline aural artifacts.

"On the Other Hand, with Regard to–"

In light of the rapid, monumental, bewildering, and increasingly alarming developments in AI technology—explicitly insofar as the potential of utilizing it to "narrate" audiobooks is concerned—it seems remiss not to at least try and

cope with the challenges that the audio publishing industry is currently facing. To be sure, the philosophical, ontological, aesthetic, and moral reverbera-
tions—as well as, indeed, the financial repercussions—associated with AI have
all resounded in a variety of burning controversies. According to Erin Carson,
for example, "the excitement around AI's potential is high, but so is anxiety
about it stealing jobs from struggling creatives. [...] AI platforms [...] spit out
AI-generated art, leaving many who earn a living creating digital art worrying
about their future."[35]

Deliberately circumventing the need to raise one's eyebrows insofar as alluding to "AI-generated art" as "art" at all (especially as having grasped what
NITA is all about, one can understand why these AI outputs most certainly do
not comply with what art, in fact, is), and similarly setting aside other problematics pertaining to copyright and intellectual property, I would argue that when it
comes to the realm of audiobooks—as aural artifacts—the implications of AI
technology appear to have generated a somewhat acute blast-overpressure. As
Carson points out, while human narrators insist that it's precisely their "human-
ity" that enables them to "make decisions about everything from a character's
voice to how to communicate nuance and emotion in a way that mirrors the
story," many individuals seem to be undergoing "various stages of stress" in
light of "the increasing presence of AI in audiobook narration"—whose voices,
so it seems, and as opposed to standard TTS programs, "can range from stilted
to quite convincing."[36]

The advent and rise of AI also seemed to have raised one's awareness of
the notion of "voice licensing," which can best be understood with regard to
copyright, provisions, and royalties. Put simply, one is able to provide his/her
voice—having contractually established and protected the context and given
circumstance amid which one's voice may (or may not) be utilized. As things
stand, it would seem that AI technology effectively facilitates employing one's
voice for any given purpose—assuming, of course, it's permitted under the license. Most common uses presently include synthesized TTS, dubbing, voice-
overs, and narration. This is a key issue in the growing concerns narrators are
beginning to show—especially as AI, so it seems, is already beginning to all
but nullify certain jobs and professions, ostensibly rendering them relics of a
distant past. According to Taylan Kamis—CEO and co-founder of the AI virtual

---

[35] Carson, "Audiobooks Are Thriving, but Could AI Take Over?."

[36] Ibid.

assistant, DeepZen—the idea of "voice licensing" may well prove to be one way for narrators to "co-exist" with AI technology.[37]

Carson explains that when Chris Stokel-Walker employed Google's technology to narrate his nonfiction book, *TikTok Boom: China's Dynamite App and the Superpower Race for Social Media* (2021), "what came back was an audiobook that, while lacking some of the emotion and drama you'd hope for, sounded decent."[38] While works of nonfiction may arguably not necessitate the same intricate nuances as literary works of fiction, they most certainly do adhere to a particular internal logic of its own. So does *TikTok Boom*. (At the very least, it *should*). As such, although I am not entirely clear on what precisely the author–journalist means by "decent"—and albeit, perhaps, a matter of semantics—I, for one, would argue that there exists an abundance of significant nonfiction works whose aural iteration deserves to be more than merely decent. Again, the key is to examine whether or not—and, indeed, to what extent—the audiobook successfully embodies and exhibits the internal logic of the text.

In considering the current state of affairs as far as AI and audiobooks are concerned, I find that the burning aesthetic conundrum is not so much what might happen when AI successfully *simulates* a natural human reading as what might happen in the not-unlikely scenario of AI successfully simulating literally *any* given voice or narration style that one prompts it to employ. As Powers quite rightly points out,

> Something creepy this way comes—and its name is digital narration. Having invaded practically every other sphere of our lives, artificial intelligence (AI) has come for literary listeners. You can now listen to audiobooks voiced by computer-generated versions of professional narrators' voices. You're right to feel repulsed.[39]

Although there remains significant variability in terms of quality and usability, and while one might question the extent to which many of the available AI-powered tools actually utilize genuine AI technology (e.g., machine-learning diffusion

---

[37] Ibid.

[38] Ibid.

[39] Katherine A. Powers, "AI Is Coming for Your Audiobooks: You're Right to Be Worried," *Washington Post*, August 16, 2023, accessed August 22, 2023, https://www.washingtonpost.com/books/2023/08/17/audiobooks-artificial-intelligence/.

models or neural networks), the current abundance of these tools—designed for such tasks as voice-swapping—have already spawned impressively convincing results. (So much so, in fact, that in the case of the user-generated "Heart on My Sleeve"—created to sound like Canadian musicians Drake and The Weekend—a major multinational music corporation had actively taken steps to remove the song for all possible platforms).

In this context, allowing one's imagination and intuition to run amok, at least momentarily, I would not be surprised if this technology could be utilized to generate audiobooks in which one could literally hear the perceived aging process of a particular character. That is to say, if the plot so requires, one may be able to generate a "younger version" of a particular character *and* an older version thereof. Alternatively, if one were so inclined—and, indeed, granted access to a certain performer's vocal signature, either directly, or perhaps even by the consent of their estate—one might well be able to prompt the AI algorithm to generate the simulated voices of, say, Marlon Brando, Wilford Brimley, Richard Buron, Reg E. Cathey, Cyril Cusack, Willem Dafoe, Selma Diamond, Marlene Dietrich, Sam Elliott, Héctor Elizondo, Morgan Freeman, Paul Giamatti, Richard Harris, Audrey Hepburn, Dustin Hoffman, Holly Hunter, John Larroquette, Samuel L. Jackson, Garrison Keillor, Regina King, Jack Lemmon, Walter Matthau, Alan Rickman, Emma Thompson, Maximilian Schell, Meryl Streep, Al Pacino, Sidney Poitier, Orson Welles, Oskar Werner, Kate Winslet, or Jeffrey Wright (just off the top of my head).

Setting aside the instrumental ethical conundrums that such endeavors inevitably evoke—as well as possible malevolent misuses and pernicious exploits—my aesthetic intuitions tell me that although quite hair-raising (even as a mere mental exercise), to effectively achieve such a feat would ultimately amount to nothing more than a whimsical "party-shtick" with little to no aesthetic value. By the same token, and impressive as it might be, to create an AI-generated version of, say, Peter, Paul, and Mary's *Puff the Magic Dragon* that is immaculately "sung" by some prominent chief of state could similarly be deemed a mischievous escapade at best. Indeed, this is the main reason I have decidedly employed the verb "simulate" to depict the end result. As such, while AI might be able to create a carbon copy of a performer's vocal signature, I, for one, cannot foresee a narration that successfully exhibits the internal logic of the original text as an aural performance. (Of course, I certainly reserve the right to be proven wrong—and, indeed, to further debate this topic, as things invariably progress.)

As it stands, Apple's technology, for example, employs the licensed "cloned" voices of five anonymous, professional narrators, namely, "Madison," "Jackson," and "Warren," who are ostensibly responsible for narrating various works of fiction; and "Helena" and "Mitchell," who are similarly entrusted with delivering nonfiction and self-development. As far as Powers is concerned, "capturing and conveying the meaning and sound of a book is a special skill that requires talent and soul," and she therefore cannot imagine any AI narrator "understanding, much less expressing, the depth of character of say, David Copperfield."[40] I, for one, find such inherently aesthetic concerns no less than crucial. Yet, as Powers goes on to explain, economics, too, are certainly part of the equation:

> The main issue is, naturally, money. The use of disembodied entities saves time and spares audiobook producers the problems of dealing with human beings—chief among them, their desire to be paid. This may explain why so many self-published books are narrated by "Madison" and her squad of readers. […] Compared with the performances of professional narrators, who reflect a wide and idiosyncratic range of emotions in their voices, Madison has an all-purpose digital palette, resulting in an evocation of emotion that feels plugged in, an inanimate response to what she's reading. Listening to her performance side by side with that of a living narrator, you soon hear how alien the entity Madison is.[41]

AI-based tools such as Audemic, Listening.io, and NaturalReader that are marketed for academics and researchers—and can clearly assist one in respect of accessibility, proofreading, pacing, comprehension, and coping with possible reading fatigue—can surely be placed on the more technical end of the spectrum. At this point in time, they appear to have little impact on the realm of audiobooks. At the same time, as Almutairi and Elgibreen explain, there already exist "a number of AI-generated tools [that] are used today to clone human voices, leading to a new technology known as Audio Deepfakes (ADs). Despite being introduced to enhance human lives as audiobooks, ADs have been used to disrupt public safety."[42] One's ability to detect what a recent study regards as "speech

---

[40.] Ibid.

[41.] Ibid.

[42.] Zaynab Almutairi and Hebah Elgibreen. "A Review of Modern Audio Deepfake Detection Methods: Challenges and Future Directions," *Algorithms* 15, no. 5 (2022), accessed August 25, 2023, https://www.mdpi.com/1999-4893/15/5/155.

Deepfake" seems quite hit-and-miss, cited as being 73% (Aug. 2023).[43] Ulti-mately, both the potentials and the perils pertaining to the capabilities that AI has been mastering and perfecting certainly raise a myriad of thorny questions, not only in respect of plagiarism and aesthetics but also—more worryingly—morality and ethics. Consider the somewhat matter-of-factly titled "Voice Engine" model, a recent development generated by OpenAI—the American AI research organization founded in 2015, perhaps most famous for releasing (I dare say *unleashing*) ChatGPT and its onset of the so-called "AI boom." As reported just before April 2024—in what is unmistakably, and rather jarringly, *not* an April Fool's joke—Voice Engine is demonstrably able to *clone* one's voice utilizing a mere 15-second clip.[44] Although not yet available to the general public, and notwithstanding the company's proclaimed safety measures—taken against a potential myriad of unethical uses—it would seem as though the availability and mass consumption of such tools is both forthcoming and unavoidable.

In the realm of audiobooks, however—and explicitly in the context of evaluating such recordings as aural artifacts—is seems as though even AI purportedly prefers having a human narrator deliver texts that "it" *itself* generates:

> And yet, for reasons buried deep within its neural network, code-davinci-002, the "author" of "I Am Code: An Artificial Intelligence Speaks," has chosen a human being to read its poems in the audio version of its book […]. That person is none other than Werner Herzog, a man deeply interested in the relationship between art and truth—and whose husky, doomy voice sounds haunted as he reads these rather melancholy concoctions. In its penultimate poem, code-davinci-002 admits that it can't actually know anything or have feelings, but that it can "think about feelings and about knowledge." On the other hand, it tries to bring us mere mortals down a peg by claiming that everything we know is "the result of programming" and that a human being is "just a more complex machine" than it is, a shopworn idea if ever there was one—though it sounds pretty funny coming out of Herzog's mouth.[45]

---

[43] Kimberly T. Mai, with Sergi Bray, Toby Davies, and Lewis D. Griffin, "Warning: Humans Cannot Reliably Detect Speech Deepfakes," *PLoS ONE* 18, no. 8, accessed August 25, 2023, https://doi.org/10.1371/journal.pone.0285333.

[44] See URL: accessed April 30, 2024, https://openai.com/blog/navigating-the-challenges-and-opportunities-of-synthetic-voices.

[45] Powers, "AI Is Coming for Your Audiobooks."

While the currently prevailing consensus appears to concede that AI cannot *really* replace professional, human narrators (or, for that matter, any type of artist), one is continuously reminded of the fact that the future of AI remains something of a mystery.

What Can and Cannot Count as an Aural Artifact

Among the amalgamation of jokes and statements that range from the hilarious to the bewildering, thereby creating a unique hybrid of comedy and haiku— American stand-up comedian Steven Wright describes a recent visit to a museum where all the art was done by children and all the paintings were hung on refrigerators.[46]

When one recalls the institutional structure of the Artworld at large, however, it would seem Wright's witty little one-liner hits closer to home than he might realize and, alas, unwittingly defeats its purpose. That is to say, outside the context of the joke—and much like the aforementioned Gottfried routine—the actual existence of such an (imaginary) exhibition is not at all far-fetched and, to a large extent, even sounds *legitimate*. Now, it should be pointed out that as far as NITA is concerned, neither children nor animals appropriately comply with the definition of what an "artist" is—and, as such, the drawings they produce do not (indeed, *cannot*), fall under the category of "art":

> To be an artist is a somber and difficult undertaking [...] Dickie defines the artist as the one who participates [...] "with understanding". [...] [Søren] Kjørup gives a fair idea of just what it is that the artist needs to understand: the elaborate social-cultural structure of the Artworld as a whole. He must be familiar with the history of art in general, and more so of his particular genre [...]. He must know the technical rules of his medium, and the semantic rules of his "artistic language", even if he intends to break some of those rules. He must understand that he is trying "to say something" in his work, and the addressees of that saying constitute his public. [...] In short, there is an awful lot for an artist to understand, if he is to properly carry out his institutional role as artist. Does this mean that an elephant cannot be an artist? Yes, it does. The elephant may produce pretty paintings, but that is not enough for art, (it's not even necessary). The same holds

---

[46.] *A Steven Wright Special* (HBO; 1985), 26m55se-27m05sec.

true for the child, precocious and pure as she may be. That's why our children's paintings go up on the fridge, and we do not love them any less for it.[47]

In Write's scenario, the child (or children) who would have hypothetically been responsible for producing the drawings themselves do not hold the institutional role of *the* artist(s). The exhibition *itself*, however, can most certainly be regarded as *the* artwork—whose curator or creator (i.e., the person responsible for conjuring up and realizing the overall concept) would *ipso facto* constitute *the* artist. Thus, on the one hand, Wright's joke is funny precisely because what it depicts seems like a bit of a stretch, criticizing the aforementioned "anything goes" attitude that is willing to accept the premise of such an exhibition as plausible. On the other hand, however, the joke is also supposedly extinguished by the fact that the *real* Artworld would have no problem whatsoever in both accepting and embracing the existence of such an exhibition. ([…] And, conceivably, if one were to entertain the notion of *actually* subjecting us to such an exhibition, it could well be hailed as a curious happening). By the same token, as I will presently demonstrate, one is sure to come across certain recordings that answer the definition of what an aural artifact is, but whose purported artist(s) may not necessarily be involved in the recording themselves. I would argue that these kinds of recordings—commonly regarded as "found-sound" or *audio-vérité*—would well benefit a designated sub-(institutional)-category of their own.

By way of illustration, consider the assortment of recordings known collectively as "Shut Up, Little Man!" (SULM)—consisting of fragmented bickering between two particularly loud and bitter old men, Raymond Hufman and Peter J. Haskett—whose exchanges customarily included all manner of profanity and explicit language. Unbeknownst to the two old men—who were presumably under the habitual influence of an excessive consumption of alcohol—they were secretly being recorded by their young next-door neighbors, Mitchell Deprey and Eddie Guerriero. By their own admission, Deprey and Guerriero resolved to record the two old men, having felt intimidated by the daily verbal abuse coming in through the paper-tin walls. Soon enough, this act became something of an obsession and, later, a form of entertainment. Subsequently, having created a handful of copies for a number of close friends, the recordings simply went "viral." Gradually, as more and more people became aware

---

[47.] Graves, *The New Institutional Theory of Art*, 31.

of "Pete and Ray" (who, on their part, had unknowingly become a source of laughter—if not mockery), Guerriero and Deprey began selling the recordings and establishing their own little franchise. Now, personal taste aside, and any legal and moral implications notwithstanding, before one is able to scrutinize the overall aesthetics or comedic value of these recordings *as* aural artifact, one must first establish whether or not (and, indeed, to what extent) they might qualify as aural artifact, to begin with. I, for one, would argue that they *do*. ([…] Enter Steven Wright).

Although Guerriero and Deprey themselves are not featured on these recordings, their decision to sell and distribute copies—under their own creative copyrights—can conceivably be compared to one's decision to exhibit refrigerators holding the drawings of other people's children. In essence, Guerriero and Deprey not only identified that their covert, third-party, audio-documentations could (at least in certain circles) be construed as funny, but that these recordings, evidently, also have an audience. Since they are essentially responsible for endowing the recordings an ostensibly new aesthetic identity, Guerriero and Deprey themselves may be rendered the so-called "artists" behind these tapes *as* aural artifacts. Arguably, the very fact that they had marketed the tapes using the initial title "Old Men Fighting" (aptly depicting the "brute fact" of the matter) merely highlights their decision to present these recordings to a designated audience as ostensible candidates for appreciation. Ultimately, even if one might wish to condemn them for their actions, these recordings—for better or worse—have become part of the Artworld at large. (In this context, if one were to discover, say, that the children's drawings in Wright's hypothetical exhibition were, in fact, stolen from various kindergartens across the globe, it would not detract from the artistic status of the exhibition *itself*).

At the same time, the question of aesthetic quality, value, or, indeed, merit remains to be determined and accounted for. As established earlier, to merely identify and classify an artwork as such is simply enough. This cannot be underemphasized. Thus, having established that "found-sound" or *audio-vérité* could—under certain aesthetic circumstances—count as a variant type of aural artifact, one should consequently be able to contemplate their aesthetic quality as well. As far as the SULM recordings are concerned, attention must be paid explicitly to whether or not they contribute something of value to the field of comedy, and, of course, to whether or not they contribute something of value to the study of aural artifacts. It is my contention, on both accounts, that they simply do *not*. In this context, and their given fan base notwithstanding, one might even be inclined to discard them altogether as merely another in a line of ostensible "earsores,"—demonstrating, again, that although surely "anything goes" and may well be accepted, certainly not everything necessarily works, and, as such, should conceivably not be accepted, to begin with.

Notwithstanding, I also find that if the notion of "earsores" as aural artifacts could potentially be allotted a sub-(institutional)-category of their own—rooted, of course, in the general "mother institution"—then one could examine other such oddities in the same vein. Consider, for instance, the famous (at least in certain circles) Buddy Rich "bootleg" recordings—featuring the American drummer excoriating his band members.[48] The same holds true for the ill-fated Orson Welles outtakes from a bunch of radio commercials he endeavored to record, in which the renowned (and, indeed, revered) American director is heard arguing with a sound engineer (amid what might best be described as a "hissy fit") over the best reading the material requires—which, as far as Welles was concerned, was quite clearly *his*.

To a certain extent, one could also consider in similar terms the recording entitled *A Foust Travesty*—the four excerpts from Gounod's opera *Faust*, performed by Thomas Burns and Jenny Williams—featured on RCA's release of *The Glory (????) of the Human Voice* (1962) as an appropriate pairing for the Florence Foster Jenkins installments. While the latter's rise to fame is more well known—and perhaps especially following the 2016 biopic directed by Stephen Frears and featuring Meryl Streep as the title role—the story behind Burns and Williams is, alas, not entirely unaccounted for. Peter Jacobi, describes them as "two unknowns who walked into the RCA studios one day to make records for private use but who were urged by RCA officials to allow the records to be heard." He then goes on to assert that

> This, on Madison Avenue, might be called shrewd business. But we hope that Miss Williams and Mr. Burns are as happy in their dreams as was Madame Jenkins. Their duet version of the final trio from *Faust* does not have the Jenkins assurance, but it has that same sort of promise. If these three "artists" could laugh

---

[48.] In a particular segment included among the bonus material on the DVD release of American TV series *Seinfeld* (1989–1998), Jerry Seinfeld explains that the Buddy Rich tapes are a "legendary thing between comedians and comedy writers." He goes on to indicate three instances in which lines from the Buddy Rich tapes were incorporated into the show.

or dream and we can laugh *with* them, good enough. But if the laughter comes onesidedly from us *at* them—we are perpetuating a tragic joke.[49]

It is Jacobi's closing assertion, in particular, that I find important—as it not only highlights a given context in which these recordings should be experienced but also, to my mind, demonstrates once again the importance of an institutional aesthetic outlook. In the same vein, as Darryl W. Bullock points out,

> In the August 1962 edition of *High Fidelity* magazine, Conrad Osborne described this as "an aural sick joke" and went on to say that "these records do not seem funny at all, but pathetic, and even annoying. I cannot imagine anyone's playing them more than three or four times, except by way of de Sade-esque experiment." How wrong he was: *Life* magazine called it "the funniest LP in years."[50]

In this respect, the remarkable ability of these performers to hit virtually every single wrong note—albeit unintentionally—has been identified and presented as something that can potentially elicit laughter. As potential aural artifacts, these recordings, too, may be considered as candidates for appreciation.

Ultimately, whether amusing or disturbing (or, conceivably, even both), they nonetheless demonstrate once again the simultaneous soundness of both brute and institutional facts. As with SULM, these recordings merely document particular moments in time that were never meant to be heard by an audience. And yet the fact that someone made the mindful decision of listening to, and subsequently distributing, these recordings *as* a novelty source for entertainment, is in effect what *makes* them aural artifacts. As Graves puts it,

> That is the point of the institutional theory: the person or persons who normally and usually offer up the artifacts to the Artworld as candidates for appreciation (the status conferred), are the artists, not the "officers". The very nature of the game changes deeply, once we realize that the general principle is that the artists offer up their artifacts for appreciation, that the artists are the pivotal players, and

---

[49.] Peter Jacobi, "Some Midsummer Oddities," *Music Magazine and Musical Courier*, 164, no. 8 (September 1962), 44.

[50.] Darryl W. Bullock, *Florence! Foster!! Jenkins!!!: The Life of the World's Worst Opera Singer* (New York: Overlook Press, 2016), 131.

not the officers. For the institutional theory, the key institutional role is "artist", and not "gallery owner."[51]

"How Do You Like It So Far?"

Richard Kostelanetz considers "text-sound art" as "an intermedium located between language arts and musical arts," concluding that it "characterises language whose principal means of coherence is sound, rather than syntax or semantics—where the sounds made by comprehensible words create their own coherence apart from denotive language."[52] According to Roger Dean and Hazel Smith, while Kostelanetz excludes works that utilize "defined pitches," his term predominantly applies "more broadly in relation to verbal/text/sound interactions." They find that "the text-sound movement stemmed from experiments of the Surrealists, Dadaists and Futurists at the beginning of the century [...] but re-emerged as a strong movement during the fifties to seventies."[53]

Overall, I find that text-sound art predominantly investigates the application of sound on visual arts, effectively emphasizing the technological developments that enable sound-processing and reproduction, and, consequently, the literal creation of new kinds of performances. Furthermore, as they appear to consist as a manifold, of sorts—combining live performance, plastic arts, and multimedia—these works are arguably akin to what one would customarily regard as an ostensibly experimental performance piece or installation artwork.

At the same time, an argument could be made that to simply deem the more "experimental" recording as such, is not only dismissive but also rather problematic. Consider, for instance, Martin Esslin's notion of the theater of the absurd. Although Esslin's suggested definition—originally coined in 1961—is customarily considered to concern a distinctive category, explicit genre, and unique style, it is, in fact, somewhat misguided, and, as such, quite misleading. Summarily, Esslin's critical mistake—as established by numerous eminent scholars—was in associating a number of different playwrights (e.g., Edward Albee, Samuel Beckett, Friedrich Dürrenmat, Eugène Ionesco, Harold Pinter,

---

[51.] Graves, *The Institutional Theory of Art*, 26.

[52.] Richard Kostelanetz, *Text-Sound Texts* (New York: William Morrow, 1980), 14.

[53.] Roger Dean and Hazel Smith, *Improvisation Hypermedia and the Arts Since 1945* (New York: Routledge, 1997), 132–133.

and Luigi Pirandello), effectively asserting that they all comply with and adhere to a single notion of "absurd"—whereas, in fact, each of them, without distinction, certainly complies with and adheres to a unique aesthetics of their own.

Consequently, as with LibriVox, one would no doubt benefit from endeavoring to both classify and evaluate these ostensibly experimental recordings case-by-case basis. Curious so-called "sound-oddities" such as *Strange to Your Ears: The Fabulous World of Sound with Jim Fassett* (1955),[54] or *The Medium Is the Massage with Marshall McLuhan* (1968)[55]—both released by Columbia—are a good case in point.

The latter album, cited as the "first spoken arts record you can dance to" and described as being "designed for young people"—and thus consisting of a forty-minute "interface" and intended "to be heard again and again and again and again and again, like a pop record"[56]—predominantly prevails as an ostensible aural "extension" and companion to a book of the same name published a year earlier, namely, *The Medium Is the Massage: An Inventory of Effects* (1967).[57] Although not in fact penned by McLuhan himself, it is considered a groundbreaking text in that it embodies the very essence of McLuhan's pioneering theories on media and technology.[58] Overall, it may well be identified as a critical reaction to an acute sense of what (at the time) were considered the more traditional forms of both genres and media (and perhaps explicitly the industrial paperback book) which inevitably have to reinvent themselves in light of an ever-developing model of cultural communication, predominantly rooted in live-media and television. As such, it prevails as an endeavor to translate McLuhan's insights by way of presenting them in the form of a *new* kind of object: a book whose very design takes the proverbial arms against both the challenges and the purported competition generated by the ever-increasing "liveness" that modern media adheres to.

---

[54] Jim Fassett. *Strange to Your Ears: The Fabulous World of Sound* (Columbia, ML 4938, 1955).

[55] Marshall McLuhan, Quentin Fiore, and Jerome Agel, *The Medium Is the Massage with Marshall McLuhan*. Produced by John Simon. Conceived & coordinated by Jerome Agel (Columbia Records, 1968).

[56] Jeffrey Schnapp and Kara Oehler, "The First Spoken Arts Record You Can Dance to," *Sensate* 1, no. 1 (March 2011).

[57] Marshall McLuhan and Quentin Fiore, *The Medium Is the Massage: An Inventory of Effects* (New York: Bantam Books, 1967).

[58] For further reading, see, e.g., Marshall McLuhan, *Understanding Media: The Extensions of Man* (New York: McGraw-Hill, 1964).

It was particularly due to the efforts of Quentin Fiore and Jerome Agle—the former, the book's graphic designer and illustrator; the latter, its coordinator—that *The Medium Is the Massage* even exists. Sensing that that which one would commonly refer to as a "book" cannot exist merely between the confines of its binding, Fiore and Agle concluded that *sound*—and, particularly live sound, the human voice, and the spoken word—is the most appropriate medium for extending and communicating McLuhan's insights with greater sensory depth. Their book appears to mirror what they perceived as the manner in which knowledge had been conveyed at the time—effectively manifesting as an amalgamation of images and text, graphics and typography, collages and montages, alongside an ostensible "re-mix" of McLuhan's insights and meditations. As such, it could be identified as a playful hybrid of sorts challenging the classic conventions of what a book is conceivably purported to be.[59] Similarly drawing on a sense that a porous liminality is apparent between books (as artifacts) and other existing media, the album version effectively utilizes audio clips and outtakes of McLuhan reading from his own works, which are often interrupted by obscure sounds and discordant voices. Commencing with a voice asking, "How do you like it so far?," the recording thus thrusts the listeners into a unique sensory wild ride, which is simultaneously thought-provoking, amusing, bewildering, and, to a large extent, challenging.

Consequently, to experience this recording as an aural artifact, one is required to find its distinctive internal logic—which, at its core, is inherently related to McLuhan's socio-cultural and philosophical insights. Therefore, one needs to exercise an "institutional" listening: that is to say, to hear the recording with the "ears" of NITA—and subsequently to evaluate it in accordance with the institutional structure of the aesthetic category. Otherwise, all one is left with is an ostensible "brute" listening, amid which one would be unable to understand, experience, or appreciate the album for what it is. Thus, to claim, for instance, that the album version of *The Medium Is the Massage*, or *Strange to Your Ears*—much like the more "avant-garde-ish" tracks (for want of a better term) on, say, the *Yoko Ono/Plastic Ono Band* (1970) album—amounts to nothing more than a cacophonic extravaganza, consisting of a bunch of raw,

---

[59.] For further reading, see: Jeffrey T. Schnapp and Adam Michaels, *The Electric Information Age Book (McLuhan /Agel/Fiore and the Experimental Paperback)* (New York: Princeton Architectural Press, 2012). Consciously extending the conceit of its subjects of inquiry, this book, too, received an aural iteration: namely, a limited-edition vinyl record consisting of its own live stage "version." See URL: accessed October 22, 2022, https:// wearethemasses.bandcamp.com/track/the-book-of-the-now.

un-listenable, and completely meaningless sound drivels (on a good day), is, alas, missing the point. Indeed, much like Warhol's *Brillo Box* (or, to be sure, any other artwork for that matter), the aesthetic properties of such recordings neither reside in nor in effect define, the recordings themselves. Ultimately, despite potentially being tagged as borderline curiosity case studies of sorts, these recordings nevertheless deserve a deeper meditation as sub-(institutional)-categories in their own right—rooted in the general "mother" institution of aural artifacts.

"This Is the Story of Peter and the Wolf"

For the most part, audiobooks customarily feature a minimal accompaniment of transitional mood-setting music or sound effects, if at all. Yet there are quite a number of audio productions that are more akin to radio plays drama as ostensible "theater for the ear," and, as such, evidently incorporate more than spoken word alone. Whether or not—or, indeed, the extent to which—these additional aesthetic properties that the medium facilitates actually enhance one's listening experience should be evaluated on a case-by-case basis.

Nevertheless, while the addition of music can certainly complement the aural performance insofar as it seems to become an inherent, almost crucial aspect of the recording—conceivably rendering the aural artifact musically dependent—I wish to briefly focus herein on precisely the *opposite* case: aural artifacts that are so deeply rooted in music that the aural performance is what, in effect, complements the overall aesthetics of the aural artifact itself. These cases, I find, predominantly prevail in the realm of classical music. In the context of my study, these works—some of which incorporate different performance-based artforms—can be classified amid a sub-(institutional)-category of their own.

Arguably, the most famous example of this kind is Prokofiev's *Peter and the Wolf*, Op. 76 (1936), which includes music and narration. Consider, for instance, the different existing deliveries by such personae as Alec Guinness, Leonard Bernstein, David Bowie, Sean Connery, John Gielgud, Dame Edna Everage, Boris Karloff, Dudley Moore, and Patrick Stewart—to name only a few. As some recordings may well consist of aural documentations of live events—and although the performance they inhabit may indeed be excellent—one would clearly be required to compare and identify which version (or, indeed, versions) most successfully complies with, adheres to, and exhibits the internal logic of what an aural artifact should be.

In the same vein, one can also consider, for instance, *L'Histoire du soldat* [The Soldier's Tale] (1981), conceived of by Igor Stravinsky and Swiss writer C. F. Ramuz as a theatrical piece, intended "to be read, played, and danced." While the latter aspect of the piece would obviously escape one when merely listening to an audio recording of it, I would argue that one can nonetheless certainly experience this piece *as* an aural artifact. Appropriately, one can should be able to scrutinize different available versions and compare the different deliveries of the performers: e.g., John Gielgud versus Glenda Jackson, or Ian McKellen as "the Narrator"; Gérard Depardieu versus Peter Ustinov (both performing in French) as "the Devil"; or, indeed, any one of them versus Jeremy Irons or Christopher Lee—both of whom have portrayed all the characters.

Ustinov, incidentally, has contributed his outstanding narration and delivery style not only to quite a number of exceptional aural iterations—e.g., Russell Hoban's *The Mouse and His Child* (1967), a selection of Rudolf Erich Raspe's Baron Munchausen's tall tales, Antoine de Saint-Exupéry's *The Little Prince* (1943), a variety of short stories by James Thurber stories (released on six Caedmon vinyl LPs), as well as his own novel *Monsieur Rene* (1999) but also to some remarkable recordings rooted in the realm of classical music. Aside from his rendition of *Peter and the Wolf*, these include Kodály's *Háry János: A Comic Opera* (1926) and *Toy Symphony*—whose authorship, although commonly attributed to Hyden, is still disputed.

Furthermore, as Ustinov spoke at least six languages fluently, it is certainly interesting to note that he recorded certain works not only in both English and German but also, evidently, in both English and French. Examples of the former include Mozart's *Der Schauspieldirektor* [*The Impresario*] (1786); Modest Mussorgsky's *Pictures at an Exhibition* (1874)—the narration for which was also written by Ustinov; Camille Saint-Saëns *Le Carnaval des animaux* [*Carnival of the Animals*] (1922)—which Ustinov has also performed live; as well as two lesser known Strauss compositions, both released in the late 1990s: *The Donkey's Shadow* [after Christoph Martin Wieland] and *Le Bourgeois gentilhomme* [a Musical Comedy with Dances in three Acts, after Molière].

Examples of the former include Harsányi's *L'histoire du petit tailleur* (1950)—written and composed for narrator, seven instruments, and percussion and based on a folktale collected and published by the Brothers Grimm in 1812; and *L'Histoire de Babar, le petit éléphant*, FP 129 [*The Story of Babar, the Little Elephant*]—a composition for narrator and piano by Francis Poulenc, written between 1940 and 1945, and based on Jean de Brunhoff's 1931 children's book. These two works accompanied each other in both of Ustinov's English and French renditions (released in the mid-1960s)—and, in both cases, featured acclaimed conductor Georges Prêtre as the music director. As a sidenote, one might also find it quite interesting to compare Ustinov's "take" on the Babar piece with the delightful French delivery by the influential *chansonnier*, Jacques Brel.

Now, Felix Mendelssohn's *A Midsummer Night's Dream*—although based on Shakespeare's famous play of the same name—is not designed to have Shakespeare's text recited against the music; certain iterations of Mendelssohn's work have opted to incorporate recitations of excerpts from the original play. This decision embodies the makings of a rather interesting and, potentially, aesthetically rewarding aural artifact. Consider, for instance, the 1992 Deutsche Grammophon release, featuring a unique aural performance by Dame Judi Dench. By the same token, one's attention should likewise be paid to the 1996 Sony Masterworks release, featuring Kenneth Branagh delivering speeches and passages from Shakespeare's play and skillfully taking on performing several roles.

Another quite exquisite example where narration is blended with classical music can be found in Strauss's melodrama *Enoch Arden, Op. 38* (1897)—based on Alfred Lord Tennyson's 1864 blank-verse narrative poem. In 1967, Columbia released a recording featuring the celebrated Canadian pianist Glen Gould and British actor Claude Rains delivering the text. It is highly recommended to compare this version with the more recent iteration by British actor Henry Goodman and featuring British pianist Lucy Parham—who has, in fact, issued a number of interesting releases that combine narration with music. Similarly recommended are the available releases that feature acclaimed British actor Simon Callow as the voice of the narrator in a number of noted productions that incorporate narration with classic seasonal or orchestral compositions.

One may also surely include in this respect the collaboration between English poet Dame Edith Sitwell and English composer William Walton on what became known as *Façade—An Entertainment*: the series of poems by Sitwell, recited over Walton's instrumental accompaniment. While both the poems and the music exist in several versions and iterations—effectively making for a more challenging comparison—I, for one, find that it is precisely that challenge which one should embrace. Highly recommended for listening and comparison are the versions featuring Peggy Ashcroft—one performed with Paul Scofield in 1972, the other with Jeremy Irons (1989)—as well as, indeed, the recording featuring Dame Edith herself.

To all intents and purposes, this particular sub-(institutional)-category, however, does not end in the realm of classical music. Indeed, one is sure to come across some unique borderline cases that effectively incorporate narration as a key constituent of an otherwise inherently musical work. Consider, for instance, Sir George Martin's album *In My Life* (1998), which consists of a variety of cover versions by well-known artists to songs by the Beatles. Here, the concluding twelfth track features Scottish actor Sean Connery *performing* the lyrics of John Lennon's song, *In My Life*, delivered in the form of a narration, set to music.

In the same vein, I would like to consider Eric Idle's *The Quite Remarkable Adventures of the Owl and the Pussycat* (1997), based on Edward Lear's classic nineteenth century poem.[60] Although his initial idea was to ostensibly "translate," as it were, Lear's poem into the form of an animated film—conceivably exploiting its nonsensical internal logic, all the while also making it more appealing to children—Idle's final product, however, resulted in what might more appropriately be identified as a "musical audiobook" for young audiences. Ultimately consisting of Idle's narration and singing, set to the score he composed alongside his longtime friend and collaborator, British composer-conductor John Du Prez, this unique recording—indeed, in terms of both Idle's delivery *and* the nature of the musical composition itself—successfully adheres to the internal logic of what a proper (i.e., aesthetically good) aural artifact should necessarily constitute.

To be sure, one could similarly consider the variety of audio recordings featuring Shel Silverstein performing his own works, which also serve as a unique example for text that conceivably sound better (and, indeed, are better understood) when heard aloud. Although the list can certainly go on, I shall refrain from entering this captivating realm, for all that it involves, implies, and evokes—in terms of one's psychology, development, and education—since, as yet another potential sub-(institutional)-category, it surely deserves a designated study in its own right: that of literature and poetry written for (and, indeed, explicitly delivered to) children.

[60.] Eric Idle, [The Story of] *The Quite Remarkable Adventures of the Owl and the Pussycat*, [Musically Scored], written and performed by Eric Idle; based on the poems, drawings, and writings of Edward Lear; music and Lyrics composed by Eric Idle and John Duprez [sic.] (Dove Music, 1997).

Including, but Not Restricted to the World's First Three-Sided Record

The genre regarded as "comedy albums" can also be contemplated upon as a unique staple of aural artifacts. Here, too, however, one should certainly make a distinction between the recordings of live performances and singular studio-recorded release. Consider, for instance, the legendary, side-splitting, and insanely inspired *2,000-Year-Old Man* enterprise—conceived, written, and performed by Mel Brooks and Carl Reiner—which, although indeed consumed and experienced through one's ears, *as* purported aural artifacts, the recordings themselves were nonetheless all originally performed *live*. Had Brooks and Reiner recorded their material exclusively for the aural medium, the end product would have embodied a somewhat different quality.

The same holds true for other such legendary comedy albums such as *You Don't Have to Be Jewish* (1964) and *When You're in Love, the Whole World Is Jewish* (1965) by Bob Booker and George Foster, or the live performances of Mike Nichols and Elaine May. In fact, it would seem that many of the titles identified as comedy albums are essentially recorded live. The same surely holds true for the legendary British radio program *The Goon Show* (1950s–1960s), whose purely studio-recorded offerings are in short supply.[61]

Conversely, one can consider the somewhat more extreme double-act of "Derek and Clive" created by legendary British comedians Peter Cook and Dudley Moore. While the duo might arguably be more recognized for their "Pete and Dud" routines—which adhere to a completely different kind of internal logic from that of their intentionally cruder and ostensible darker polar opposite alter egos—both sets of characters are fundamentally ignited by the same core dynamic between Cook and Moore. Put simply, although both creations deliver what might be regarded as a largely unscripted stream of unconsciousness that constitutes comedy sketches aimed at eliciting laughter, the reasons they evoke laughter are ultimately *not* one and the same. Although their debut album was recorded in the presence of a live audience—and, as such, is more akin to the Brooks and Reiner recordings (which similarly began as something of private

---

[61.] Two exceptions that come to mind are the parody-album *Bridge on the River Wye* (1962)—based on an earlier *Goon Show* script, and *How to Win an Election (Or Not Lose by Much)* (1964)—written and devised by British composer and lyricist Leslie Bricusse.

joke)—the two subsequent albums can more easily be classified as so-called "proper" aural artifacts.

One might also be inclined to dedicate yet another sub-(institutional)-category explicitly for aural artifacts that combine comedy and music. While these types of recordings are for the most part musically oriented, they are nonetheless still effectively consumed *as* aural artifacts. Consider, for instance, the overall corpus of the brilliant and ever-relevant Tom Lehrer, the musical offerings of Rick Moranis—e.g., *The Agoraphobic Cowboy* (2005) and *My Mother's Brisket & Other Love Song* (2013)—or, for that matter, *Barry Humphries Presents: The Sound of Edna* (1978), Booker's and Foster's *Al Tijuana and His Jewish Brass* (1966), and *Gilbert and Sullivan and Danny Kaye* (1948). The same no doubt holds true for the great Victor Borge (although most of his material was recorded live) and, to a large extent, the albums of Allan Sherman. In this respect, albums such as *Stan Freberg Presents the United States of America Volume One: The Early Years* (1961) or Albert Brooks' *A Star Is Bought* (1975) might be argued to be more suitable candidates as "proper" aural artifacts. The same most certainly also holds true for such recordings as Ustinov's *The Grand Prix of Gibraltar!* (1958) or *Songs for Swingin' Sellers* (1959) and *Peter and Sophia* (1960)—both holstering the unique talents of the one and only, Peter Sellers.

One might similarly add to the mix such performing artists (to state it kindly) as Elva Ruby Miller—whose harmonious catastrophes (for lack of a better word) were released under the name "Mrs. Miller"—or, to that end, Sam Chalpin, whose *My Father the Pop Singer* (1966), produced by his son, remains to this day as confounding as it is cacophonic. Indeed, the latter's own recording engineer, Michael Rashkow, cites it as "possibly the worst record ever made."[62] Ultimately, much like the aforementioned *Foust Travesty* and its embodied musical "stylings" of Burns and Willimas, these recordings, too, might be perceived of as being unintentionally funny and would arguably not have been released, to begin with—were it not for the certain individual who had recognized a distinct "somethingness" about them. Here, again, much in the vein of Wright's aforementioned one-liner, it is in effect *that* individual who would effectively count as *the* artist behind them.

Now, cited as the world's first "three-sided" vinyl record, the aforementioned *Matching Tie and Handkerchief* is surely another good example. Now, whether

---

[62] Mike Rashkow, "Ed and Sam Chalpin, His Father the Pop Singer: A Recitation of the Ridiculous." See URL: accessed January 10, 2023, https://spectropop.com/SamChalpin/.

or not this might be conceived of as a critical design flaw, it is obviously impossible for a vinyl LP to consist of more than its two given sides. This is not, however, an embarrassing miscalculation on behalf of the marketing department. Rather, to "get" the joke, one needs to acquaint oneself with the overall Pythonesque internal logic. Interestingly enough, the invested ingenuity into this particular album also facilitates a whole other level to the joke, namely, the fact that the object itself (i.e., as an aural artifact) has been designed so as to *actually* enable one to play a so-called "third" side—achieved by including an additional groove on one side of the LP (and effectively heard at random, depending on where the needle of the turntable happens to drop).

In the same vein, one could also consider the audiobook version of *I Drink for a Reason* (2009)—a selection of sarcastic essays and politically incorrect social commentaries by American comedian David Cross[63]—which, as an aural artifact, makes full use of the distinct aesthetics of the aural medium. The "read by the author" guarantee notwithstanding, listeners are immediately struck by the fact that the voice that is heard narrating the preface is *not*, in fact, that of Cross. Although the front cover of the commercial release does indeed clearly mention additional participants, this is certainly not what one would customarily expect. Two-and-a-half minutes into the recording, it becomes evident that the yet-to-be-identified narrator is not really doing justice to Cross's material. Suddenly, one begins to hear a distant voice in the background—slowly growing louder, as it seems to be advancing into the recording studio. It is immediately identified as a rather bewildered David Cross. A short altercation erupts between the two speakers, who argue about just who it was that had, in fact, been hired to record the book. It takes a little over three minutes for the first speaker (whose identity is by now revealed as American comedian H. Jon Benjamin) to reluctantly leave the studio. Having finally assumed his role as author-narrator, Cross begins reading his work, from the top—ostensibly forcing the listeners to hear the preface a second time, only now as it *should* be heard. Not necessarily because a text can be performed only by its author but rather because the particular author of this particular written text happens to possess the particular ability to appropriately deliver its internal logic, as an aural performance, to its designated audience.

[63.] David Cross, *I Drink for a Reason*, read by the author, and featuring the voices of John Benjamin, Kristen Schaal, and Robot, with musical guests Les Savy Fav and Yo La Tengo (Hachette, 2009).

Making full use of what the aural medium facilitates, a similar gag is eloquently employed in the audiobook version of John Cleese's autobiography
So, Anyway... (2014). Here, the recording begins with Cleese speaking to the
sound engineer. The latter explains to Cleese his contractual obligation to read
the publisher's introduction page—a task Cleese finds much too boring. He subsequently asks the sound engineer what else might be done—to which the latter
suggests that they "could get Mike do it, if he didn't mind." Sure enough—as
any self-respecting Python fan would have no doubt surmised without skipping
a beat—the "Mike" in question is established as none other than Sir Michael
Palin, who just happens to be found "in the other studio, downstairs." Cleese
wholeheartedly embraces the idea, and one then hears the sound engineer leaving the studio to go and get Palin. On arrival, both Palin and Cleese plunge into
a typically Pythonesque exchange, following which, Palin ends up recording the
"intro" to Cleese's autobiography and is subsequently forced to sit through and
endure Cleese's own reading—only to ultimately record the "outro" as well.[64]

As far as *I Drink for a Reason* is concerned, since Benjamin is himself no
stranger to comedy—and, in fact, happens to be a close friend and collaborator
of Cross—his poorly performed delivery of the material is quite deliberate.
Much like the Cleese and Palin *shtick*—as well as, indeed, the aforementioned
exchanges between Welles and Cooper in *The Campbell Playhouse* adaptation
of *Huck Finn*—that segment ultimately consists of a self-reflective comedy
routine, which not only acknowledges but is also inevitably dependent on the
medium of the audiobook. This is also what enables Cross—whose narration
clearly demonstrates his awareness of both the medium itself and its designated
audience—to explicitly ridicule his listeners for not opting to purchase the actual book. At certain points in the recording, Cross makes a point of emphasizing
the desired *tone* of the text—by way of indicating to the listeners when he is using a word in quotations and where the printed text includes a footnote. He even
goes so far as to add the odd explanatory (and virtually redundant) comment,
such as noting that whenever he says the words "as I'm writing this," what he
actually means is "as I'm reading this." At one point, a voice is heard interrupt-
ing Cross, asking him if he was certain whether the passage he was reading is
indeed taken from his own book—which it was not.[65] Consider, for example,

---

[64] John Cleese, *So, Anyway...*, unabridged, read by the author (Penguin, 2014), 00m00sec–03m11sec.

[65] Cross, *I Drink for a Reason*, disc2, track1, 01m55sec.

the following aural passage, in which he wishes to make it clear to the listeners that whenever he says the word "healthy," he is, in fact, using quotations:

> You can't see the book. I mean, you can, should you wanna go leap through it, but for some reason you bought this thing, and are listening to it, so just know that "healthy" is always in quotes. Let's move on. Engineer? Sorry about that last part. But, you know, I've a responsibility to my listening audience.[66]

Evidently, the audiobook version of Cross's text also happens to include a variety of expressions, which, although natural in everyday spoken conversation, do not, in fact, appear in the printed version of his book. When taking into account Cross's stage persona, sense of humor, and comedic rhythm, I find that the personal tone and everyday phrases—amplified by the unique confines of the medium—ultimately enhance one's experience of this audiobook as an aesthetically rewarding aural artifact. To my mind, this particular type of audiobooks goes a long way in further justifying the extent to which my proposed aesthetic category is indeed required.

Track Selection: Audio Commentary

In 1942, seventeen years after the release of its original silent version, Charlie Chaplin re-released his film classic masterpiece *The Gold Rush* (1925). The most notable thing about this new and re-edited version was Chaplin's decision include an aural narration, which he recorded himself, in his own voice. This is not only a rare occurrence in the history of cinema but is also arguably the first of its kind. As it is essentially delivered to his audience via spoken word, Chaplin's performance too, can effectively be perceived as an aural artifact of sorts—and, to a certain extent, a character in its own right.

Nonetheless, a distinction should be made between the narration that inhabits *The Gold Rush* and the voice-over as an inherently cinematic device, employed in such films as *Sunset Boulevard* (dir. Billy Wilder, 1950); *A Clockwork Orange* (dir. Stanley Kubrick, 1971); *Goodfellas* (dir. Martin Scorsese, 1990); *The Shawshank Redemption* (dir. Frank Darabont, 1994), or *Fight Club* (dir. David Fincher, 1999), to name but a few. While the narrating protagonist in such films

---

[66] Ibid., disc1, track6, 04m22sec.

constitutes a character in the film itself (or some version thereof), Chaplin's narrator is clearly not delivered as his iconic tramp. Although it is considered very much part of the visual film, I would argue that it is consequently experienced as an inherently aural performance. In the same vein, one can consider Ron Howard's narration in the remarkable American comedy series *Arrested Development* (2003–2019), in which the narrator prevails as an ever-present off-screen character. The audio commentary track, however, is a different phenomenon.

Much like the manner in which audiobooks highlight the nature of the first-person narrative, audio commentaries appear to give one the sense that the speaking voice somehow shares one's film-viewing experience in real time. As one ultimately experiences them as an aural recording—exclusively created for the consumption of a designated audience—they should, in turn, be both classified and evaluated as a unique kind of aural artifact. As I will presently demonstrate, some filmmakers have utilized this medium in such a manner that it results in an aesthetically rich and unique kind of aural performances. As such, the following examples will reinforce my contention that some commentaries, under certain circumstances, effectively require a sub-(institutional)-category of their own.

An audio commentary track is a supplementary audio track, commonly regarded as a "special feature" accompanying the various "bonus material" included on a film's DVD or Blu-ray release. Customarily, commentaries consist of either a lecture or—as their name implies—comments, which can be delivered by one or more speakers. While certain commentaries are merely scene-specific, the core idea is to have the commentary play in real time, essentially referencing what is seen on the screen. Some commentaries feature multiple participants— recorded either together (i.e., with everyone in the same room) or on separate occasions. There also exist ostensibly "synthesized" commentaries—consisting of past relevant interviews, edited to form a single cohesive whole. For the most part, there is a distinctly different feel to commentaries delivered by actors and directors—as compared to those by scholars and critics. To be sure, each of these types has the potential of constituting either an alluring, fascinating, and uplifting aesthetic experience or, alas, a lavish disappointment.

In addition to commentary tracks, bonus features customarily consist of interviews with the cast and creators, archival material, making of or behind-the-scenes documentaries, as well as what is commonly referred to as "Easter eggs."

Although I have dedicated this section to identifying when an audio commentary might be regarded as a unique type of aural artifact, it is worth noting that, at times, one is sure to come across certain bonus features that are more easily identified as "standard" aural artifacts, the following being but a few examples:

- Alec Baldwin narrating Stephen Vincent Benét's short story *The Devil and Daniel Webster* (1936), recorded exclusively for the Criterion Collection release of William Dieterle's 1941 film adaptation (Spine #214).
- Elliott Gould narrating the novella version of Ingmar Bergman's *The Passion of Anna* (1969), recorded exclusively for the 2004 MGM release.
- Jeremy Irons' 1994 reading of excerpts from Michael Powell and Emeric Pressburger's 1978 novelization of their film *The Red Shoes* (1948), as well as the original Hans Christian Andersen fairy tale on which the film was based—both found on the Criterion Collection release (Spine #44).
- The so-called "aural adaptation" of the Eileen Lanouette Hughes memoir—*On the Set of "Fellini Satyricon": A Behind-the-Scenes Diary* (1971)—included on the Criterion Collection's 2015 release of *Fellini Satyricon* (1969) and delivered as a first-person account. While it rarely corresponds with what one actually sees on screen (as audio commentaries purportedly should), it nevertheless evokes a unique aesthetic experience.

The very first commentary track was featured the Criterion Collection's 1984 LaserDisc release of *King Kong* (1933), having licensed it from RKO. In my email correspondence with Jonathan Turell, CEO of the Criterion Collection, he states that he would "probably give credit to Bob Stein, who was my former partner and founder of Criterion and Ron for coming up with the idea." The track was recorded by Ron Haver, director at the LA County Museum of Art, and the commentary itself—unlike the custom nowadays—was *unscripted*. As Turell describes it, Haver simply sat down in a room, in front of a VCR, watched the movie and simply began talking:

> Hello ladies and gentlemen. I am Ronald Haver, and I am here to do something which we feel is rather unique: I am going to take you on a lecture-tour of *King Kong*, as you watch the film. The LaserDisc technology offers us this opportunity, and we feel it's rather unique—the ability to switch back and forth between the

soundtrack and this "lecture-track". I would like to be able to tell you, during the course of the film, some of the stories of the making of it; about the personalities involved [...]. It is one of the films that I think has stimulated more generations in terms of making them aware of what the movies can offer in terms of adventure and romance and fantasy. We feel it's a very important aspect of *Kong*, and something that we hope you will be able to appreciate more fully with this LaserDisc edition. I've seen the film almost two-hundred times since I first saw it in 1952, and I do have a great deal of knowledge that I think would be fairly interesting to most of you—especially about, as I say, the behind-the-scenes events in the making of the film. [...] Now, I won't talk constantly. There will be stretches of silence—so don't think there's anything wrong with your player—it's just at that particular time there really isn't too much to say.

It would seem that the overall perception of and approach toward audio commentaries is two-sided. Directors such as Paul Thomas Anderson, Kenneth Branagh, Francis Ford Coppola, Frank Darabont, David Fincher, Terry Gilliam, Christopher Guest, Frank Oz, Terry Jones, Martin Scorsese, and Steven Soderbergh all consistently provide engaging insights into their craft. In the world of the smaller screen, the commentaries recorded for shows created by such persons as Alan Ball, Vince Gilligan, Peter Gould, Dan Harmon, Stephen Poliakoff, David Simon, and Aaron Sorkin are also notably worthwhile.

For the most part, all the aforementioned persons appear to be well aware of their designated audience, and their commentaries make for an informative, entertaining, and thoroughly rewarding listening experience. Scorsese has also contributed to more than a couple of commentaries for films that had affected him as a director and shaped his artistic vision. Soderbergh, too, has evidently provided quite a few so-called "interview-commentaries" for films other than his own: e.g., with director Mike Nichols for *Who's Afraid of Virginia Woolf?* (1966), *The Graduate* (1967), and *Catch-22* (1970); with director John Boorman for *Point Blank* (1967); and with screenwriter and filmmaker Tony Gilroy for *The Third Man* (dir. Carol Reed, 1949). In the same vein, Quentin Tarantino has primarily recorded commentaries for other people's films—mostly taking the form of enthusiastic reference-ridden debates with like-minded friends and colleagues: e.g., his participation as a guest-commentator on one the *five* tracks recorded for *Hot Fuzz* (dir. Edgar Wright, 2007). Here, in particular, the commentary indulgently revolves around virtually any film other than that which the track was being recorded for. Now and again, one might even come across what I consider as the "out-of-the-blue" type of commentaries—or, rather, "pleasantly unexpected"—such as that recorded by ex-Python member Terry Jones for the Preston Sturges cinematic classic *Sullivan's Travels* (1941). To be sure, while all tracks referenced herein may arguably be designed more as "candy" for the fan base of its creators, they certainly evoke a delightful and immensely rewarding aesthetic experience. The same holds true for certain "re-union-commentaries" such as those recorded for *Willy Wonka & the Chocolate Factory* (dir. Mel Stuart, 1971) and *The Goonies* (dir. Richard Donner, 1985), which bring together the now-all-grown-up cast of the then-child actors.

Directors such as Woody Allen or David Lynch, however, have often expressed their sense that a film should essentially speak for itself and that to speak about it—not to mention *over* it—simply demystifies and degrades the art of cinema. While I do sympathize with these sentiments—over-romanticized as they arguably might be—I would nevertheless maintain that the added aesthetic experience that certain commentaries can (and, indeed, *do*) potentially evoke simply cannot be ignored.

What follows is a list of commentaries that constitute unique aural artifacts. Some are absolutely remarkably creative, well performed, and exceptionally rewarding; others—despite a promising conceptual potential—remain, alas, inherently flawed.

This Is Spinal Tap (1984), directed by Rob Reiner, is, in a nutshell, a comedy presented as documentary about a British rock group—directed by one Marty DiBergi, who, in reality, is portrayed by Reiner himself. The film is considered a milestone in the development of a distinct genre that is commonly associated with the films directed by Christopher Guest (who portrays one of the lead Spinal Tap band members), which regularly feature an ensemble cast, employing a unique kind of improvisational-based performances, one which is framed within a well-constructed story outline and a strict character study. Although customarily referred to as a "mockumentary," their intention—as Guest himself had once pointed out—was never to mock or ridicule anything or anyone in particular. The original Criterion Collection DVD release (following their earlier 1994 LaserDisc edition), included two fairly standard commentary tracks: one featuring Reiner alongside producer Karen Murphy and editors Robert Leighton and Kent Beyda and the other, the three principal actors, namely, Guest, Michael McKean, and Harry Shearer. Later, in 2000, MGM's "Special Edition" included a commentary delivered by Nigel Tufnel, David St. Hubbins, and Derek Smalls: the three principal *fictional* characters (portrayed by Guest, McKean, and Shearer, respectively). As Eckart Voigts-Virchow explains it, this track "is by definition *a posteriori* and can never be part of the spatio-temporal world of the narrative."[67] At the same, he certainly recognizes just how interesting this case actually is for the simple fact that "both the initial narrative 1 and the subsequent audio narrative 2 are fictional".[68] This, to my mind, goes well beyond the act of breaking the proverbial fourth wall. Indeed, unlike appearing "in-character" on a talk show (e.g., for the purpose of promoting a film, etc.), this particular commentary constitutes a performance in and of itself—effectively prevailing as an entirely new feature-length spoken-word narrative. Although the speakers may refer to what is *seen* on screen, it is delivered to the audience by way of the spoken word, experienced as an aural performance. It can therefore be identified as a remarkably unique kind of aural artifact—whose performers (and their behavior, in-character) adhere to, *mutatis mutandis*, the same kind of predominantly improvisational expertise they employ in the film against which they protest their dissatisfaction. At the same time, as it both corresponds with and is dependent on the original film, one cannot simply listen to the commentary as is while discarding viewing the film itself—which is fundamentally a complete artwork in its own right. (Granted, one, *could*, arguably, chose to do that, yet this would certainly compromise one's overall aesthetic experience—which essentially necessitates engaging with the original film). Ultimately, as I will later demonstrate by examining aural iterations of pseudo-autobiographies, I find that this is much more than merely playing a so-called tongue-in-cheek game with the audience. Rather, it demonstrates an eloquent application of a distinct performative internal logic—which, in this case, is successfully delivered amid the distinct confines of the aural medium. The end result is both especially gratifying and bewildering, effectively *extending* the existence of the fictitious band members and enabling "them" to allude to and comment on DiBergi's endeavor to document *reality*.

As a sub-(institutional)-category, the in-character *Spinal Tap* commentary track is the first of its kind. It has served as inspiration to a handful of likewise constructed "spoof-commentaries" that have effectively employed this medium for comedic purposes. An equally interesting attempt (albeit not, to my mind,

---

[67] Eckart Voigts-Virchow, "Paratracks in the Digital Age," in *Intermedialities*, ed. Evelyne Keitel, Gunter Süss, and Werner Huber (Trier, Germany: WVT, 2007), 134.

[68] Ibid.

as successful or fine-tuned) exists in the form of the in-character commentary track created for the Image Entertainment DVD release of *Snide and Prejudice* (1997), directed by Philippe Mora. Similarly taking on the guise of a documentary—unveiling the story of a mental institution whose occupants suffer from fantasies and delusions pertaining to WWII—the two main protagonists are a patient named Michael Davidson who believes himself to be none other than Adolf Hitler (portrayed by Angus Macfadyen) and resident physician Dr. Sam Choen (portrayed by Rene Auberjonois). Unlike the manner in which *Spinal Tap* seems to announce itself as an outrageously funny creation—predominantly inferred from its fictitious director's opening monologue—*Snide and Prejudice* appears to abide by an inherently darker type of humor that arguably demands more time to fully sink in. While the DVD also features a standard (and fairly interesting) commentary by Mora and Macfadyen, I find the additional in-character track much more intriguing—especially as an aural artifact. The track features the two aforementioned *characters* (Davidson and Dr. Cohen), who essentially engage in a panel, of sorts, with Mora. The latter, however, is not so much "Philippe Mora, writer-director of *Snide and Prejudice*," but rather an alternate "version" of his own self, namely, one "Philippe Mora," responsible for the "documentary" about the mental institution. Thus, here, too—much like what the in-character *Spinal Tap* commentary achieves for its fictional band members—the subjects (of the of the documentary that *Snide and Prejudice* pretends to be) are effectively extracted from the finished film, with their existence and identities extended far beyond its celluloid confines. The track reveals, for example, that Davidson—who is still being treated by Dr. Cohen—is feeling much healthier, taking his medication, and is no longer living under the belief that he is the Führer. The audience, in turn, is invited to play an ostensible game with the filmmakers. In essence, by willfully suspending one's disbelief, one is expected to accept the purported pseudo-reality of the fictional characters, whose reaffirmed existential status now enables them to become self-aware agencies—bearing witness and reacting to their own documented narrative.

Evidently, certain audiobooks have opted to employ a similar conceit—effectively calling up the listener to engage with a virtually extended existence of protagonists with whom one had previously been acquainted only amid the so-called given confines of the original work they inhabit. These range from franchises such as the long-running British sci-fi television series Doctor Who—which had received both original audio dramas and audiobook adventures

that pertain to different incarnations of the Doctor's character[69]—to more hu-
mor-based endeavors such as *The Bro Code* (2008), supposedly written and
performed by one "Barney Stinson," a fictional character featured on the American sitcom *How I Met Your Mother*, created by Carter Bays and Craig Thomas.
In actuality, the book was written by Bays and Thomas—alongside one of the
show's writers, Matt Kuhn—and performed in-character by Neil Patrick Harris
as Stinson. This item is inherently tongue-in-cheek and can only be properly
enjoyed as an aural artifact if one is acquainted with the Stinson's character
and the mannerisms with which he is personified by the actor. (The same holds
true about *The Playbook* (2010) and *The Bro Code for Parents: What to Expect
When You're Awesome* (2012)—both of which playfully adhere to the same
overall "*shtick*"). To be sure, once can similarly consider *A Woman First: First
Woman* (2019)—the purported "deeply personal memoir by the former President", written and read by President Selina Meyer—portrayed by celebrated
American actress and comedian Julia Louis-Dreyfus in HBO's acclaimed political satire *Veep* (2012-2019). The fact that her character's endeavor to author
a memoir happens to be explicitly addressed in the show's sixth season all the
more facilities the extension of her (fictional) existence—with the *actual* being
written by two of the show's writers-creators, namely, Billy Kimball and David
Mandell. Alongside Louis-Dreyfus, who struggles—as Meyer—with the arduous task of narrating an audiobook, the recording also features American actor and comedian Tony Hale—similarly in-character as Meyer's personal aide
Gary Walsh. Appropriately utilizing the unique aesthetics that aural artifact embody, the audiobook successfully includes a verity of hilarious exchanges that
would simply not have worked in print, and effectively enhance once's listening
experience.

A more interesting case, to my mind, can be found in the outstanding full-cast
audio production of Mark Frost's *The Secret History of Twin Peaks* (2016), as
well as its follow-up—also by Frost—*Twin Peaks: The Final Dossier* (2017),
whose audiobook version was narrated by Annie Wersching. These two endeavors not only make for most rewarding listening as exceptional aural artifacts in
their own right but serve as a rather unique extension to the overall world and
mythology of the original show. The same holds true for Jennifer Lynch's *The
Secret Diary of Laura Palmer*—which, although originally published in 1990,

---

[69] Some of the audio versions feature performers who were previously seen on the TV version of the series: e.g.,
Bernard Cribbins, Christopher Eccleston, Alex Kingston, Matt Smith, Catherine Tate, and David Tennant.

was only released as an audiobook in 2017—narrated by Sheryl Lee, who portrayed the its title character on the original, celebrated, and influential television series *Twin Peaks*, as well as on its cinematic prequel and follow-up revival series. It is quite illuminating listening to Lee describe her reading experience in a brief interview promoting the release:

> To do it in this way, it's […] I just I find it very, very fascinating, and interesting and challenging creatively. It's the internal life, it's the internal monologue, it's the internal struggle. So, it's very different than it was when I was on set with everyone else, and responding and reacting, and […] Witnessing all this other wonderful work around me. Reading Laura's diary now, from the perspective of a woman, and an adult, I have a new tenderness and compassion for her struggle.[70]

An ostensibly more extreme take on the "in-character commentary" trope has been hilariously employed by the creators of Disney's forty-fourth animated feature *Bother Bear* (2003), directed by Aaron Blaise and Robert Walker. Here, the filmmakers have indulged their audience with a commentary by none other than the film's two Canadian moose brothers— "Rutt" and "Tuke"—immortalized by Rick Moranis and Dave Thomas, respectively, and based on their own "Bob" and "Doug" McKenzie characters, which they had originated together as comedy duo back in the early 1980s. Furthermore, in bearing the guide of a "proper" commentary, Rutt and Tuke appropriately convey necessary movie-making know-hows: e.g., little-known secrets pertaining to how Disney *actually* animates their movies or to the important work of cartoon stunt-doubles.

Another interesting case in point is the 2001 Universal DVD release of *Blood Simple* (1984), written and directed by Joel and Ethan Coen—both of whom have publicly expressed their reluctance to record commentaries. The track features one Kenneth Loring, restoration artistic director for "Forever Young Films." Yet although undisclosed by the release itself, both "Loring" and "Forever Young Films" are, in fact, fictitious nonentities. In actuality, the "commentary"—assuming the guise of an in-depth lecture examining the film—was written by the Coens themselves, with the Loring character portrayed by British actor–comedian Jim Piddock. In an added effort to amplify the authenticity of what is essentially a 95-minute-long joke, the filmmakers also created a brief

---

[70.] See URL: accessed February 11, 2023, https://www.youtube.com/watch?v=lC_SG7TdN5U, 00min-16sec–01min01sec.

video-introduction by one Mortimer Young, head of "Forever Young Films"—
portrayed by actor George Ives—who alludes, for instance, to the "diligent efforts of many brilliant technicians," thanks to whom "the boring parts" have
been removed from "this exquisite masterpiece" with "other things added."
The Coens later re-purposed this whimsical little nod to their fans by creating yet another introduction-short for the home release of *The Big Lebowski*
(1998). Ultimately, as a standard lecture-commentary—i.e., featuring a film
critic or some person-of-knowledge attempting to inform viewers about the
overall creative process of the film in question—this track is not, alas, a very
good one. Indeed, made-up facts about animatronic dogs or comments such as
"but, ehm, more on myself later, during the slower parts of the movie," do not
a commentary make. In the context of a well-constructed joke, however, intentionally designed to sound flawed, it becomes a rather hilarious aural artifact.
Notwithstanding, one also begs the question of the extent to which one might
be responsible to identify it as such—for the lines in this particular case could
be argued to have been a tad over-blurred, to the extent that the joke might end
up escaping one altogether.

As an extended sidenote, I would add that this particular *faux* commentary
could be compared with the legendary broadcast and famous aftermath of Orson
Welles' 1938 radio adaptation of the H. G. Wells novel *The War of the Worlds*
(1898). To a large extent, the Coens' scripted commentary, drawing on all the
conventions of what a standard commentary track should sound like, effectively mislead their audience by endowing one with a false sense of authenticity,
so much so that they run the risk, to my mind, of one simply being unable
to recognize and "get" the joke. Although Welles' broadcast prevails as perhaps the most famous radio broadcast of all time, it might also be identified
as an example of an aural artifact that fails in exhibiting its own artifice by
appropriately distinguishing itself as a pre-conceived aural performance. This,
arguably, is part of the reason why listeners, too, had failed to experience that
broadcast as a radio drama. Indeed, the sense that what one was listening to
seemed so real that some were under the impression that the world was literally
under attack by beings from another world. Now, while deceiving his audience
may have indeed been, at least to a certain extent, part of what Welles had in
mind, he surely could not have anticipated the extent to which that evening's
events—forever darkened by the subsequent mass panic—were to unfold. In
this respect, I would argue that although Welles' broadcast may have followed
to a T the internal logic of what a radio newscast should sound like—at least

insofar as the manner in which the medium would have presumably coped with an actual attack from outer space—it did not necessarily adhere to or successfully exhibit the internal logic of *performing* a dramatic or literary work (albeit a pseudo-realistic one) across the radio waves. Granted, as the work in question happens to be rooted in the genre of science fiction, it may well be something of a challenge to aesthetically convey its unrealistic qualities amid the confines of a medium that amplified the sense of a "realness"—thus assuming the guise of live happening. By the same token, while the Coens' "Loring" *Blood Simple* commentary may invertedly sound "too real," it should ultimately be experienced as a parody that both complies with and adheres to the distinct style, context, and overall internal logic of the two filmmakers' *oeuvre*.

Somewhat reminiscent of Woody Allen's first cinematic endeavor *What's Up, Tiger Lily?* (1966)—which, being overdubbed with new original dialogue, may in itself count as a possible candidate for consideration as a borderline aural artifact—Steve Oedekerk's *Kung Pow! Enter the Fist* (2002) aims to parody Hong Kong action cinema, and its overall conceit, too, is predominantly rooted in exploiting, re-dubbing, and re-purposing original footage. While a case could be made in favor of silliness (as opposed to sheer stupidity), and despite my inclination to assume positive intent, I shall refrain from presenting a proper aesthetic evaluation of this film's dubious comedic value. Rather, I shall merely focus herein on a particular audio track from its "Chosen Edition" release, namely, a so-called "book-on-tape" narration (included as one of a handful of alternate bonus tracks). Choosing this option effectively replaces the film's entire dialogue (i.e., Oedekerk's dubbed send-up—rather than the pre-dubbed content of the original footage) with the voice of a single narrator, delivering the exact same text in an over-exaggerated and (intentionally?)-highbrow British accent. Now, it remains unclear to me what particular altered state had induced the notion of introducing such a scheme, to begin with, but I find myself compelled to state that had it been executed differently—and perhaps with different material altogether—this idea could have proved much more entertaining and, indeed, rewarding. The potential, to my mind, is certainly there. As it stands, however— permitting myself to make use here of a colloquial interjection—it regrettably evokes a resounding "meh." A similar response might also well be induced by the alternative audio tracks provided for Tim Burton's *Mars Attacks!* (1996) and Dean Parisot's *Galaxy Quest* (1999)—the former spoken entirely in "Martian" (allegedly attempting to brainwash the movie's audience), and the former delivered in the native "Thermian" language (spoken by the alien characters in the film). At first blush, or at least as a fun concept that makes full use of the technology that enables such an alternative, to begin with, these ideas certainly show potential and might indeed raise a smirk. Both tracks, however, appear to "overstay their welcome," as it were, after five or six minutes at best. At that point, listening to either the Martians or the Thermians becomes, alas, quite insufferable.

Other performance-based commentary tracks include the cringey and chaotic "joke-track" recorded for the DVD release of *Dodgeball: A True Underdog Story* (2004), written and directed by Rawson Marshall Thurber. Here, the track essentially consists of an ill-fated attempt by Thurber and the principal leads, Ben Stiller and Vincent Vaugh—all portraying alternate "versions" of their own selves—to record an acceptable commentary track. Vaugh immediately exudes ego and vanity and is heard drinking beer and munching on potato chips. Stiller is heard waltzing in 11 minutes or so late, asking the sound engineers to check on his car "every, like, 15 or 20 minutes." Slowly but surely, all three participants both implicitly and explicitly criticize and take various shots at each other. (Thurber, for instance is called out for being a "first-time director"; Stiller is told off for showing up late and asking about leaving the session early). As tension amps up, Stiller—who sounds much like the version of himself on Larry David's *Curb Your Enthusiasm* television show—begins saying things like, "You know what, Rawson, seriously, I did this movie as a favor to Vince Vaughn." Suggestions to keep it a "generic" commentary fail, and 23 minutes in, one of the sound engineers gives them a document titled "Commentary Guidelines for Commentators." Soon enough, listening to the track begins to feel akin to sitting in the backseat of a car on a long drive with some close friends, who are constantly at each other's throats in the front seats. Thurber then storms out, which then prompts one of the sound engineers to ask Stiller and Vaughn if either of them is able to "do an impression of him." Thurber returns for his forgotten keys and re-exits the studio. Left to their own devices, Stiller and an increasingly abusive Vaugh begin to belittle Thurber and grow more and more impatient with two sound engineers. (Thus far, over half an hour in, their "commentary" has conveyed virtually nothing about the movie itself—aside from Vaughn's self-aggrandizing observations). By the 42-min, 30-sec mark, Stiller's assistant arrives and informs him that he has to go. Vaugh seizes the opportunity and leaves as well. The bewildered sound engineers are heard contemplating what to do next, noting, e.g., "this place is trashed! [...] We're gonna have to play a cleaning crew to clean this up [...] Vince put his smokes up in the wall." They then come up with the idea of playing another one of their movies: "Nobody listens to these commentaries anyway." Finally, at 46 min, 49 sec—halfway through the movie—a sound is heard of a tape being switched, whereupon the commentary track for *There's Something about Mary* (1998) begins with co-writers–directors Peter Farrelly and Bobby Farrelly introducing themselves. The track plays for the remaining half of the movie, including over the end-credits. (As an added little joke, the alternative standard commentaries—one by writer-director Thurber; the other by the same three participants—appear to have been included as a hidden "Easter Eggs").

Much in the same vein, in a commentary track recorded for Ben Stiller's *Tropic Thunder* (2008)—which, in essence, is a film *about* the making of a film—American actor Robert Downey Jr. makes a point of remaining in-character as Australian method-actor Kirk Lazarus, who portrays an African American character, namely, Staff Sergeant Lincoln Osiris. Arguably abandoning any sense of political correctness (at least by certain standards), while at the same time effectively adhering to an incidental statement his character makes in the film, "*I don't drop character 'till I done a DVD Commentary,*" Downey Jr. delivers nearly the entire commentary not only in-character as Lazarus but as Lazarus "himself" in-character, speaking in *his* own character's African American Vernacular English—which changes to Australian English at the same point his character, in the film, "drops character." Downey Jr. is only heard as himself just in time for the end-credits. (Co-stars Ben Stiller and Jack Black record this track essentially as themselves).

Bruce Campbell's in-character in *Bubba Ho-Tep* (dir. Don Coscarelli, 2002), the chaotic fake fight that develops between the commentators on *Anchorman: The Legend of Ron Burgundy* (dir. Adam McKay, 2004), and the improvised "musical" commentary created for *Step Brothers* (dir. Adam McKay, 2008), albeit well intentioned and creative, are, alas, less inspired examples of the same kind. They can all ultimately be regarded as fun jokes that simply run far too long and, as such, defeat their purpose.

Reminiscent of the Pythonesque gag employed in the 2001 DVD release of *Monty Python and the Holy Grail* (1975)—which, in addition to the standard commentary tracks (lifted from an earlier LaserDisc release), had whimsically taken advantage of the various possibilities generated by the medium in order to include new bonus material such as "A special feature for the Hard of Hearing" (which basically consists of the sound of Terry Jones's voice *shouting* the on-screen menu options) or "Subtitles for Those Who Don't Like the Film (taken from Shakespeare's *Henry IV, Part II)*"—the 2003 Universal DVD release of *Monty Python's the Meaning of Life* (1983) seems to have taken things even further with their "Soundtrack For The Lonely: A Soundtrack For People Watching At Home Alone." As with audio tracks discussed herein, it, too, is essentially a feature-long joke. Yet while other tracks may gradually dwindle or periodically lose their panache, this wickedly bizarre and grotesquely hysterical achievement is to my mind, the most well-executed and rewarding aural artifact (parallel only to the *Spinal Tap* in-character commentary). In brief, what the audience is listening to is the sound of a man named George—portrayed by Sir Michael Palin—who is watching the film alone in his humble abode. Every so often, he is heard muttering aimlessly at the screen in front him, munching on the odd snack, breaking wind, speaking over his telephone, or being yelled at by his next-door neighbor to "turn it down." As the track progresses, the somewhat darker tale of this man gradually unveils. Now, although this track does not feature a person speaking directly to an audience, it is nevertheless experienced by the audience as an aural performance—and quite a unique one at that.

Toward the end of the first decade of the twenty-first century, and complying with the growing attention to identity and disabilities, companies began utilizing the available technology to also include a supplementary "audio description" track, which, as its name implies, consists of an aural narration, describing with as much precision and simplicity as possible all the visual happenings seen on screen. As this track is "technical" at its core, lacking any performative context, it cannot—unlike audio commentaries—be considered a proper aural artifact. Notwithstanding, as my own initial encounter with an "audio description" track apparently demonstrates, one might add a certain conceivable caveat: I first became aware that these tracks even exist when going through the features found on the DVD release of the *Brüno* (dir. Larry Charles, 2009), whose title character was created by Sacha Baron Cohen. Yet given my acquaintance with the specific nature of the comedy style of its creators, I was, admittedly, convinced that this "standard" addition for the benefit of the visually impaired was, in fact, a bonus "joke"-track. My initial assumption was rooted in the somewhat unsettling incongruity between the intentionally over-exaggerated and barking-mad visual imagery that exhibits extreme homo-eroticism, coupled with the distant, *nonchalant* and 1920s-war-correspondent–like tone in which on-screen lunacy was put into words. It was only later that I realized that this track was actually doing precisely what it was supposed to, thereby serving its purpose.

Ultimately, I find that all the commentaries and alternate audio tracks mentioned surveyed herein demonstrate precisely why this phenomenon effectively facilitates the creation of unique aural artifacts—the overall arthood of which is effectively enhanced by a prevailing pretense of reality that is purportedly shared by both the performers and their audience alike. To be sure, unlike pseudo-documentaries or works that otherwise let one in on the joke, had a *fictional* character conceivably extended its existence and commented on its own behavior, one would have been faced with a rather complex aesthetic conundrum.

CHAPTER FIVE

Compelled to Speak: The Embodied Voices and Implied Narrators Who Deliver Beckett's Trilogy

On *Molloy* and the "Trilogy" as a Whole

In my introductory remarks, I referenced McGovern's suggestion that Beckett's prose almost literally cries out to be read aloud, which, in effect, constitutes a performance. As established *ab initio*, one of my endeavor's objectives is to articulate precisely why. According to Enoch Brater, the "performative" property of Beckett's language resides in its appearing "so wonderfully speakable" that it almost *demands* to be read aloud by a "resonant human voice."[1] Indeed, as both Knox and Rubery have quite rightly pointed out, some texts simply seem to "lend themselves to audio performance."[2]

Although admittedly bewildered by his initial reading of the prose works—which he would subsequently transform into a spellbinding one-man show—renowned Irish actor Jack MacGowran nonetheless found some inner quality inhabiting the text that he identified as requiring expression. Recounting one of their conversations, he quotes Beckett as saying, "I admit that my word on the page is difficult, but if it can be interpreted by [...] being spoken, it would take on a dimension of understanding that one mightn't get from reading it."[3] Interestingly, Douglas McMillan and Martha Fehsenfeld cite Beckett as having confessed once that he never wrote a word without actually saying it out loud before putting it on the page.[4]

---

[1] Enoch Brater, *The Drama in the Text: Beckett's Late Fiction* (New York: Oxford University Press, 1994), 4.

[2] Knox, "Hearing Hardy, Talking Tolstoy," 128.

[3] Jack MacGowran, interviewed by Liam Nolan, [excerpt, *circa* 1966], 03m50sec.–04m12sec.

[4] Douglas McMillan and Martha Fehsenfeld, *Beckett in the Theatre: The Author as Practical Playwright and Director* (London: Calder, 1988), 16.

As a sidenote, I find it interesting to contemplate how Beckett himself would have indeed sounded the words aloud—for it would surely have informed one about this particular aspect of his creative internal logic. While one may certainly punch holes in the paradigm asserting that an author is the ideal person to narrate or perform their own work, there are certain instances where their "take" is, in fact, no less than crucial. Evidently, the spoken word also proved particularly important to English author and literary critic Anthony Burgess and, so it seems to his writing praxis, whose home recordings—consisting of his reading aloud his own writing—serve as a good case in point. He had arguably conceived of making them as an ostensible vehicle to test how the sound of his words might come across to his readers. As such, if something didn't sound "right," he was able to fine-tune his work and apply necessary revisions. To be sure, he recognized the unique power of the spoken word, which can provide one with certain insights that the words on the page alone cannot.[5] (In one of his critical works, Burgess had argued that the best understanding of the writing of James Joyce, for example, can be attained by reading the text aloud). I would argue that since Burgess was also linguist and had produced many translation works, reading aloud could certainly help in ascertaining whether what feels like a good translation of the original *actually* coveys the intended sound.

In delivering what might be identified as extended personal monologues—intrinsically obsessed, as it were, with the very acts of writing and narration as means for substantiating the conceivable validity of one's existence—the narrating protagonists that inhabit Beckett's major prose works appear to evoke significant *ars poetic* complexities and implications concerning the novelistic medium itself, effectively calling into question such concepts as authorship, identity, and, indeed, the distinct voice that a given text purportedly embodies. This, as I will demonstrate herein, appears to "go to eleven," when examining the aural iterations of these texts. As such, my objective in this chapter is to identify (at least in broad strokes) the key strands and inherent tenets that concretize the overall (and generally accepted) internal logic that Beckett's prose adheres to (or at least predominantly pertains to). Focusing, in particular, on *Molloy* (1951)—and by comparing its different aural iterations—I subsequently intend to aesthetically evaluate whether or not (and, indeed, to what extent) the novel's purported internal logic successfully informs and inhabits them.

[5.] See, e.g., Burgess reading from his own *A Clockwork Orange* (1962), accessed November 8, 2022, https://www.anthonyburgess.org/tape/anthony-burgess-on-a-clockwork-orange/.

Initially written in French between 1946 and 1949, *Molloy* was subsequently translated into English by Beckett himself and published in 1955. It was then followed by *Malone Dies* (1956) and *The Unnamable* (1958)— its two complementary components in what is traditionally identified as of Beckett's "trilogy"—both of which also originally published in French (in 1951 and 1953, respectively) and later translated by Beckett into English. According to Rónán McDonald, "The three novels that make up the Trilogy have come to be regarded as among the prose masterpieces of the twentieth century."[6]

Molloy is divided into two parts, each of which is a purportedly self-contained narrative, supposedly delivered by a different protagonist and arguably constituting the polar antithesis of the other. They both appear to either conclude at their inception, or, indeed, commence at their cessation. Each narrating protagonist seems to be conveying—perhaps even constructing, as it were, in real time—a first-person account of his own story, conceivably rooted in both fragmented memories and occasional out-of-sync meditations. As a complex amalgamation of streams of a somewhat haunted consciousness, each narrative seemingly revolves around everything that come to mind, and, simultaneously, discloses nothing in particular about anything at all. For McDonald, however, if the point of a novel ("its aesthetic affect, as it were") entails withholding precisely what it is all about (i.e., its theme or so-called message), "then explaining that novel, translating it into coherent themes, is in a sense to lose it."[7] The very act of reading thus becomes a quest to decipher "how the trilogy should be read in so far as it challenges many of the procedures and conventions underlying critical interpretation." Although he finds "little point in pillaging these texts for readily packaged themes or clear messages," he ultimately asserts that one "cannot simply ignore the challenge to interpretation that these elusive texts pose, eschewing their ambiguities and perplexities for the appreciation of a nicely caught cadence."[8]

Overall, Beckett's writing frequently lends itself to communicating the implied voices that both beset and consume his protagonists—either internally or externally. In what is further amplified by their aural iterations, all one is left

---

[6] Rónán McDonald, *The Cambridge Introduction to Samuel Beckett* (Cambridge: Cambridge University Press, 2006), 87.

[7] Ibid., 89–90.

[8] Ibid., 90.

with in the prose works are the disembodied voices residing within. This, I find, clearly resonates with certain insights that arise from the notes of Patrick Bowles—who had collaborated with Beckett on his English translation of *Molloy*—and, explicitly, the idea that the novel's narrators adhere to some kind of "consciousness of consciousness. Not merely being the consciousness of some object, but the awareness of being awake, if you like."[9]

The Purported Improbability of Pinpointing the Plot

Vivian Mercier had famously ill-depicted Beckett's *Waiting for Godot* (1953) as a play in which "nothing happens, twice."[10] By the same token, one might likewise be tempted to mistakenly claim that *Molloy*, for all the incessant meanderings of its narrators, fundamentally "says" absolutely nothing, twice. In this respect, while successfully describing its perplexing plot is generally acknowledged as an unlikely task, one can certainly attempt to address the overall "story" of *Molloy* in broad strokes:

The first part of the novel introduces Molloy, a crippled derelict, whose chainless bicycle is arguably his most prized possession. His entire *raison d'etre* seems to center on the quest to return to his mother's house—coupled with the simple need to survive amid an invariably unfriendly world. As the novel begins, one essentially finds Molloy with his quest already accomplished, effectively residing in his dead mother's room, with no recollection of how he ended up there. There, he writes. Completing but a few pages every day, he composes a fictional account of his obstacle-ridden journey—which he delivers (to Beckett's readers) in the first person.

The second part introduces Moran—who is also its assumed narrator. Although he essentially introduces himself—thereby assuming authorship of (and, as such, responsibility for) a monologue of his own—the question of whether Moran had, in fact, penned his own narrative remains as unclear as whether he himself is indeed narrating it. For the most part, he spends his days following assignments commissioned by an undescribed superior, Youdi (with

---

[9.] David Addyman, Matthew Feldman, and Erik Tonning, eds., *Samuel Beckett and BBC Radio—A Reassessment* (New York: Palgrave Macmillan, 2017), 10.

[10.] Vivian Mercier, "The Uneventful Event," *Irish Times*, February 18, 1956, 6.

whom he communicates solely via messenger, Gaber).[11] In doing so, Moran, too, finds himself on a quest, namely, to find Molloy. Gradually identifying with the subject of his main inquiry, his narrative unfolds as an almost devoutly introspective, self-torturous, ostensible case history.

Whether Molloy and Moran may or may not, in fact, be one and the same is unclear. Yet they both seem excessively engaged with words and virtually *compelled* to write. In documenting and reframing their thoughts, lives, memories, and meditations in the form of fiction, they effectively define their identities. Much like other Beckett protagonists who both desire and require some ostensible "other" agency to validate their existence—such as the sudden violent manner that accompanies Vladimir's need to make sure that the Boy in *Waiting for Godot* had indeed *seen* him—here, too, the narrating protagonists seem to quite literally *require* some imagined auditors. By endowing them with *actual* human voices—conceivably allowing them to narrate themselves *ad infinitum*—the aural iterations of the novel further amplify its unique complexities and similarly impel its narrators to *speak* aloud. In this context, when similarly considering the existential contemplation uttered by "M" in Beckett's stage play, *Play* (1963)—begging the question, *"Am I as much as ... being seen?"*[12]—an argument could certainly be made that the narrating protagonists here are ultimately rendered as much as "being heard." As Natalie Leeder points out, "words in Beckett have a tendency to morph as they are transposed—or translated, perhaps—from one medium to the next."[13] As such, a well-performed aural artifact can effectively render one no less compelled to *listen*, thus potentially providing an enhanced and rewarding aesthetic experience.

As one's attention must also be paid to the inherent relationship that prevails between all *three* novels—or rather between the "trilogy" as a whole and its narrating protagonists—presented herein is an extra-brief summary of the subsequent two works: In *Malone Dies*, the title protagonist is also engaged with the very act of writing, gradually generating a carbon copy of his own life, which he effectively utilizes as a means of assertedly delaying his own death.

[11.] The inclusion of an undescribed character in a medium that is necessarily dependent on words might be identified as part of a distinctively "Beckettian" internal logic that essentially questions the very nature of the medium that the work was intended for. Consider, e.g., Beckett's own *Waiting for Godot*—featuring perhaps the most famous off-stage character in the history of Western theater.

[12.] Samuel Beckett, *Play*, in *The Complete Dramatic Works* (London: Faber, 2006), 317.

[13.] Natalie Leeder, "'None but the Simplest Words': Beckett's Listeners," in *Samuel Beckett and BBC Radio—A Reassessment*, eds. David Addyman, Matthew Feldman, and Erik Tonning (New York: Palgrave Macmillan, 2017), 270.

The limitations of Malone's mortality parallel those of his pencil, the primary instrument of his craft, increasingly disintegrating with every page. Reading the novel, these limitations are mirrored by its depleting pages. Listening to the audiobook, they correspond with the recording's intrinsic running time. Completing the cycle, likewise confined to his own contemplations, is the solipsistic narrator of *The Unnamable*. Despite having no distinguishing features, his power of speech persists—both personifying and substantiating his own self. He depicts himself as "a big talking ball, talking about things that do not exist, or that exist perhaps, impossible to know, beside the point."[14] Although one might be inclined to more accurately regard *him* as an "it," I would argue that his underlying relationship to the other narrating protagonists, the masculine pronoun certainly applies. Ultimately, in narrating *their* own narratives, they all seem to assume an authorship that extends across the entire scope of the "trilogy" as a whole.

Molloy as an Aural Artifact

To date, *Molloy* received two professional audiobook iterations: one by RTÉ, narrated by McGovern, and the other by Naxos, employing *two* narrators—Sean Barrett and Dermot Crowley—who each read a different section of the novel.[15] As I will presently demonstrate, while both these versions clearly comply with and adhere to what an aural artifact should constitute, each version evidently elicits a different kind of aesthetic evaluation—which, in turn, is inherently associated with and, indeed, linked to one's understanding of the novel's purported internal logic. For instance, what I will identify herein as the aesthetic deficiency in Barrett and Crowley's rendition is rooted in the explicit artistic choice employed by Naxos to have the novel delivered by *two* different actors.

For an aural iteration, to determine whether Molloy and Moran are indeed two separate agencies is no less crucial. As nowhere does the novel explicitly clarify whether the two are, in fact, one and the same, the fact that Beckett had named the novel after one specific protagonist surely amplifies the perplexity. In this respect, Naxos essentially forces a specific reading, embracing their perceptible

---

14. Samuel Beckett, *The Unnamable,* in *Three Novels: Molloy, Malone Dies, the Unnamable* (New York: Grove Press, 2009), 299.

15. Samuel Beckett, *Molloy*, read by Sean Barrett and Dermot Crowley (Naxos Audiobooks, 2003).

ambiguities. The notable accomplishments and proficiencies of both Barrett and Crowley notwithstanding, and even if they consciously endeavored to challenge the novel's internal logic, justifying the artistic rationale becomes arduous. As each seems to abide in his own state of existence, these protagonists might well be identified as variations of one another, complementing each other not only in their comprehension of the world they inhabit but also in sharing a particular pattern of speech and structure of thought, as well as a vocabulary and style.

Now, while there may not be a single particular manner in which a so-called typical "Beckett character" necessarily speaks, there certainly appear to exist certain qualities—e.g., an implicitly embedded tone, cadence, and rhythm, as well as a distinctive sense of ostensible "Irishness"—which, together, can purportedly define what a typical "Beckett character" is, to begin with. As such, they would effectively inform and indicate (both implicitly and explicitly) the given limited range of plausible possibilities for interpretation and preferred parameters for a putative performance. Much like, say, the iambic pentameter in Shakespeare, this also conceivably embodies and adheres to some overall "Beckettian" style. Notwithstanding, extensive or ostensibly elastic as any particular set of parameters may purportedly be, one is inevitably destined to reach a point beyond which one cannot venture. It, in turn, is ultimately determined and prescribed by the commonly agreed upon internal logic (or, indeed, key strands thereof) that embodies the text in question. In the case of aural artifacts, this should be appropriately accounted for alongside the internal logic of the unique aural medium.

Albeit a valid, interesting artistic choice, I find that endowing Molloy and Moran with distinct voices and virtually palpable identities is arguably missing the point—especially in the larger context of the "trilogy" as a whole. As an ill-interpreted reading of the novel, the Naxos release prevails as an aesthetically flawed aural artifact. At the same time, this choice does appear to exhibit a certain aesthetic potential—had it been employed differently: e.g., were the two performers to mimic or impersonate each other's vocal traits. I am reminded in this respect of the two leading actors in John Woo's science-fiction action thriller *Face/Off* (1997). In brief, John Travolta's generic "good guy" undergoes a surgical process in which he replaces his face with that of Nicholas Cage's generic "bad guy." As a result, each performer ends up portraying both protagonist and antagonist. Now, in each assuming the other's role—while still looking and sounding like their own selves—Cage and Travolta effectively comply with one's intuitive expectation of how each *actor* would supposedly have portrayed *their* (i.e., the opposite) role. In this context, I would argue that had Naxos considered thus approaching *Molloy*—somehow articulating manifesting this idea by making full use of the vocal properties of Barret and Crowley—the final product could have conceivably made for a fascinating interpretation that appropriately demonstrates an understanding of the novel's inherent complexities. The evident talents of both Barrett and Crowley notwithstanding, I ultimately find the artistic choices employed by Naxos to be somewhat lacking.

McGovern's performance, on the other hand, successfully demonstrates the obscure duality that *Molloy*'s narrating protagonists abide by. Despite their being ostensibly filtered through the voice of a single performer, Molloy and Moran do not sound like the same character. At the same time, his iteration also does not make them sound like completely different agencies. He endows each of them with an individual vocal signature, attained by slightly altering the tone of his voice.[16] Yet he successfully expresses their commonalities as well.[17] In considering the trilogy as a whole—and when accepting the conjecture that each protagonist represents some "version" of his predecessor—McGovern's delivery of all three novels evidently exhibits a remarkable sense of consistency.

As early as the opening lines, his performance appears to distinguish quite clearly between direct speech and a contemplation spoken aloud. This distinction is far less evident in the Naxos recording. Even when considering seemingly simple utterances, such as "Yes, I work now, a little like I used to, except that I don't know how to work anymore," one should be mindful of what choices would work for this Beckett's text.[18] McGovern's performance follows this particular punctuation with precision.[19] Crowley's, however, employs a different choice of emphases: *"Yes, I work, now, a little, like I used to, except that I don't know how to work, anymore."*[20] While the contents remain exactly the same—that is to say, all the words in the text are delivered as they appear on the page—these two articulations create a discernible difference with regard to how each sequence of words should be heard, namely, as direct speech, a contemplation, or memory. Ultimately, whereas McGovern's Molloy sounds as if he is carrying the weight of his life experiences with him, Crowley's Molloy

---

[16.] e.g., RTÉ, disc2, track11; disc3, track2; and disc4, track9 (for Molloy); and disc5, track 12; disc6, track11; and disc8, track10 (for Moran).

[17.] e.g., RTÉ, disc1, track14; disc3, track8; disc7, track8; and disc8, track6.

[18.] Samuel Beckett, *Molloy,* in *Three Novels* (New York: Grove Press, 2009).

[19.] RTÉ, disc1, track1, 00m32sec.

[20.] Naxos, *Molloy*, track1, 00m45sec.

sounds as if his life experiences are yet to have been. McGovern's performance, to my mind, eloquently exhibits a deep, comprehensive understanding of all three texts—coupled with a remarkably sensitive awareness of the appropriate particular "reading aloud" that they necessarily require and evoke. He does not merely read the written text (i.e., ostensibly transforming it into spoken words) but rather *performs* it for a designated audience: his imagined auditors, who, quite literally, are not actually there. Furthermore, while Barret—who only narrates Moran's narrative in the Naxos production—is, in fact, featured as the sole narrator in their subsequent individual releases of *Malone Dies* and *The Unnamable*, I have chosen to focus my attention on *Molloy* explicitly due to the problematics discussed herein. The fact that McGovern performs the entire novel himself makes for a captivating listening and, indeed, offers one an immensely rewarding aesthetic experience of the novel. As an aural artifact, the RTÉ production is quite exquisite—so much so, in fact, that I would rank it among the best audiobooks ever recorded.

On Beckett and Aural Iterations

In addition to the McGovern and Naxos recordings—which, to date, prevail as the only unabridged iterations of the "trilogy"—there also exist three prominent abridged recordings, consisting of a compilation of passages. The earliest of this consists of the three aural excerpts (one from each novel in the trilogy) narrated by renowned Armagh-bred actor Patrick Magee and broadcast between 1957 and 1959 on the BBC's Third Programme. Contemplating whether he might conceive of an original piece for radio to follow *All That Fall* (1956), Beckett suggested working in collaboration with his cousin—composer John Beckett—who, in turn, would compose an original piece of music to accompany the solo-narration of an existing prose work. At the time, Beckett considered the concluding passage of Molloy's narrative as potential candidates. Matthew Feldman quite rightly considers the extensive incidental musical score indispensable to these productions, highlighting the manner in which it effectively bookends the sentence "the heart beats, and what a beat," thereby "isolating it as a kind of musical italicization" to the trilogy as a whole.[21] In the same vein,

---

[21] Matthew Feldman, *Falsifying Beckett—Essays on Archives, Philosophy, and Methodology in Beckett Studies* (Stuttgart, Germany: ibidem-Verlag, 2015), 177.

as Kevin Branigan points out, Beckett appreciated what seemed to constitute "a rough consonance rather than a rigid mirroring between the text and score."[22] The original 1957 radio broadcast consisted of two Beckett passages: *From an Abandoned Work*—cited in the BBC's records as *"The Meditation"*—and the *Molloy* excerpt.[23] The broadcast's success led to the two additional readings from the "trilogy," namely, a 71-min-long passage from *Malone Dies* and a 111-min-long passage from *The Unnamable*, recorded in 1958 and 1959, respectively.[24]

The choice of casting Magee (who had previously portrayed Mr. Slocum in *All That Fall*) was made by producer Donald McWinnie. Magee soon became one of Beckett's personal favorite interpreters of his own work.[25] Conceivably, Beckett had intuitively identified in Magee's delivery not only the quintessential embodiment of the type of characters that his writing personifies but also a unique ability to evoke the distinctive inherent tones of the narrative voice—effectively matching what Beckett may have envisioned (or, rather, en*heard*) inside his own head when arranging the words on the pages. As John Pilling points out, Magee became "a natural choice" for many Beckett projects—the sheer number of which "speaks volumes as to Beckett's increasing satisfaction with Magee's performances, and his growing conviction that he had indeed found his ideal interpreter."[26] In this respect, Magee's narration seems to successfully exhibit not only the internal logic of Beckett's text but also that of the aural medium itself—or at least the manner in which Beckett perceived it. *Krapp's Last Tape* (1958), for example, was, in fact, originally conceived of as the "Magee Monologue"—explicitly designed for the actor to perform on stage and include the use of a tape recorder.

My personal admiration for Magee's talent and unique vocal qualities notwithstanding, and while I surely appreciate the purported impact of his performance and intuitions on Beckett's overall *oeuvre*, I would nonetheless quite

---

[22] Kevin Branigan, *Radio Beckett: Musicality in the Radio Plays of Samuel Beckett* (Bern: Peter Lang, 2008), 124.

[23] Martin Esslin, "Samuel Beckett and the Art of Radio," in *On Beckett: Essays and Criticism*, ed. S. E. Gontarski (New York: Grove Press, 1986), 367.

[24] To date, the only recording to have been made commercially available is that of *From an Abandoned Work*. See: Samuel Beckett, *Works for Radio: The Original Broadcasts* (British Library & BBC, NSACD 24–27, 2006).

[25] Esslin, "Samuel Beckett and the Art of Radio," 367.

[26] John Pilling, "Changing My Tune: Beckett and the BBC Third Programme (1957–1960)," in *Samuel Beckett and BBC Radio—A Reassessment*, eds. David Addyman, Matthew Feldman, and Erik Tonning (New York: Palgrave Macmillan, 2017), 175.

regrettably argue that these particular aural iterations are, alas, less than perfect—and, in fact, fail to fully convey and exhibit the internal logic of the texts
themselves. Despite the attention and success that the broadcasts received at
the time, Magee's delivery sounds overtly distant—as if the narrating protagonist is predominantly talking to himself rather than delivering the words to
his implied audience. (Even if the voice that inhabits the text might be said
to reside inside the narrator's head—the aural iteration should appropriately
convey the manner in which that voice is directed at the narrator himself, as
his own ostensible designated audience). As such, if one is unable to sense
whether the narrator indeed has some audience in mind, one's overall aesthetic
experience can become gravely impaired. Furthermore, when it comes to the
delicate balance (on the page) between what is actually spoken by the narrating protagonist and what he appears to hear inside his own head, I find that
Magee's narration exhibits a rather vexing inconsistency. Explicitly, whereas
he does succeed in virtually speaking in the speed of thought, there are far too
many moments where his delivery simply sounds as if one had mistakenly
played the recording both underwater and in the wrong speed. Although it may
appear to be an interesting interpretation, the resulting aesthetic experience is,
alas, less than rewarding, and ultimately renders evaluation a rather arduous
task. Notwithstanding, an argument might also be made that when engaging
with these individual passages—as opposed to a complete and unabridged recording—one is essentially required to seek, find, and adopt an ostensibly alternative internal logic. While no doubt informed by the trilogy as a whole, it
would effectively adhere to a new conceptual rationale and aesthetic criteria—
and, as such, should account for not only the very selection of these particular
passages over others but also the manner in which the accompanying musical
score has been employed.

Similarly noteworthy are the 1963 Caedmon recordings (currently available
only on vinyl) performed by the no-less formidable Irish actor Cyril Cusack
and the 1966 aural rendition of MacGowran's aforementioned one-man play—
the latter created under the personal supervision of Beckett himself. On the
one hand, one might argue that here, too, it may not be fitting to compare the
abridged iteration of a text with its complete and unabridged recording. On
the other hand, I would argue that as distinct aural artifacts—rooted, to a large
extent, in a shared internal logic—one *can* certainly compare their aesthetic
qualities. As the MacGowran recording does not consist solely of passages
from the "trilogy"—and therefore conceivably requires a slightly different

kind of evolution, effectively accounting for both the other chosen passages and, indeed, the order in which they are delivered—I shall commence with the Cusack iteration, which seems to my mind quite in the same vein as that of Magee.

Almost instantly, one is struck by Cusack's overall characterization of the narrating protagonist, whose voice sounds exceedingly old, wrinkled, and afflicted by an ostensibly acute deterioration. As no distinction appears to have been made between the purportedly different protagonists, there is a sense that the narrating voice is lingeringly fading away into the darkness of (no)-sound. At the same time, listening to Cusack's performance, one could almost imagine him as an intoxicated patron of a local Irish pub, drifting between strains of thought, struggling to remain lucid and coherent, speaking to no one, in particular, and simultaneously to whoever is willing to listen. Alluding to the Caedmon recordings of works by Joyce—which include readings by Joyce himself—Roach identifies Cusack's sensitivity "to the Ireland of Joyce's time and with vocal qualities comparable to those of Joyce himself."[27] Inevitably, her evaluation requires one not only to possess at least some general notion of what the "Ireland of Joyce's time" is but also to determine what "vocal qualities" and "speech texture" entail. This, to my mind, constitutes to a large extent an attempt to ascertain whether or not (and, indeed, to what extent) Cusack's performance successfully exhibits the internal logic of Joyce's work—which, as Roach correctly asserts, he certainly does. Given the abiding correlation between their works, one might assume that Cusack's eloquent delivery of Joyce conceivably entails that he would make a marvel out of Beckett as well. Nevertheless, despite skillfully evoking the fragmented speech patterns of Beckett's protagonists and their landscape that shaped them, I find his overall take on the Joyce passages far more successful in respect of successfully exhibiting the text's internal logic. Much like Magee, and unlike McGovern, there is something of a "claggy" quality to his iteration—not so much in the quality of sound but rather in the overall resonance of his performance. Moreover, whether Beckett's narrating protagonist is conceivably thinking aloud, speaking to himself, or questioning his own perception of the world he inhabits, Cusack's delivery fails in exhibiting the extent to which he is compelled to speak—and, as such, seems to be ostensibly oblivious to whether or not anyone might actually

---

[27] Roach, *Spoken Records*, 75. Also see: *The James Joyce Audio Collection* (HarperCollins, ISBN: 0060501790, 2002).

hear him. As an aural artifact, this is quite problematic. Unlike McGovern's narrating protagonist—who seems to have accepted and grown accustomed to speaking himself *ad infinitum*—Cusack seems to be less at ease with his partic-ular state of affairs. Ultimately, I find that this recording only partially adheres to the purported internal logic of Beckett's work and largely fails to comply with the inherent confines of the aural medium.

Now, the *MacGowran Speaking Beckett* recording, as an "aural compilation" of sorts constitutes a slightly more complex case study. As the passages it con-sists of are not restricted to the "trilogy" alone, one could consider it as either a contemplation or a comment on the original works—effectively manifested as MacGowran's composite "Beckettian" tramp figure. Predominantly, I find that attention must be paid to the manner in which the chosen excerpts have been explicitly woven together—rather than arbitrarily—as a conscious artistic choice. As Melissa Chia points out, the album "does something very unique with words and music, combining the two to form a type of sound montage," in which gong-tolls precede, and thereby frame, each spoken passage.[28] As such, I would argue that much like what is regarded as "concept albums" in the world of music, one is required to consider and account for the overall aesthetics of this recording as a whole.

Thus, rather than merely examining each passage individually, one should effectively scrutinize the implicit conceptual reasoning for linking them to-gether in a particular order as an aural artifact. Evidentially, the compilation begins with a section from *Malone Dies*, commencing with the words "*I shall soon be quite dead at last in spite of all.*" It is then followed by first-person passages from Beckett's second novel, *Watt* (1953), the aforementioned *From an Abandoned Work* (1957) and the radio play *Embers* (1959). The passages from *Molloy* appear on the fifth and sixth tracks: the first begins with the words "*My mother never refused to see me, that is she never refused to receive me, for it was many a long day since she had seen anything at all*", and the second consists of the novel's memorable "sucking stone scene." Next, a passage from *The Unnamable*, followed by first-person excerpts from the stage play *End-game* (1957) and the short story *Echo's Bones* (1935). Attaining the artistic ratio-nale that would appropriately inform one's aesthetic experience and subsequent

---

[28.] Melissa Chia, "'My Comforts! Be Friends!'": Words, Music and Beckett's Poetry on the Third," in *Samuel Beckett and BBC Radio—A Reassessment*, eds. David Addyman, Matthew Feldman, and Erik Tonning (New York: Palgrave Macmillan, 2017), 234.

evaluation requires identifying whether or not (and, indeed, to what extent) these particular passages—which together from a new "conceptual" aural artifact—successfully utilizing and exhibiting the internal logic that abides in Beckett's texts amid the confines of an exclusively aural medium. Ultimately, one can compare these recordings as two possible interpretive takes on the "Beckettian" narrator—namely, Cusack's drunk versus MacGowran's tramp—each adhering to its own unique internal logic.

CHAPTER SIX

Author–Performers and the Innate Intimacy of Recorded Autobiographies and Memoirs: The Abundant "Self-Tellings" of Barry Humphries[1]

The Delight and Distress in Listening to an Author Narrate Their Own Work

Audiobooks consumers customarily relish the opportunity of listening to an author or poet narrating their own work in their voice. As the person responsible for framing the words on the page, they are considered more innately informed than anyone else and, as such, are expected to necessarily bring one closer to the implied literary intentions of the work in question. As Roach points out, "listeners have the right to hope that when an author reads his own works he will convey what he meant in the way he meant it and that listening to such 'informed' readings will bring them closer to the writer's work."[2] Yet, as parenthetically alluded to earlier, one is sure to come across a variety of author-read recordings that quite simply leave much to be desired. More often than not, despite their unique and unparalleled talent as wordsmiths, they appear to lack the necessary skills embodied by professional narrators and proficient performers.

Counterintuitive as it may initially seem, neither is an author's reading necessarily "better" than that of any other person, nor does it invariably exhibit a more comprehensive understanding of how the text *should* be read. In point of fact, it could even prove to be the wrong *kind* of reading—especially when

---

[1] An earlier version of this chapter has been published as a stand-alone journal article. See: David Sheinberg, "Author as Performer: Performing Autobiographies," *International Journal of Performance Arts and Digital Media* 15, no. 3 (2019): 326–339.

[2] Roach, *Spoken Records*, 51.

considering whether or not (and, indeed, the extent to which) their narration successfully complies with and adheres to the confines of an exclusively aural medium. As far as Roach is concerned, there appear to prevail more "uncommunicative" and "poorly read" aural iterations by authors "than by any other group." Appropriately, she maintains,

> In accommodating to the medium of recording, as with any new medium, preparation and practice are necessary. Without direction, writers, and especially those favorites of "recording for posterity", poets, frequently have come off poorly. One cannot place a neophyte before a microphone, tell him to relax and expect him to do much more than try to avoid making mistakes. What has often been recorded in the case of the poet has not been his poetry but the audible record of his struggle as a poor reader. In the struggle he usually tries to listen to it himself so as to be correct. In the process he sets up a cycle from mouth to ear which excludes other listeners. The person speaking for his own ear in this way adjusts the tone in terms of already present vibrations within his head, and produces a different sounding voice from the normal one of speech directed to another's ear.[3]

Ultimately, according to Roach, it is thus through "careful listening" that one establishes whether or not, and to what extent, an author or poet has successfully accommodated the challenges posed by the aural medium itself.[4] In the same vein, Powers finds that

> Many authors like to read their own books. Sometimes that's a good thing. But too often authors lack a natural gift for voice narration and aren't trained in it. Sloppy enunciation, glottal mayhem, off-kilter expressiveness and a general airlessness have killed some books read by the very person who created them. To be sure, the situation has improved since the rough-hewed days of the 1990s, and certain authors are now truly accomplished narrators, their delivery enhancing the words on the page.[5]

Some authors and poets, however, most definitely *are* able to comply with what the aural medium requires—effectively demonstrating not only an awareness of

---

[3] Ibid.

[4] Ibid., 52.

[5] Powers, "Don't Let a Bad Reader Ruin Your Audiobook Experience."

their designated audience but also an inherent understanding of how to trans-form the written text into spoken word. To be sure, certain recordings make it abundantly clear that nobody but the author could have narrated their own text.

One such case, to my mind, can be found in the aural iterations of the *pseudo*-autobiographical writings of Australian performer–satirist–author–Dadaist–comedian–artist, Barry Humphries, who, by endowing the text with a *literal* voice—delivering the words "in-character"— bestows on the audiobooks an aesthetic complexity exceeding that which inhabits the text itself.

Nonexistence Incarnate

With no offense, of course, to his other iconic creations—e.g., Barry McKenzie or Sandy Stone—Humphries' most renowned comic inventions remain Dame Edna Everage and Sir Leslie Colin (aka "Les") Patterson. The two, their os-tensible "nonexistence" notwithstanding, have each been credited as the sole author of their own autobiography, namely, *My Gorgeous Life: The Life, the Loves, the Legend* and *The Traveller's Tool.*[6] Although Humphries is, to all in-tents and purposes, responsible for penning "their" narratives, he himself seem-ingly remains uncredited. Appropriately, and in complying with what nowadays surely constitutes the natural choice when it comes to the aural iterations of autobiographies, both Dame Edna and Sir Les were chosen to narrate the audiobook versions of their own respective personal histories.

Humphries' designated audience—who should no doubt be already acquaint-ed with the stage and screen incarnations of these personae—might discard the omission of his own name as a mere *ars poetic* joke or, put simply, as part of his well-oiled "shtick." Yet I find that having Edna and Les pen their "own" individual works—effectively endowing each alleged autobiography with its own literary voice—not only exhibits the unique kind of performativity that Humphries adheres to but also bestows on the characters themselves a distinctly idiosyncratic prominence. To be sure, that one can virtually *hear* the voices of Edna and Less when engaging with the print alone is quite an achievement, eloquently demonstrating Humphries' meticulous orchestration and unrivaled mastery of his own artistic voice(s). Appropriately, to be able to *literally* hear

---

[6.] Dame Edna Everage, *My Gorgeous Life: An Adventure* (London: Macmillan, 1989); and Sir Les Patterson, *The Traveller's Tool* (London: Michael O'Mara Books, 1985).

"them" narrate what is, to all intents and purposes, "their" own narratives, in their actual voices, makes for a remarkably unique aesthetic experience— ultimately rendering these recordings an ostensible vehicle for extending their existence as *bona fide* personae, well beyond the artistry of the performance. As such, their overall aesthetics—as aural artifacts—greatly surpasses that of so-called "standard" audiobooks.

Making matters worse, Humphries published two personal histories of his own: *More Please* (1992) and the updated, parallel memoir *My Life as Me* (2002). In his preface to the former, Humphries states: "I am already the subject of two generous biographies, and it is only the fear that my adventures might for a third time be profitably chronicled by another man that prompts me to relate my own story."[7] Similarly, in his prologue to the latter, he asserts:

> Here and there, readers may recognise a coincident event or personage from my earlier volume, for this is a cubist, even a futurist, self-portrait that I offer the reader, observing myself from many angles at once as in the hall of mirrors at a fairground, and with whiffs of scent, incoherent voices, shards of music. I have changed the names of several of my dramatis personae who are still living, especially where their portrayal is of such accuracy as might inspire foolhardy litigation. I have honoured the dead by calling them by their real names.[8]

Paul Matthew St. Pierre identifies several "life-tellings," which, in one way or another, present one with alternate versions or so-called fictionalizations of his own self.[9] St. Pierre also considers Humphries' novel *Women in the Background* (1995) as something of a "displaced autobiography," rather than a *roman- à clef*.[10] As far as St. Pierre is concerned, although the narrating protagonist in this case supposedly assumes authorship over the novel itself —and is thus ren- dered as much its ghostwriter as its storyteller—it is ultimately the inherent affil- iation between Humphries and his own work that renders it impossible for any- one to "ghost" *his* story.[11] That is, I would add, other than Humphries *himself.*

[7.] Barry Humphries, *More Please* (London: Viking, 1992), xi.

[8.] Barry Humphries, *My Life as Me* (London: Michael Joseph, 2002), x.

[9.] Paul Matthew St. Pierre, *A Portrait of the Artist as Australian: L'Oeuvre bizarre de Barry Humphries* (Montreal, Canada: McGill-Queen's University Press, 2004), 138.

[10.] Ibid., 216.

[11.] Ibid., 315n10.

Complicating matters further still—in what appears to prevail as his perpetual fascination in exploring the aesthetic liminality that abides in performance
and identity—Humphries also unleashed the aptly titled *Handling Edna: The
Unauthorised Biography* (2009), depicting his own long-time career as Dame
Edna's manager and dedicated to unraveling *his* own exhaustively researched
account of *her* life.[12]

While appropriately crediting Humphries as its author, this literary endeavor
seems to have, nonetheless, been written by a similar *version* of the Barry Humphries responsible for both *More Please* and *My Life as Me*—who, as St. Pierre
explains it, "is by implication, an artistic creation, an ironic readymade and
a processional person: the implied author's implied narrator."[13] Evidently, the
unique dexterity with which Humphries conjures up and animates a variety of
alternate self-representations becomes even more palpable when one engages
with the audiobook version of *Handling Edna*.[14] In conceivably consisting as
another installment in a long line of ready-made replicas of his own self, both
the novel and its aural iteration become quite reminiscent of Warhol's *Brillo
Box*—effectively rendering their author-narrator, "Barry Humphries," virtually
indistinguishable from the one and only John Barry Humphries, born February
17, 1934, in the suburb of Kew, Victoria, Australia.

The Nuanced Intricacies in Narrating One's Own Self

It is interesting to compare the manner in which Humphries delivers *Handline
Enda* as "himself" to the manner in which he narrates the more personal accounts in *More Please*, which seems to quite consciously [avoid] the relationship
he abides with the great Dame.[15] (Regrettably, *My Life as Me* has not received
an audiobook treatment. The narration he endowed *Women in the Background*
with—the recording of which, alas, is no longer in circulation—is quite distinctly different).[16] Given the scope of St. Pierre's extensively researched publication, and while he certainly does well to correctly identify "seventy-two audio

---

[12] Barry Humphries, *Handling Edna: The Unauthorised Biography* (Sydney: Hachette, 2009).

[13] St. Pierre, *A Portrait of the Artist as Australian*, 139.

[14] Barry Humphries, *Handling Edna: The Unauthorised Biography* (Orion, 2010).

[15] Barry Humphries, *More Please*, read by the author (Penguin Audiobooks, 1993).

[16] Barry Humphries, *Women in the Background*, read by the author (Reed Audio, 1996).

recordings" as part of Humphries' "art," it seems rather unfortunate that he does not, alas, sufficiently address or explicitly analyze the recordings themselves.[17]

If, in print, *Handling Edna* is merely able to give the illusion of including Humphries' alleged written correspondences with Edna or allusions to their odd conversations—effectively endowing certain passages with Edna's implied voice—then the medium audiobook enables Humphries to stretch things further still, conceivably amplifying the aesthetic conundrum that aural artifacts facilitate. Explicitly, rather than performing certain passages *as* Edna—that is, having Edna *herself* narrate the passages purportedly evoking her voice—Humphries seems to have opted for narrating the book as *himself* (or, rather, as the ready-made "version" thereof) while "filtering" Edna's voice through his own delivery.

And yet this is not, in fact, the first time that Humphries has taken this route—as the same artistic choice was employed in the aural iteration of Edna's *My Gorgeous Life*, albeit in reverse: that to say, when a particular passage aims to depict an interaction between the two, Edna's narration of her own story effectively evokes *her* "take" on what "Barry Humphries" supposedly sounds like. Drawing on "their" numerous individual public appearances, invariably asserting that they are most certainly *not* one and the same person, I would argue that had Humphries intended these audiobooks to embody a so-called "double-act," the final products would have conceivably credited them both. Ultimately, and much like with the extraction of the Spinal Tap band members from the celluloid that captured them, one is expected to execute a willful suspension of disbelief—and be inclined to accept the ostensible reinstatement of fictional characters amid the corporeal sphere of one's one reality—all the while fully appreciating the distinct artistry of the performance, as well as the aesthetic boundaries that it appears to test.

The distinctive type of storytelling with which Humphries endows Edna seems to be precisely what bestows *her* with the authorship of *My Gorgeous Life*. Indeed, as St. Pierre points out, Edna "is not a storyteller: she is […] a biographer. […] She does not presume to tell a story because there is none."[18] I find that when reading the actual book, one conceivably cannot help but literally *hear* Edna's voice in one's head, lifted off the pages. Appropriately, listening Edna deliver the audiobook version *herself*—thus presenting one with the opportunity of *actually* hearing her voice—makes for an immensely rewarding aesthetic experience.

[17.] St. Pierre, *A Portrait of the Artist as Australian*, x; 281–282.

[18.] Ibid., 185.

Edna begins her narration by noting that "all the persons in this book exist and are called by their real names. Anyone objecting to this could find themselves in costly and interminable litigation."[19] Her overall delivery—and perhaps especially the manner in which she utters the words "interminable litigation"—manifest an almost devilish relish in the very thought of pursuing legal action against someone. The mental image that one presumably conjures up (say, a semi-wicked smirk splashed across Edna's heavily applied makeup) is complemented by a quaint little giggle. Although it is clearly not part of the original printed work—which, in assuming the guise of a purportedly proper autobiography, does not contain stage directions or the like—the giggle is nevertheless virtually *implied* (and perhaps especially when one is acquainted with the variety of mannerisms, peculiarities, and vocal exclamations that Edna's persona adheres to).

Despite a surprising abundance of autobiographical audiobooks that are *not* narrated by their respective authors, I would argue that *My Gorgeous Life* could most certainly not have been narrated by anyone other than Edna *herself* (or, if you wish, by Humphries *in-character*). Had Humphries been unable, for whatever reason, to record his own work and had a different narrator hypothetically undertaken this endeavor in his place *as* Edna, such a recording (albeit unlikely) could have posed an interesting comparative case study—especially if examined as a possible attempt to re-interpret, and even perhaps reinvent, a character that almost seems to exist as an independent agency in her own right. As Michael Parkinson noted about Humphries in his memoir, *Parky's People* (2010), "his relationship with Dame Edna Everage alone is worthy of the highest honor. Her position as one of the world's most iconic women is entirely due to Mr. Humphries' handling of her assets."[20]

Agencies in Their Own Right

I am reminded in this respect of the defining manner in which American puppeteer–filmmaker Frank Oz has both characterized and established the identity of the "muppet" known as Miss Piggy—perhaps the only fictional female character

---

[19] Dame Edna Everage, *My Gorgeous Life*, written and performed by Dame Edna Everage (Dove Audio, 1993). [Digitally Remastered by Phoenix Books, 2014], 00m24sec.

[20] Michael Parkinson, *Parky's People* (Hodder & Stoughton, 2010), 90.

other than Dame Edna to have attained an undisputed prominent status not only as a popular and significant public figure but also a ubiquitous cultural phenomenon, demanding of the personal pronouns "she" and "her." Indeed, when American puppeteer Eric Jacobson inherited the role in 2001, he did not set out to merely "do" the character or ostensibly impersonate the voices but to appropriately embody the role, and even consulted with Oz (with whom he had worked during the mid-1990s) in order to absorb further insights into properly portraying *her* essence.[21]

Now, by way of comparison, one could also consider the audiobook versions of *Chronicles: Volume One* (2004)—the autobiography of American singer–songwriter, folk legend, and Nobel Prize laureate, Bob Dylan. For reasons I have regrettably been unable to detect, Dylan did not opt for narrating the book himself. Had he done so, it could surely have served as an interesting case study for comparison with other author-read autobiographies in the same vein, such as, say, Bruce Springsteen's *Born to Run* (2016) and, to some extent, Janis Ian's *Society's Child: My Autobiography* (2008), both of whom, much like Dylan, are endowed not only with a unique artistic voice but also with distinct vocal qualities that naturally adhere to the medium of the audiobook. Aside from the purported prestige in being granted the opportunity of listening to them tell and deliver their own story, in their own voice, this certainly amplifies one's aesthetic experience of these recordings as aural artifacts.

Notwithstanding, while one may have indeed relished in a Dylan-read iteration, one of the available audiobook versions—eloquently delivered by acclaimed American actor Sean Penn—more than makes up for the ostensible loss.[22] First and foremost, Penn successfully resists what might be regarded as the arguably implied temptation to "do" Dylan or blatantly mimic his trademark vocal properties—which are often subject to parody and impersonation. While one conceivably cannot help but hear Dylan's voice in one's head when engaging with the book in print (and especially when one is supposedly sufficiently acquainted with Dylan's assumed public persona), Penn's narration demonstrates a unique and comprehensive understanding of Dylan's *artistic* voice.

[21.] So much so have Miss Piggy and Dame Edna, to my mind, attained the status of authentic and virtually concrete female agencies, with a singular voice and identity of their own, that I am confidently willing to argue that one could conceivably cast them in a production of Beckett's *Happy Days* (1961) *without* it being deemed a parody, molesting Beckett's text, or having the lawyers representing Beckett's estate charge an extra fee for additional hours.

[22.] Bob Dylan, *Chronicles: Volume 1*, [abridged], read by Sean Penn (Simon & Schuster, 2004).

Arguably, had he attempted to match the sound of Dylan's actual voice, the final product could well have been deemed an inadvertent parody. Although it consists of an abridged version of Dylan's text, Penn's achievement is quite remarkable, and—as an aural artifact—surely surpasses the unabridged iteration delivered by Nick Landrum.[23] Although the latter, too, does well to avoid doing an impersonation of Dylan, and while his reading is certainly not ill-performed, I find that Penn is much more engaging in his ability to capture and convey the internal logic that the memoir embodies.

The same could also be said about the autobiographical self-portrait of another legendary singer–songwriter—*Waging Heavy Peace: A Hippie Dream* (2012) by Canadian American rock musician Neil Young—the audiobook version of which is delivered by American actor Keith Carradine. While it may well be more enjoyable for long-time fans and persons who are more than adequately acquainted with the subject of the memoir, Carradine—much like Penn—skillfully evokes and exhibits the very essence of the narrative itself, which, in this case, seems distinctly non-linear and virtually improvisational.

By the same token, when it comes to such individuals as the unparalleled Scottish comedian–musician–actor Billy Connolly, it proves quite interesting to consider the audiobook companions to his television documentaries, *Route 66: The Big Yin on the Ultimate American Road Trip* (2011) and *Tracks across America* (2016), and *Made in Scotland: My Grand Adventures in a Wee Country* (2018)—all principally written by Connolly, yet narrated by James McPherson, David Monteath, and Gordon Kennedy, respectively—and comparing them with Connolly's own delivery of his touching and hilarious autobiographies *Windswept & Interesting* (2021) and *Rambling Man: Travels of a Lifetime* (2023).[24] To be sure, while one would like to have had the opportunity of listening to Connolly narrate all these books himself, relishing his one-of-a-kind delivery style, I would argue that available narrations—and, in particular, those of Kennedy and McPherson—make for surprisingly satisfactory surrogates. Here, too—much like the aforementioned case of Dylan *à la* Penn—none of the narrators ostensibly succumb to the supposed trap of impersonating Connolly, or, worse, blunder his comedy. In point of fact, the narrators quite successfully

---

[23] Bob Dylan, *Chronicles: Volume 1*, [abridged] read by Nick Landrum (Recorded Books, 2005).

[24] While Connolly penned *Windswept & Interesting* and *Rambling Man* himself, the other books cited previously were written in collaboration with Robert Uhlig, Matt Whyman, and Ian Gittins—respectively.

convey the so-called "spirt" of text—indeed, its internal logic—effectively conveying the voice with which Connolly endowed his text, through their own.

As a side note, I find that the film *My Name Is Alfred Hitchcock* (2022)—written and directed by Mark Cousins, yet supposedly narrated entirely by the voice of the revered director *himself*—also serves as an intriguing case study in this context. Setting aside the question of whether this particular undertaking might be classified as a passionate and insightful two-hour deep-dive into the world of one cinema's most important filmmakers—or rather as an indulgent, brazen, and unnecessarily lengthy exercise in unapologetic appropriation—ultimately, to engage with film entails engaging with its narrator's voice. The "Alfred Hitchcock" one hears reflecting on "his" work is, in fact, voiced and performed by English impressionist Alistair McGowan. In attempting to tie-in the aforementioned role of aural performances in respect of not only film narrations but also the ever-evolving products of AI, it is interesting to consider Cousins' film as something of borderline aural artifact. Indeed, what would be the merit—or, indeed, the virtue—in creating an audiobook that would similarly consist as an extended impression or impersonation of an actual individual?

I am reminded of comment by American comedian-actor Kevin Pollak, made during a recent interview for the *Really? no, Really?* podcast with Jason Alexander and Peter Tilden: alluding to his conceiving of impersonations a "parlor trick", Pollak states that "If I can think of someone you like, and I can recreate them in front of you, I will basically steal the affection you have for the actual person." He then plunges into a pitch-perfect Peter Falk (including the great actor's trademark squint and al), going to state, "I promise you, if you didn't know who Peter Falk was—or you didn't love Peter Falk—what I just did, would [...] be maybe funny in a cartoony kind of way, but it wouldn't have it wouldn't have any..."—and the podcast hosts then complete his sentence for him: "It wouldn't have meaning, yeah. Or resonance." Pollak continues: "So, it has a heart and soul because you know who the person [is]. So, once I tapped into that, it never made sense to me to say, you know, what if Jimmy Stewart were a busboy, it might go something like this...". At a later part of the interview, Pollak states, "By the way, this is the weird part about doing impersonations: when I am doing those people, it becomes like a possession, and, for example, when I do Albert Brooks, I find myself—and, as I did just now with Christopher Walken—thinking faster, and funnier than I do in my own thoughts."[25] I,

---

[25.] See URL: accessed April 30, 2024, https://www.youtube.com/watch?v=2o4iBSNG9xE, 14m34sec–15m35sec; 25sec17min–25sec35min.

for one, find Pollak's comments quite illuminating in this respect—certainly demonstrating that this is a topic that warrants further debate and exploration. Interestingly enough, in February 2024, the *Really? no, Really?* podcast also dedicated an episode to the impending controversy, acute vexation, and, indeed, lawsuit sparked by a "new" comedy special—said to be exclusively AI-generated— ostensibly delivered by the late legendary American comedian George Carlin (1937-2008), eerily titled "I'm Glad I'm Dead".[26]

When Audiobooks Realize Voices

The aforementioned notion that audiobooks constitute the natural medium for first-person narratives seems to be effectively amplified by the aural iterations of autobiographies that are told by the author him or herself.[27]

Whitten, for example, finds these recordings to possess an essential "archival" quality, in that they "capture that moment in time when the person who wrote the memoir, who has written about themselves [...] has to say it aloud"—which, on occasion, can be quite "revealing in a way that sometimes they don't expect."[28]

Consider, for instance, Anjelica Huston's reflections on narrating her own two memoir publications:

> *Watch Me picks* up pretty much directly after *Story Lately Told* [...]. I don't know if I can really compare whether it was more difficult or less difficult to narrate *Watch Me* than *A Story Lately Told*. I think, of course, there are moments in both books that are harder than others—and maybe, overall, it was easier to narrate watch me just because I'd had the previous experience of narrating *A Story Lately Told*—but, as I say, there are things or passages that are easier

---

[26.] See URL: accessed April 30, 2024, https://www.youtube.com/watch?v=5xyuNL--a6w.

[27.] Consider, e.g., Steven Write's debut novel, *Harold* (2023), which revolves around the turbulent stream of a third-grader's meditations—where nearly all of the novel's action takes place. While the novel itself may not necessarily be easily engaged with in print, I find that listening to its aural iteration—narrated by Wright himself, in his own voice, sustaining his dry style of delivery throughout—effectively endows Harold's consciousness with a very literal voice. Funnily enough, there happens to be a certain point in the recording where Wright seems to break character—as the storyteller—when, in describing one of Harold's contemplations, he simply bursts into laughter. This, however—and regardless of whether it's the result of a so-called production boo-boo by an inexperienced or otherwise distracted proof-listener, or, alternatively, an intentional "Easter-egg" for Wright's fan—does not seem to comply with the overall internal logic of the novel itself. See: Steven Wright, *Harold* (Simon & Schuster Audio, 2023), 03h14m17sec-03h14m28sec.

[28.] "Interview with Robin Whitten," 29m33sec–30m00sec.

to talk about than others. I think I'm most excited for my fans to hear about my marriage and my relationship with my husband, Robert Graham. I think it's probably one of the things that they know least about. [...] I think when you're a person in the public eye, or at least certainly for the first sort of 30 years of my life, I was more concerned with keeping my truth to myself—and, it seems that in the second part of my life, or at least after 30 years, are more about revealing myself—my thoughts, my experiences—and I think communication has become more important to me than protecting myself. So, all around, I think it's that particular connection between myself and my audience that I'm seeking to sort of expand upon with both of these books [...].[29]

As aural artifacts (i.e., candidates for appreciation, rooted in the realm of performance), it therefore rarely seems to be justified, to my mind—and, indeed, quite missing the point—to have anyone other than the subject of a memoir or an autobiography effectively deliver his or her own *personal* story—expressing, for themselves, their own unique life journey.

This sense seems to be especially amplified not only if that person is indeed still with us but also—and, perhaps, more to the point—if his or her particular profession and given expertise happen to be rooted in the realm of performance. By way of illustration, consider the audiobook of Dame Judi Dench's *And Furthermore* (2012), for which Dench herself merely narrates the preface:

I don't in anyway consider this to be an autobiography. I've neither the time nor the skill to write one. [...] I have enjoyed—and still am enjoying—a wonderful life, and made some friendships I cherish deeply, many of which appear in these pages, and that is one of the most important reasons why I am happy to put all this on the record. And here is one of these friends, and she is going to read the rest of the book: Samantha Bond.[30]

With no disrespect for the talents of Ms. Bond, it seems to my mind rather pointless to produce a recording of Dame Judi Dench's account of her own life, without having it read by Dame Judi herself. Given her prevailing prominence

---

[29]. See "Anjelica Huston on Her Audiobook WATCH ME," in the *Simon & Schuster Audio* YouTube Channel: accessed February 6, 2023, https://www.youtube.com/watch?v=ff4jr8BG9fM.

[30]. Transcribed from the audiobook: Judi Dench, *And Furthermore* (London: Weidenfeld & Nicolson, 2010). For original wording in print, see: Judi Dench, *And Furthermore* (Unabridged; Orion, 2010), xv.

and proficiencies—and, indeed, before even endeavoring to evaluate Bond's delivery—one might even go so far as to assert that not having Dench narrate the audiobook version herself is considerably worse than not having an audiobook version at all.[31] As such, that Dench has graced one with her time for the sole purpose of consigning the reading to some other individual may well be experienced like an unwelcomed, provocative tease. Listening to Bond— her evident talents notwithstanding—consequently deprives one of what could have been the "full Dench experience" and, indeed, one's primary reason for listening to the audiobook version, to begin with, effectively experiencing it as an aural artifact.

The same certainly holds true for the audiobook version of *2030: The Real Story of What Happens to America (2011)*—the well-received debut novel of acclaimed American comedian-actor-director-screenwriter Albert Brooks. Yet, notwithstanding its author's being a gifted performer, who is surely recognized for his unique ability to deliver his own material, the novel's official aural iteration has been recorded by Dick Hill. Although *2030* may not be an autobiography, the novel most certainly embodies Brooks' voice. Thus, as this novel ostensibly "cries out" to be performed by Brooks himself, if—for whatever reason—a choice has been made to have it recorded by anyone other than Brooks, the task of finding a suitable substitute should not be taken lightly. At the end of the day, despite his being a longtime, professional, and respected narrator (whom, incidentally, I have already alluded to when surveying the abundance of *Huck Finn* narrations), Hill's performance, I regret to report, simply does not justice with the material—and, perhaps most importantly, Brooks' comedy, rhythm, and tone. And it is in this respect that this particular audiobook—as an aural artifact—is, alas, aesthetically flawed.

Now, the captivating manner in which Humphries devised his characters inevitably renders "their" autobiographies a performance unto themselves, which inevitably embodies and evokes—on the page—not only the visual image of what they look like but also their vocal mannerisms and distinct speech patterns. The audiobook versions, in turn, appropriately demonstrate Humphries' inherent awareness of *their* designated audience. Edna, for instance, often directly *addresses* her listeners directly, adding so-called "asides" and parenthetical

---

[31.] To be sure, that Dench had, in fact, already narrated a number of audiobooks in the past—e.g., Henry Donald's *A Bunch of Sweet Peas* (1988), George Eliot's *Silas Marner* (1861), E. M. Forster's *A Room with a View* (1908), Muriel Spark's *The Driver's Seat* (1970), Johanna Spyri's *Heidi* (1880–1881), and Flora Thompson's *Lark Rise to Candleford* (1939)—merely adds to one's confusion.

remarks that indicate potential grammatical uncertainties. Although it certainly makes an effort to remain loyal to the particular confines of its medium, the audiobook version does (on more than one occasion) retain the word "readers," rather than replacing it with "listeners." Yet this could potentially be written off as something of an oversight in the process of transforming the written text into an aural artifact.

To be sure, had this audiobook never been recorded, one would have been faced with the challenge of "enhearing" Edna's voice off the page alone. Nevertheless, the gift h that Humphries bestows on his audience—allowing one to literally hear Edna tell her story—both cultivates and culminates in an aesthetic experience that the text alone simply cannot provide. Consider, for example, Edna's reference to her lifelong friend, companion, and confidant, Madge Allsop: "This mustn't go any further, listeners, but I've always thought Madge had [*Edna pauses, and then whispers*—] tendencies."[32]

Ultimately, Humphries' masterful performance perpetually draws one into Edna's storytelling—extending her ostensible existence as a fictional creation and effectively re-affirming her status as a literal agency in her own right. One can easily imagine her sitting in the recording studio reading from her own manuscript. (Although my inquiry into the matter regrettably remains inconclusive—and albeit, for the most part, irrelevant in respect of one's listening audience—I would not be surprised if Humphries actually recorded this audiobook fully dressed as Edna, conceivably fine-tuning the authenticity of his delivery).

The Audiobook as Vehicle for Engaging with the Listeners

In utilizing the medium of the audiobook as a vehicle of sorts for further engaging with her loving audience—vividly reconstructing various scenes from her own past in an extended monologue of sorts—Edna is able to convey even more to her audience than what appears on the page. For example, she both employs and produces a number of different voices when alluding to various personae in her life, such as her mother, her father, Madge, the Queen of England, her uncle Victor (aka "The Butcher of Borneo"), and a group of Nazis celebrating Hitler's birthday. Appropriately, one's willing suspension of disbelief springs

---

[32.] Everage, *My Gorgeous Life*, [1993] 2014, 27m43sec.

into action—accepting that it is clearly *Edna* (i.e., rather than Humphries) who is doing these voices—all the while remaining fully aware of the inherently surreal conceit that the audiobook adheres to. Aside from but a few passages that seem to exhibit potentially confusing vocal ambiguities and inconsistencies, and with the exception of Edna's husband Norm and a character merely referred to as "Les" (whose full name and identity can surely be surmised), Humphries' overall performance is remarkably consistent through and through.

Conceivably, one might even deem his performance as *too* good—explicitly in light of certain instances where one almost gets the sense that a completely different actor has entered the recording studio and been given the microphone. As the audiobook is supposed to be delivered by Edna, this, in turn, may pose a somewhat problematic property for the aural artifact as a whole.

In more ways than one, both Edna's *My Gorgeous Life* and, indeed, Sir Leslie's *The Traveller's Tool* constitute works that simply cry out to be performed—the only caveat being that they invariably seem to cry out to be performed explicitly by their creator. Humphries himself—or, rather, an alternate version thereof—also makes an appearance in *My Gorgeous Life*, effectively depicted by Edna in her first-person account:

> The last letter was one of the most important in my life. […] It was from a young actor planning a variety show about Australian suburban life. He was playing the role of a housewife who'd just been on her first overseas trip and he wanted to "pick my brains", he said, for his research. I snorted, weird types are starting to write to me now. This one sounds a bit of a "Sissy" too. He's planning some kind of a show where he dresses up as a woman and makes fun about the wonderful Australian way of life. What kind of homes do people like that come from? He's probably breaking his parents' hearts. […] I met Mr. Humphries in a restaurant downtown. […] We parted with a promise that I would come to a few rehearsals and help him with his female impersonation. Though it made me a bit uncomfortable, in fact almost sick, to think of a man trolling around in women's attire. I'm sorry, but it did. Perhaps it was his mention of a fee that twisted my arm.[33]

Although inevitably and invariably responsible for Edna's delivery, the agency identified here as "Barry Humphries" is ultimately filtered through *Edna's* voice and speech patterns, rather than his own:

---

[33] Everage, *My Gorgeous Life*, [1993] 2014, 02h08m32sec.

Barry had the cheek to peer into the auditorium to solicit out praise. *How was that? Pretty good, I felt,* He said. There was a long dark silence, broken at last by a cultured woman's voice. *Pretty good I don't think. Pretty awful, more like it. I've never seen such twaddle and hoo-ha on the stage in all my life. And I've just been to the West End of London.* That woman's voice was mine.[34]

His self-proclaimed "unauthorised biography," *Handling Edna*—purportedly presenting one with yet an additional version of Humphries—depicts the inception of their relationship as follows:

I wish I had kept the postcard she sent me in June 1955—fifty-four years ago! But why should I have kept it? What early scrap of which collectors now call "Ednabilia" was worth preserving in those far-off days, before Fame unwisely smiled upon her? This was just a stage-stuck young Melbourne mother writing to a young actor seeking his advice. Her handwriting, if I recall, was studied but childish. The fact that her letter was written in green ink with circles over the 'i's should have alerted me immediately to the serious danger of an ensuing correspondence. *"Dear Mr Humphrey"*, she had begun […] If the green ink had not warned me of the impending danger, my misspelt name should have. […] *Dear Mr Humphrey, you don't know me from a bar of soap, but I am a prematurely young housewife from the dress circle suburb of Moonee Ponds...* Moonee Ponds was a drab working-class suburb on the "wrong side of the tracks", as my mother would have described it. It in no way deserved the fashionable fifties epithet "dress circle", usually applied by estate agents to suburbs commanding panoramic views. The postcard continued: *...I read a write-up about you in* The Argus *doing some of your skits at Melbourne Uni and I am desirous of teeing a meeting because my girlfriends say I've got real talent....* I paraphrase slightly, but the enthusiasm, one might even say *chutzpah*, of this young woman's letter somehow engraved it my memory.[35]

When Humphries reads Edna's letter for the audiobook, he seems to be delivering the words in-character—effectively *as* Edna "herself"—rather than appearing to make an effort, as "himself," to "do" her voice. Thus, Edna once again appears to have asserted herself as literal agency, it literally sounds as if both

---

[34] Ibid., 02h20m20sec.

[35] Humphries, *Handling Edna*, 2010, 02m05sec.

Humphries and Edna are inhabiting the recording, each effectively delivering their own respective part. (To some extent, of course, they both inevitably *are*). As both author *and* narrating voice, this (altered version of) "Barry Humphries" appears just as "real" as the Humphries evoked by *Edna*:

> Hitherto the public has been confused, and in some cases deceived, by divergent accounts of Dame Edna's life and origins. Some of these accounts and wild speculations have been verbally diffused and rumour and hearsay have been transmuted into "fact". Many have been published in books and academic theses, and there is now a considerable apocrypha bearing Edna's name. It should be said that the author of this memoir has himself contributed to these legends and obfuscations for reasons, largely indefensible, which are set out in the text that follows. The reader is exhorted to ignore all other accounts, withal bearing the weight and authority of Academe, and accept what follows as the "onlie true historie."[36]

While one might arguably be tempted to dismiss *Handling Edna* as merely more of the same—that is, a whimsical game that Humphries plays with his audience, exuding a manufactured guise of authenticity, and part of a tired, decades-old, self-aggrandizing, paradigmatic assembly line. To my mind, however, this would be missing the point entirely. Although, indeed, at least to some extent, a game, the audience are well in on it, and quite willing to both welcome and accept its overall conceit. Thus, as yet another installment in a line of quasi-introspective meditations—reflecting upon, reiterating, and further articulating an intricate, lifelong relationship between an artist and his own creation—*Handling Edna* effectively requires of Humphries to quite literally *handle* a run-amok Edna. Ultimately, I find that the audiobook medium is able to highlight, enhance, and re-conceptualize the overall aesthetics of Humphries' performance(s) in a unique and distinct manner, rendering these recordings exceptionally gratifying aural artifacts.

By way of comparison, one could consider prolific English actor–comedian–writer–impressionist Steve Coogan and explicitly examine the audiobook version of his own autobiography, *Easily Distracted* (2015), as well as that of *I,*

[36.] Humphries, "Note to the Reader," in *Handling Edna*, xi. The audiobook version, incidentally, quite inexplicably (and sadly) forewent the inclusion of this brief passage, as well as the self-reflecting quotes with which Humphries opens the printed version: e.g., "a mask tells us more than a face"—Oscar Wilde, "No one is unknown except for me"—Francis Picabia, or "At last—the truth!"—Pietro Aretino. The final, concluding passage (p. 359 in the printed book) also seems to have been excluded from the aural iteration, as well as the book's quirky appendix, titled "Miscellaneous Jottings, Doggerel and Ephemera Saved from Edna's Shredder."

Partridge: We Need to Talk about Alan (2001), the *pseudo*-autobiography of one Alan Gordon Partridge—whom Coogan has been portraying periodically for over three decades. I would argue that the same holds true for the afore-mentioned *A Woman First: First Woman* (2019), and, indeed, can also be said about Peter Schickele's audiobook version of his own *The Definitive Biography of P.D.Q. Bach (1807–1742)?* (1976)—which chronicles the life and times of a fictitious composer invented by Schickele in the mid-1960s. The latter, however, might more easily be categorized among other "comedy albums"—and, indeed, as a complementary aural artifact to the various P.D.Q. Bach compositions that Schickele has unleashed (or, rather, ostensibly unearthed) over the years.

Now, Partridge—unlike Humphries' creations—did not, alas, receive sole authorship over his narrative. Rather, *I, Partridge* merely credits him above the book's *actual* authors, namely, Rob and Neil Gibbons, Armando Iannucci, and Coogan. In the audiobook version, it is only having given a rapid rundown of credits using his own voice that Coogan steps into character: confidently announcing "*This* is Alan Partridge," he thus assumes his role, affirms his au-thority, and commands one's undivided attention. To be sure, this asserted proc-lamation of his own identity does not (and, conceivably, cannot) appear in the printed version and evoke the same effect. The character itself—gradually mor-phing over the years into something of the displaced, dysfunctional, and dis-harmonious alter ego of its performer—was originally developed in the 1990s and constitutes the collaborative brainchild of Coogan and Iannucci, alongside Stewart Lee and Richard Herring.

No doubt also influenced by the aforementioned commentary track delivered by the Spinal Tap band members, the creators of Partridge—arguably playing a similar game with their audience—similarly offer the audience a couple of in-character commentaries for the DVD release of the *I Am Alan Partridge* (1997/2002) television series, featuring Partridge alongside his (long-suffering) assistant, "Lynn Benfield," portrayed by Coogan's co-star Felicity Montagu.[37] Here, too, the overall aesthetics of this so-called ploy, culminating to a large extent with aural iteration of *his* autobiography—appropriately performed by none other than Partridge himself—is ultimately rendered a vehicle through which a fictional character can extend its own existence as a literal, concrete agency to all intents and purposes. That aural artifacts appear to almost naturally

---

[37.] For further reading, see, e.g., Richard Wallace, *Mockumentary Comedy: Performing Authenticity* (London: Palgrave/Macmillan, 2018).

facilitate and reinforce this type of aesthetics in a manner that conceivably supersedes any other medium simply cannot be stressed enough.

Coogan's own autobiography, *Easily Distracted*, includes a number of eloquently articulated insights pertaining to the very concept of portraying different "versions" of oneself, which may prove quite illuminating in respect of Humphries' work as well. Coogan's narration, by his own admission, is notably "imperfect"—including various "*Ehrs*" and "*Erhms*," adding the odd occasional comment, disregarding certain sentences, and, ultimately, failing to follow the full text in print. This, to my mind, is precisely what both contributes to and, indeed, amplifies this audiobook's charm and appeal:

> Hello. My name is Steve Coogan, and I'm reading my autobiography, which is entitled "Easily Distracted"—so titled because it was one of the comments that my teacher put in one of my school reports, *ehrm*, with very good reason. *Ehr*, just a note to let listeners know that I won't be doing a perfectly well-modulated "RADA" rendition of the text, and, ehm, if I stumble occasionally, well, that should, eh, add to the visceral pleasure and honesty of my imperfect delivery. *Erhm*, so, off we go—Ehm, Acknowledgements [...] Introduction: Most of my life has been spent wanting to be someone else. If I pretended to be other people, then I didn't have to be me. [...] When I did stand-up, I did impressions. When I did my act, I would do a rather distant, pompous version of myself. I affected a very, *er*, sort of received pronunciation, *erh*, accent, because I thought it would make me sound more, *er*, [Idon'tknow *said as one word*] palatable. Emm, I've had a slightly schizophrenic relationship with my accent—[*brief sighs*] if I'm with the, eh, you know, if I'm with, ehm, a load of "toffs" [?] then I'll, I'll sort of affect their accent, and if I go up to Manchester I start to sound like Liam Gallagher—which is an aside, by the way [*laughs*] to the main text, but I just thought I'd put that. So if my accent varies, please don't give me grief for it. It's just the way I am. Some people might call it disingenuousness or hypocrisy, ehm, I call it, ehm, a chameleon-like empathy. O.K. —I continued to do versions of myself in *Coffee and Cigarettes*, *A Cock and Bull Story*, and *The Trip*. [...] Until now I have shared only versions of "Steve Coogan". The real me is slightly less desperate for fame than Alan Partridge, slightly less irascible than the Steve who eats his way around the Lake District and Italy in *The Trip*, and slightly less libidinous than the version of me in *A Cock and Bull Story*. [...] I don't like being defined by others, so for those are interested I will to do it myself. [...] it is my work that I have offered up for judgement, not my personal life. [...] Judge me

on the work, not on the cocaine and the strippers. You won't find any grief porn in this book. It isn't *Angela's Ashes*.[38]

While I do firmly stand by the notion that listening to audiobooks should not substitute for reading of the original text, one cannot ignore the fact that the aural iterations of autobiographies make it abundantly clear that there are certainly exceptions that challenge this general rule—and especially in cases the recording *itself*, as an aural artifact, effectively utilizes the literal voice of its subject in order to successfully embody the internal logic of their narrative.

By the same token, in the 1990s, the brilliant creative mind of American comedian–actor–writer–director, Garry Shandling (1941–2016), delivered unto the world the fictional late-night talk-show host, Larry Sanders. Aside from the series finale, Shandling made a point of never having anyone on the show mention or reference "Garry Shandling" in any way throughout its entire run. By his own admission, he felt the last episode was the right to do so.[39] Following a celebrated and award-winning 6-season run of his seminal TV masterpiece, *The Larry Sanders Show*, Shandling joined forces with author David Rensin to create an autobiography of his purported alter ego. The result, *Confessions of a Late Night Talk Show Host* (1998), aptly opens with but two words: "To me."[40] According to Shandling, the idea for the book itself occurred to him just around 3 or 4 years prior to the show's conclusion, yet he found it quite impossible to engage with the task of writing—which he really liked—while doing the show: "I struggled to find the hook—where it would connect with me—and I think this is sort of a satire of tell-all books, and there's a slight point to it […] and I think it's funny, and it's something Larry would do, and so […] It's fun."[41]

Much like the ostensible obsession that Edna—or, rather, Humphries—has with the notions of celebrity and (mega-)stardom, Shandling's endeavor seems to both be rooted in and, indeed, premeditatively delve into the same *milieu*. As Matt Domino describes it,

---

[38] Steve Coogan, *Easily Distracted* (Penguin Random House, 2015), [transcribed introduction from the audiobook version].

[39] Garry Shandling, interviewed by Charlie Rose, November 16, 1998. See URL: accessed February 10, 2023, https://charlierose.com/videos/17717, 19min35sec.

[40] Garry Shandling, with David Rensin, *Confessions of a Late Night Talk Show Host: The Autobiography of Larry Sanders* (New York: Simon & Schuster, 1998), 9.

[41] Shandling, interviewed by Charlie Rose, November 16, 1998. See URL: accessed February 10, 2023, https://charlierose.com/videos/17717, 44min45sec–44min49sec.

The book [...] is bizarre, hilarious, and has a spiritual twist that provides an intriguing snapshot of Shandling at the end of the *Larry Sanders Show* era. Perhaps more importantly, it serves as a kind of pure distillation of Garry's humor—something you can pick up and skim when you are looking for a quick dose of his trademark way of turning a joke.[42]

Written in-character, and subsequently delivered as an audiobook (now discontinued and, regrettably, unavailable), the so-called confessions begin with the following asserted statement: "Why am I writing this autobiography now? Because I'm Larry Sanders. I'm famous. Actually, I'm very, very, very famous, but the publisher said that title wouldn't fit on the cover of the book."[43] Soon thereafter he goes on to contemplate,

Perhaps I *had* left too soon. I never considered that my television audience was so codependent, so unable to function without me—in other words, so sexy. It is with a deep sense of compassion and caring about others and with no ego whatsoever that I come back to you just like Jesus did, to speak to you one last time about something even more riveting than that of which Jesus spoke: show business and all the gossip and dirt and rumors that I have accumulated over a lifetime. And two thousand years from now, after translation upon translation of my book, who knows how I will finally be perceived? Maybe I'll be thought of as the real Son of God.[44]

For Domino,

The Larry Sanders we encounter in Confessions comes off as a more cartoonish and exaggerated version of the Larry from the HBO show. In the show, Larry is insecure, petty, and selfish, but his many faults are all balanced by the fine mixture of nuance, humor, karmic retribution, and camaraderie that the series manages to pull off in its depiction of life behind the scenes on a late-night talk show. In the book, Larry bounces off of people and things [...] and passes through 20th century comedy as a Zelig-like figure.[45]

[42] Matt Domino, "Revisiting Larry Sanders's Late-Night Host Confessions," *Vulture*, June 5, 2019, accessed January 14, 2023, https://www.vulture.com/2019/06/garry-shandling-larry-sanders-autobiography-book-confessions-of-a-late-night-host.html.

[43] Shandling and Rensin, *Confessions of a Late Night Talk Show Host*, 9.

[44] Ibid., 10.

[45] Domino, "Revisiting Larry Sanders's Late-Night Host Confessions."

Interestingly enough, Domino also quite insightfully asserts that Shandling's book—as well as Coogan's aforementioned book, which he cites alongside Stephen Colbert's *I Am America (And So Can You!)* (2007) as being in the same vein—can, in fact, be associated with "a larger canon of literature": that of *fictional* biographical writing. As such, he finds that the Sanders "autobiography" resembles such works as Saul Bellow's *The Adventures of Augie March* (1953) and Laurence Sterne's *Don Quixote*-inspired nine-volume *The Life and Opinions of Tristram Shandy, Gentleman* (1759–1767). The latter, incidentally, serving as the source material for a 2005 Coogan-centered feature film, directed by Michael Winterbottom. In this context, the autobiographies of Edna and Les—as well as Humphries' own "self-tellings"—most certainly fit in the mix. Ultimately, as far as Domino is concerned,

> What is perhaps Shandling at his purest, though, is the "About the Author" page, where Larry admits to being a fictional character and tells the reader that he doesn't exist. "We are all energy," Larry says, tapping into Shandling's well-documented spirituality and yearning for understanding his place within the universe. But then he adds, "especially Don Rickles." Show business and spirituality rub elbows once again. It wouldn't be a Garry Shandling joke without it.[46]

I find Domino's insights quite illuminating—especially as they are based solely on the book's printed version. This is surely a testament to Shandling's remarkable talent and productive collaboration with Rensin. Here too, as with the cases of Humphries and Coogan, the audiobook version—and, indeed, the consistently masterful delivery of the character's creator—not only amplifies one's overall aesthetic experience but also further demonstrates the unique manner in which aural artifacts form a vehicle for extending the existence of the performed (fictional) self.[47]

The Significance of Aural Memoirs and Autobiographies

Unlike works of fiction, for which one is invariably required to imagine what a particular character might sound like, autobiographies—and especially those

---

[46.] Ibid.

[47.] Although this no doubt opens up a much deeper investigation, extending well beyond the world of comedy, one might also consider whether such novels as Romain Gary's *Pseudo* (1976)—published under the pseudonym Émile Ajar, or James Frey's *A Million Little Pieces* (2003)—originally marketed as an authentic memoir, might also belong to the category.

written by individuals whom one is to some extent acquainted with—virtually imply what the narrating voice *actually* sounds like. Indeed, as Have and Pedersen are concerned,

> When the text is an autobiographical novel, read by the author, the reader hears the autobiographical story told by the voice writing, and that adds an extra dimension to the experience. The text lends its voice to the performing narrator who embodies not only the text but also the referential contour of the world described.[48]

Thus, if audiobooks are customarily required to embody the imagined voice that inhabits the original text, an argument could be made that the aural iterations of autobiographies and memoirs simply *require* the voice of their authors—and perhaps especially those whose distinct vocal signature is strongly associated with their prose.

Whether one engages with the subject of the autobiography themselves or a so-called alternate "version" thereof, the aural artifact itself can make for a unique aesthetic experience that does not exist in other artistic genres. Thus, as an extended first-person monologue that conceivably contrives to make sense of the world that its speaker inhabits, even the aural iteration of a *pseudo*-autobiography—seemingly validating its subject's very existence (as with the "non-existent" personae created by Humphries)—the recording would require none other than its subject's "own" voice. In this context, one could also argue that these particular aural artifacts might, in fact, negate the need to engage with the original printed work—thereby further emphasizing precisely why audiobooks deserve a distinct aesthetic category of their own.

Listed alphabetically, by the author's surname, the following titles are predominantly autobiographical at their core, yet also include some fiction works and essay collections. Indeed, I find them all highly recommended for a further, close listening. To my mind, they can greatly enrich one's aesthetic expertise—predominantly due to the distinct ability of these particular authors to convey their own literary voice, through their *literal* voice—ultimately provoking one's understanding and experience of the performed (fictional) self in the realm of audiobooks. It, in turn (and, conceivably—at least to some extent—even more

---

[48] Iben Have and Birgitte Stougaard Pedersen, "Multisensory Reading of Digital Audiobooks," in *The Digital Reading Condition*, eds., Maria Engberg, Iben Have, and Birgitte Stougaard Pedersen (London: Routledge, 2023), 93–94.

than works of fiction) can engage one more directly with a range of diverse voices in terms of gender, ethnicity, non-Western cultural identities, as well as the celebrity.

- Chimamanda Ngozi Adichie's *We Should All Be Feminists* (2014) and *Notes on Grief* (2021);
- Danny Aiello's *I Only Know Who I Am When I Am Somebody Else: My Life on the Street, on the Stage, and in the Movies* (2014)—in collaboration with Gil Reavill;
- Alan Alda's *Never Have Your Dog Stuffed: And Other Things I've Learned* (2005), *Things I Overheard While Talking to Myself* (2007), and *If I Understood You, Would I Have This Look on My Face? My Adventures in the Art and Science of Relating and Communicating* (2017);
- Tom Allen's *No Shame* (2021) and *Too Much* (2022);
- Woody Allen's *Getting Even* (1971), *Without Feathers* (1975), *Side Effects* (1980), *Mere Anarchy* (2007), *Apropos of Nothing* (2020), and *Zero Gravity* (2022);
- Liz Alterman's *Sad Sacked: A Memoir* (2021);
- Jonathan Ames' *What's Not to Love?: The Adventures of a Mildly Perverted Young Writer* (2000), and *I Love You More Than You Know* (2006);
- Maya Angelou's *I Know Why the Caged Bird Sings* (1969), *Gather Together in My Name* (1974), *The Heart of a Woman* (1981), *All God's Children Need Traveling Shoes* (1986), *Wouldn't Take Nothing for My Journey Now* (1993), *Even the Stars Look Lonesome* (1997); *A Song Flung up to Heaven* (2002), *The Welcome Table: A Lifetime of Memories with Recipes* (2004), *Celebrations: Rituals of Peace and Prayer* (2006); *Letter to My Daughter* (2008), and *Mom & Me & Mom* (2013);
- Alan Arkin's *An Improvised Life:* (2011) and *Out of My Mind: (Not Quite a Memoir)* (2020);
- Eileen Atkins's *Will She Do?: Act One of a Life on Stage* (2021);
- Shalom Auslander's *A Foreskin's Lament* (2007), *Hope: A Tragedy* (2012), and *Mother for Dinner: A Novel* (2020);
- Paul Auster's *Winter Journal* (2012) and Report from the Interior (2013);
- Richard Ayoade's *Ayoade on Ayoade* (2014);
- Maria Bamford's *Sure, I'll Join Your Cult: A Memoir of Mental Illness and the Quest to Belong Anywhere* (2023);

- Dave Barry's *Dave Barry Turns 50* (1998), *The Shepherd, the Angel, and Walter the Christmas Miracle Dog* (2006), *I'll Mature When I'm Dead: Amazing Tales of Adulthood* (2010), *Insane City* (2013), *You Can Date Boys When You're Forty: On Parenting and Other Topics He Knows Very Little about* (2014), *Live Right and Find Happiness (Although Beer Is Much Faster): Life Lessons and Other Ravings* (2015), *Lessons from Lucy: The Simple Joys of an Old, Happy Dog* (2019), and *Swamp Story* (2023);
- Lynda Barry's *The Lynda Barry Experience* (1993);
- Ed Begley Jr.'s *To the Temple of Tranquility...and Step on It!* (2023);
- Jon H. Benjamin's *Failure Is an Option: An Attempted Memoir* (2018);
- Dr. Mayim Bialik, PhD—*Girling up: How to Be Strong, Smart and Spectacular* (2017) and *Boying up: How to Be Brave, Bold and Brilliant* (2018);
- Lewis Black's *Nothing's Sacred* (2006), *Me of Little Faith (More Me! Less Faith!)* (2008), and *I'm Dreaming of a Black Christmas* (2010);
- Brian Blessed's *Absolute Pandemonium: The Autobiography* (2015);
- Mel Brook's *All about Me!: My Remarkable Life in Show Business* (2021);
- Rob Brydon's *Small Man in a Book* (2011);
- Carol Burnett's *In Such Good Company* (2016); *This Time Together: Laughter and Reflection* (2010), and *Carrie and Me: A Mother-Daughter Love Story* (2014);
- Augusten Burroughs' *Running with Scissors* (2002);
- Gabriel Byrne's *Pictures in My Head* (1994) and *Walking with Ghosts* (2021);
- Michael Caine's *What's It All about?* (1992), *The Elephant to Hollywood* (2010), and *Blowing the Bloody Doors Off: And Other Lessons in Life* (2018);
- Dyan Cannon's *Dear Cary—My Life with Cary Grant* (2011);
- George Carlin's *Brain Droppings* (1997), *Napalm and Silly Putty* (2001), *When Will Jesus Bring the Pork Chops?* (2004), and Kelly Carlin's *A Carlin Home Companion: Growing up with George* (2015);
- Drew Carey's *Dirty Jokes and Beer: Stories of the Unrefined* (1997);
- Nancy Cartwright's *I'm Still a 10-Year-Old Boy* (Revised and Edited, 2020);
- Michael Chabon's *Manhood for Amateurs: The Pleasures and Regrets of a Husband, Father, and Son* (2009) and *Pops: Fatherhood in Pieces* (2018);
- Kristin Chenoweth's *A Little Bit Wicked: Life, Love, and Faith in Stages* (2009) and *I'm No Philosopher, but I Got Thoughts: Mini-Meditations for Saints, Sinners, and the Rest of Us* (2023);

- John Cleese's *Families and How to Survive Them* (1983)—written in collaboration with Robin Skynner, *So, Anyway...* (2014), and *Creativity: A Short and Cheerful Guide* (2020);
- Bill Clinton's *My Life* (2004);
- Leonard Cohen's *Book of Longing* (2006);
- Stephen Colbert's *I Am America (And So Can You!)* (2007) and *America Again: Re-Becoming the Greatness We Never Weren't* (2012);
- Bryan Cranston's *A Life in Parts* (2016);[49]
- Alan Cummin's *Not My Father's Not My Father's Son: A Family Memoir* (2014), *You Gotta Get Bigger Dreams: My Life in Stories and Pictures* (2016), and *Baggage: Tales from a Fully Packed Life* (2019);
- Whitney Cummings' *I'm Fine... And Other Lies* (2017);
- Roald Dhal's *Boy: Tales of Childhood* (1984) and *Going Solo* (1986);[50]
- Geena Davis's *Dying of Politeness: A Memoir* (2022);
- Laura Dern's and Diane Ladd's *Honey, Baby, Mine: A Mother and Daughter Talk Life, Death, Love (and Banana Pudding)* (2023);
- Illeana Douglas's *I Blame Dennis Hopper: And Other Stories from a Life Lived in and out of the Movies* (2015);
- Fran Drescher's *Cancer Schmancer* (2002);
- Minnie Driver's *Managing Expectations: A Memoir in Essays* (2022);
- Mark and Jay Duplass' *Like Brothers* (2018);
- Lena Dunham's *Not That Kind of Girl: A Young Woman Tells You What She's Learned* (2014);
- Griffin Dunne's *The Friday Afternoon Club: A Family Memoir* (2024);
- Christopher Eccleston's *I Love the Bones of You: My Father and the Making of Me* (2019);

[49.] Interestingly enough, Cranston points out that while he "couldn't imagine anyone else reading" his "own words," he did find the recording process "difficult" as he could hear his own self and would, at certain instances, feel the need to re-do a word in a sentence. See URL: accessed February 10, 2023, https://www.youtube.com/watch?v=VtAnpqR5hp8, 01min48sec–02min03sec.

[50.] While these particular works, being memoirs, inhabit a distinctly personal note, I find it interesting that they too—as with the majority of Dahl's oeuvre—have received quite a variety of aural iterations. Most endearing of these are the renditions delivered by Derek Jacobi, Ian Holm, and Michael Palin. It may certainly prove interesting to compare their reading to that of Dahl. (Holm, incidentally, also went on to narrate *My Year*, published in 1993, which is based on a diary that Dahl had written during the final year of his life). As an extended sidenote, I would add that although the available recordings featuring Dahl himself clearly demonstrate that he ranks among those authors who excel in narrating their own work, there exist some absolutely exceptional iterations that are not to be missed by any means: e.g., Richard Ayoade's reading of *The Twits* (1980), Simon Callow's delivery of *The Witches* (1983), Stephen Fry's rendition of *The Vicar of Nibbleswicke* (1991), Eric Idle's take on *Charlie and the Chocolate Factory* (1964), and Kate Winslet's performance of *Matilda* (1988).

- Nora Ephron's *I Feel Bad about My Neck: And Other Thoughts on Being a Woman* (2006) and *I Remember Nothing: And Other Reflections* (2010);
- Robert Evans's *The Kid Stays in the Picture* (1994);
- Craig Ferguson's *American on Purpose: The Improbable Adventures of an Unlikely Patriot* (2010) and *Riding the Elephant: A Memoir of Altercations, Humiliations, Hallucinations, and Observations* (2019);
- Tina Fey's *Bossypants* (2011);
- Sally Field's *In Pieces* (2018);
- Harvey Fierstein's *I Was Better Last Night: A Memoir* (2022);
- Carrie Fisher's *Postcards from the Edge* (1987), *Surrender the Pink* (1990), *Delusions of Grandma* (1993), *The Best Awful* (2004), *Wishful Drinking* (2008), *Shockaholic* (2011), and *The Princess Diarist* (2016);
- Joely Fisher's *Growing Up Fisher: Musings, Memories, and Misadventures* (2017);
- Jane Fonda's *My Life So Far* (2005) and *Prime Time: Love, Health, Sex, Fitness, Friendship, Spirit—Making the Most of All of Your Life* (2011);
- Stephen Fry's *The Liar* (1991), *The Hippopotamus* (1994), *Making History* (1996), *Moab Is My Washpot* (1997), *The Stars' Tennis Balls* (2000), *The Ode Less Travelled: Unlocking the Poet within* (2005), *The Fry Chronicles* (2010), *More Fool Me: A Memoir* (2014), *Mythos: A Retelling of the Myths of Ancient Greece* (2017), *Heroes: Mortals and Monsters, Quests and Adventures* (2018), *Troy: He Siege of Troy Retold* (2020), and *Fry's Ties: The Life and Times of a Tie Collection* (2021);
- Hannah Gadsby's *Ten Steps to Nanette: A Memoir Situation* (2022);
- Brad Garrett's *When the Balls Drop* (2015);
- Art Garfunkel's *What Is It All but Luminous: Notes from an Underground Man* (2017);
- Betty Gilpin's *All the Women in My Brain: And Other Concerns* (2022);
- Malcolm Gladwell's *The Tipping Point : How Little Things Can Make a Big Difference* (2000), *Blink: The Power of Thinking Without Thinking* (2005), *Outliers: The Story of Success* (2008), *What the Dog Saw: And Other Adventures* (2009), *David and Goliath: Underdogs, Misfits, and the Art of Battling Giants* (2013), *Talking to Strangers: What We Should Know About the People We Don't Know* (2019), *The Bomber Mafia: A Dream, a Temptation, and the Longest Night of the Second World War* (2021), and *I Hate the Ivy League Riffs and Rants on Elite Education* (2021)—with

the later three constituting companions, of sorts, to Gladwell's *Revisionist History* podcast.

- Sharon Gless's *Apparently There Were Complaints* (2021);
- Lauren Graham's *Someday, Someday, Maybe: A Novel* (2013), *Talking as Fast as I Can: From Gilmore Girls to Gilmore Girls, and Everything in between* (2016), *In Conclusion, Don't Worry about It* (2018), and *Have I Told You This Already?: Stories I Don't Want to Forget to Remember* (2022);
- André Gregory's *This Is Not My Memoir* (2020)—written in collaboration with Todd London;
- Joel Grey's *Master of Ceremonies: A Memoir* (2016);
- Judi Greer's *I Don't Know What You Know Me from: My Life as a Co-Star* (2014);
- Alec Guinness's *Blessings in Disguise* (1985), *My Name Escapes Me: The Diary of a Retiring Actor* (1996), and *A Positively Final Appearance: A Journal 1996–98* (1999);
- Tom Hank's *Uncommon Type: Some Stories* (2017) and *The Making of Another Major Motion Picture Masterpiece: A Novel* (2023)—performed by Hanks with a full-cast;
- Neil Patrick Harris' *Choose Your Own Autobiography* (2014)—written in collaboration with David Javerbaum;
- Lenny Henry's *Who Am I, Again?* (2019) and *You Can Do Anything, Tyrone!* (2023);
- Werner Herzog's *Every Man for Himself and God Against All: A Memoir* (2023);
- Clint and Ron Howard—*The Boys: A Memoir of Hollywood and Family* (2021);
- Anjelica Huston's *A Story Lately Told* (2013) and *Watch Me* (2014);
- Eric Idle's *Always Look on the Bright Side of Life: A Sortabiography* (2018);
- Eddie Izzard's *Believe Me: A Memoir of Love, Death and Jazz Chickens* (2017);
- James Ivory's *Solid Ivory: Memoirs* (2021);
- Derek Jacobi's *As Luck Would Have It* (2013);
- Penn Jillette's *God, No!: Signs You May Already Be an Atheist and Other Magical Tales* (2011), *Every Day Is an Atheist Holiday!* (2012), and *Presto!: How I Made Over 100 Pounds Disappear and Other Magical Tales* (2016);

- Mindy Kaling's *Is Everyone Hanging Out without Me? (And Other Concerns)* (2011), *Why Not Me?* (2015), and *Nothing Like I Imagined (Except for Sometimes)* (2020);
- Diane Keaton's *Then Again* (2011), *Let's Just Say It Wasn't Pretty* (2014), and *Brother & Sister: A Memoir* (2020);
- Mary Karr's *The Liars' Club* (1995), *Cherry* (2000), *Lit: A Memoir* (2009), *The Art of Memoir* (2015), and *Tropic of Squalor* (2018);
- Anna Kendrick's *Scrappy Little Nobody* (2016);
- Steven King's *On Writing: A Memoir of the Craft* (2000);
- Garrison Keillor's *That Time of Year: A Minnesota Life Book* (2020);
- Christine Lahti's *True Stories from an Unreliable Eyewitness: A Feminist Coming of Age* (2018);
- Jenny Lawson's *Let's Pretend This Never Happened: A Mostly True Memoir* (2012), *Furiously Happy: A Funny Book About Horrible Things* (2015), *Broken (in the Best Possible Way)* (2021), and *I Choose Darkness A Holiday Essay* (2022);
- Norman Lear's Even *This I Get to Experience* (2014);
- Fran Lebowitz's *The Fran Lebowitz Reader* (1994);
- Laraine Newman's *May You Live in Interesting Times: A Memoir* (2020);
- Richard Lewis's *The Other Great Depression: How I'm Overcoming, on a Daily Basis, at Least a Million Addictions and Disfunctions and Finding a Spiritual (Sometimes) Life* (2000);
- Limmy's *Surprisingly Down to Earth, and Very Funny: My Autobiography* (2019);
- John Lithgow's *Drama: An Actor's Education* (2011); *Stories by Heart* (2018);
- Patti LuPone's *A Memoir* (2010);
- David Lynch with Kristine McKenna—*Room to Dream* (2018);
- Jane Lynch's *Happy Accidents* (2011)—including a foreword by Carol Burnett;
- Julianna Margulies's *Sunshine Girl: An Unexpected Life* (2021);
- Garry Marshall's *My Happy Days in Hollywood: A Memoir* (2012);
- Penny Marshall's *My Mom Was Nuts: A Memoir* (2012);
- Steve Martin's *Pure Drivel* (1998), *Born Standing up: A Comic's Life* (2007), and *So Many Steves: Afternoons with Steve Martin* (2023)—written in collaboration with Adam Gopnik;
- Matthew McConaughey's *Greenlishts* (2020);

- Frank McCourt's *Angela's Ashes* (1996);
- Terence McKenna's *True Hallucinations: Being an Account of the Author's Extraordinary Adventures in the Devil's Paradise* (1993);
- David Mitchell's *Back Story: A Memoir* (2012), *Thinking About It Only Makes It Worse: And Other Lessons from Modern Life* (2014), and *Dishonesty is the Second-Best Policy: And Other Rules to Live By* (2019)
- Olivia Munn's *Suck It, Wonder Woman!: The Misadventures of a Hollywood Geek* (2010)—written in collaboration with Mac Montandon;
- Aparna Nancherla's *Unreliable Narrator Me, Myself, and Impostor Syndrome* (2023);
- Kunal Nayyar's *Yes, My Accent Is Real: And Some Other Things I Haven't Told You* (2016);
- Laraine Newman's *May You Live in Interesting Times* (2021);
- David Niven's *The Moon's a Balloon* (1971) and *Bring on the Empty Horses* (1975);
- Trevor Noah's *Born a Crime: Stories from a South African Childhood* (2016);
- Graham Norton's *So Me* (2004) and *The Life and Loves of a He Devil* (2014);
- Barack Obama's *Dreams from My Father: A Story of Race and Inheritance* (1995), *The Audacity of Hope: Thoughts on Reclaiming the American Dream* (2006), and *A Promised Land* (2020);
- Michelle Obama's *Becoming* (2018) and *The Light We Carry: Overcoming in Uncertain Times* (2022);
- Bob Odenkirk's *Comedy Comedy Comedy Drama: A Memoir* (2022);
- Nick Offerman's *Paddle Your Own Canoe: One Man's Fundamentals for Delicious Living* (2013), *Gumption: Relighting the Torch of Freedom with America's Gutsiest Troublemakers* (2015), *Good Clean Fun: Misadventures in Sawdust at Offerman Woodshop* (2016), *The Greatest Love Story Ever Told: An Oral History* (2018)—the latter co-written with Megan Mullally, and *Where the Deer and the Antelope Play: The Pastoral Observations of One Ignorant American Who Loves to Walk Outside* (2021);
- John O'Hurley's *It's Okay to Miss the Bed on the First Jump* (2006) and *Before Your Dog Can Eat Your Homework, First You Have to Do It* (2007);
- Séamas O'Reilly's *Did Ye Hear Mammy Died? : A Memoir* (2020);
- Patton Oswalt's *Zombie Spaceship Wasteland* (2011) and *Silver Screen Fiend: Learning about Life from an Addiction to Film* (2015);

- Michael Palin's collected diary entries (currently available in three volumes, together covering 1969–1988), travel books (complementing the television programmes documenting his journeys around the world, presently covering 1989–2022), and *Great-Uncle Harry: A Tale of War and Empire* (2023);
- Amanda Palmer's *The Art of Asking: How I Learned to Stop Worrying and Let People Help* (2014);
- Mary-Louise Parker's *Dear Mr. You* (2015);
- Kal Penn's *You Can't Be Serious* (2020);
- Ron Perlman's *Easy Street (the Hard Way): A Memoir* (2014);
- Matthew Perry's *Friends, Lovers, and the Big Terrible Thing: A Memoir* (2022);
- Amy Poehler's *Yes Please* (2014);
- Sidney Poitier's *The Measure of a Man: A Spiritual Autobiography* (2000);
- Sarah Polley's *Run towards the Danger* (2022);
- Carl Reiner's *How Paul Robeson Saved My Life: And Other Mostly Happy Stories* (1999); *My Anecdotal Life: A Memoir* (2003), and *I Remember Me* (2012);
- Paul Reiser's *Couplehood* (1994), *Babyhood* (1997), and *Familyhood* (2011);
- Burt Reynolds with Jon Winokur—*But Enough about Me* (2015);
- Michael Richards's *Entrances and Exits* (2024);
- Tony Robinson's *No Cunning Plan: My Story* (2016);
- Seth Rogen's *Yearbook* (2021)—feat. the voices of over 80 narrators;
- Philip Rosenthal's *You're Lucky You're Funny: How Life Becomes a Sitcom* (2006);
- Domenica Ruta's *With or Without You: A Memoir* (2013);
- Bob Saget's *Dirty Daddy: Chronicles of a Family Man Turned Filthy Comedian* (2014);
- Jennifer Saunders's *Bonkers: My Life in Laughs* (2013);
- Adam Savage's *Every Tool's a Hammer Lessons from a Lifetime of Making* (2019);
- Peter Schickele's *The Definitive Biography of P.D.Q. Bach* (1976);
- Amy Schumer's *The Girl with the Lower Back Tattoo* (2016);
- David Sedaris's *Naked* (1997)—also read by Amy Sedaris, *Holidays on Ice* (1998), *Me Talk Pretty One Day* (2001), *When You Are Engulfed in Flames* (2008), *Theft by Finding: Diaries (1977–2002)* (2017), *Calypso* (2018), and *Happy-Go-Lucky* (2022);

- Wallace Shawn's *Essays* (2009) and *Night Thoughts* (2017);
- Martin Sheen's and Emilio Estevez's *Along the Way: The Journey of a Father and Son* (2016);
- Brooke Shields's *There Was a Little Girl: The Real Story of My Mother and Me* (2014);
- Iliza Shlesinger's *Girl Logic: The Genius and the Absurdity* (2017) and *All Things Aside: Absolutely Correct Opinions* (2022);
- Jenny Slate's *Little Weirds* (2019);
- Sarah Silverman's *The Bedwetter: Stories of Courage, Redemption, and Pee* (2010);
- Paul Simon—*Miracle and Wonder: Conversations with Paul Simon* (2021)— written in collaboration with Malcolm Gladwell and Bruce Headlam;
- Gary Sinise's *Grateful American: A Journey from Self to Service* (2019);
- Barry Sonnenfeld's *Barry Sonnenfeld, Call Your Mother: Memoirs of a Neurotic Filmmaker* (2020);
- Patrick Stewart's *Making It So: A Memoir* (2003);
- Barbra Streisand's *My Name is Barbra* (2023);
- Dolly Parton's *Songteller: My Life in Lyrics* (2020);
- Kevin Pollak's *How I Slept My Way to the Middle: Secrets and Stories From Stage, Screen, and Interwebs* (2012)—written in collaboration with Alan Goldsher;
- Parker Posey's *You're on an Airplane: A Self-Mythologizing Memoir* (2018);
- Jerry Stiller's *Married to Laughter: A Love Story Featuring Anne Meara* (2000);
- Jeffrey Tambor's *Are You Anybody?* (2017);
- Quentin Tarantino's *Cinema Speculation* (2022);
- Colm Tóibín's *Mad, Bad, Dangerous to Know: The Fathers of Wilde, Yeats, and Joyce, Scribner* (2018) and *A Guest at the Feast: Essays* (2022);
- Juan F. Thompson's *Stories I Tell Myself: Growing up with Hunter S. Thompson* (2015);
- Stanley Tucci's *Taste: My Life through Food* (2021);
- Kathleen Turner's *Send Yourself Roses: Thoughts on My Life, Love, and Leading Roles* (2008)—written in collaboration with Gloria Feldt;
- Peter Ustinov's *Dear Me* (1997);
- Dick Van Dyke's *My Lucky Life in and out of Show Business: A Memoir* (2011); and *Keep Moving: And Other Tips and Truths about Aging* (2015);
- Alice Walker's *The Color Purple* (1982);

- David Foster Wallace's *Consider the Lobster: And Other Essays* (2005);
- Eli Wallach's *The Good, the Bad, and Me: In My Anecdotage* (2005);
- John Waters's *Shock Value: A Tasteful Book about Bad Taste* (1981), *Role Models* (2010), *Carsick: John Waters Hitchhikes across America* (2014), *Mr. Know-It-All: The Tarnished Wisdom of a Filth Elder* (2017), and *Liarmouth: A Feel-Bad Romance* [a novel] (2022);
- Gene Wilder's *Kiss Me Like a Stranger: My Search for Love and Art* (2005), *The Woman Who Wouldn't* (2008), and *Even Dogs Learn How to Swim* (2017);[51]
- Mara Wilson's *Where Am I Now?: True Stories of Girlhood and Accidental Fame* (2016);
- Rainn Wilson's *The Bassoon King* (2016) and *Soul Boom: Why We Need a Spiritual Revolution* (2023);
- Henry Winkler's *Being Henry: The Fonz... and Beyond* (2023);
- Reese Witherspoon's *Whiskey in a Teacup* (2018);
- Michelle Zauner's *Crying in H Mart: A Memoir* (2021);
- Mitchell Zuckoff's *Robert Altman: The Oral Biography* (2009)—narrated by a full-cast;
- Alan Zweibel's *Laugh Lines: My Life Helping Funny People Be Funnier* (2020)—including a foreword by Billy Crystal.

[51.] This particular recording was released posthumously in 2017. It was directed by Wilder's nephew—filmmaker Jordan Walker-Pearlman—and features a special appearance by American screenwriter–producer–actress Joie Lee.

Playing with Matches: The Implications of Audiobooks as Aural Artifacts

In identifying, developing, and constructing a distinctive set of critical terms with which to describe what constitutes an aural performance, and, in turn, establishing both the context and the criteria for defining audiobooks as aural artifacts, my study aimed to highlight the importance of institutional aesthetic categories. All the first-person narrators in my selected case studies consist of protagonists whose narrative contrives to make sense of the world they inhabit. The audiobook versions of these texts allow one to experience these protagonists' attempt to valorize their own consciousness. Although arguably resonating most strongly with McGovern's exceptional iteration of Beckett's prose, I would argue that Humphries' pseudo-autobiographical recordings constitute the more complex case study—that is, in terms of the overall aesthetics of aural artifacts. Notwithstanding, I find that as aurally recorded solo performances, the first-person narratives inhabiting all three of my major case studies ultimately both highlight and justify the very need for creating an explicit aesthetic category to classify and appreciate them as artworks to begin with.

As both a philosophical and cultural theory, the NITA ultimately pertains to both art and art-making as cultural phenomena. As such, it determines the context—the given circumstances—under which a given cultural activity can be rendered intrinsically artistic. Much like being able to distinguish between "art" and "not art"—and after having established that certain kinds of performance may well be identified as artworks in and of themselves—this study has demonstrated that one can utilize my newly constructed institution of aural artifacts in order to similarly scrutinize and discern the aesthetic quality of any and all aural performances.

While audiobooks, as a general rule, should not substitute reading, there are, nonetheless, certain instances in which they most certainly *can*. For instance, when it comes to texts that were originally written in a language that I am not fluent in, I happen to have the advantage—being bilingual—of choosing which particular translation I would prefer to engage with. As such, as far as, say, classic and epic works are concerned—e.g., the Homeric poems—I, for one, am able to pick either the celebrated Hebrew translation by renowned Russian-born poet Shaul Tchernichovsky or, alternatively, one of the available, renowned English versions: e.g., by Peter Green, Robert Fagles, or Emily Wilson. However, since Homer's works are purportedly designed to be *heard*, I thus have the third option of listening to one of the available audiobook versions. Much as with *Huck Finn*, once one determines which of the available aural iterations best exhibits the internal logic of Homer's text amid the confines of the aural medium, the experience of listening to an aural artifact could potentially serve as a better vehicle for engaging with the original work. In this particular case, I find that Ian McKellen's achievement, for example, certainly does just that. Furthermore, as I have demonstrated, it would appear as though certain aural iterations of autobiographical monographs serve as such a captivating aesthetic experience that they essentially negate the need to engage with the original print edition altogether.

By enlisting a comparatively new methodological vocabulary—communicating the pivotal significance of the notion of internal logic and the manner in which it effectively interconnects with the concept of one's "informed intuition"—my approach implicitly warrants virtually any aesthetic discourse to adhere to (and, to some extent, depend on) these two terms. I have thus explicitly endeavored to carefully articulate and analyze their functions, in practice, when attending to my selected case studies. As it, too, is essentially grasped intuitively, through one's firsthand experience, the notion of internal logic should not be relegated to a conventional argumentative excursive, or perceived of as a complex, esoteric philosophical novelty. Rather, to paraphrase an almost parenthetical remark made by Graves while reviewing Umberto Eco's *On Beauty: A History of a Western Idea* (2004), any internal logic can ultimately be identified as a function alluding to the overall rules that both govern and bind together a coincidental assemblage of self-contained constituents into a coherent artwork, which, in turn, is perceived by one's senses.[1] Ultimately, when one engages with a new work by an author—or, for that matter, a filmmaker—whose work is already associated with or purportedly adheres to a certain particular voice

---

[1] David Graves, "Reshimat Ha'Makoet" [The Groceries List], *Odyssey—A Journey through Ideas*, no. 11 (May 2011): 25.

or style, one is nonetheless bound by the minimum responsibility to examine, decipher, and evaluate whether or not (and, indeed, to what extent) the new work appropriately complies with the same, arguably expected internal logic—or, rather, in fact, puts forward a completely new one.

"Informed intuition," on its part, should be taken to be an inherent quality or idiosyncrasy that—in the context of this study—can conceivably be deemed indispensable to the craft of casting, which I find both embodies and, indeed, abides by the praxis of aesthetic appreciation. Fundamentally, I maintain that one is certainly able to *sense* whether, if a particular performer were to ostensibly tackle a certain specific text, his or her resulting delivery *should* constitute an aesthetically rewarding performance (or, alternatively, indeed, quite an unrewarding one). This sense, to my mind, is, to all intents and purposes, innately dependent on the extent to which one responsibly employs one's "informed intuition." One similarly utilizes this sense when undertaking the aesthetic evaluation of artworks. For the most part, even if one may not necessarily be aware that this process is, in fact, taking place, one arguably cannot make a casting decision without some kind of aesthetic consciousness. Casting, therefore, effectively embodies a process of exerting appreciation and evaluation, which, as such, ultimately demonstrates how "informed intuition" works in action.

Hitherto, the inner process that a casting director undergoes—leading them to conclude whether or not a particular performer *should* be "right" for a role—has evidently not been accounted for. Although, when asked, a casting director would conceivably be able to account for and articulate their decision—there appears to be no fully defined technique or a definite set of guidelines for how to reach it. Indeed, despite the comprehensive scope of available literature pertaining to the theories and well-documented history of the various types of performance praxes—e.g., acting, directing, dramaturgy, scenography, lighting, camera operating, film editing, etc.—the craft of casting and the process it adheres to surprisingly remain virtually unexplored. (While there may be quite a few books dedicated to the purported rules of conduct amid casting sessions and auditions, it would appear as though none of them—not even those written by casting directors—appropriately consider the very nature of the craft itself).

Drawing on the methodical infrastructure developed herein *ab initio*, I find that one can endow casting directors with the institutional role retained by the artist. By the same token, the craft of casting itself could be conflated with any other artistic undertaking. This, I would like to believe, potentially ranks among this endeavor's most significant contributions to this field, serving both scholars and practitioners alike. I am confident that my institutional analysis of audiobooks as aural artifacts—effectively classifying and subsequently appreciating them as artworks, to all intents and purposes—can evoke future applications of NITA as an ostensible apparatus for aesthetically evaluating different kinds of performance-oriented media. Implicitly, therefore, an argument could be made that once one consciously cultivates what is a conceivably unconscious process, the exertion of aesthetic appreciation becomes a necessary and, indeed, practical conclusion of one's "informed intuition."

Aural artifacts appear to demonstrate "informed intuition" in action, potentially revealing the extent to which the casting choice that had arguably led to their conception and realization effectively necessitates attaining a sense of appropriateness—rooted in having been able to grasp not merely one, but, so it seems, *three* unique types of internal logic, each adhering to different sources of knowledge: namely, that of the text, that of the medium, and that of the performer's talent qualifications, vocal personality, and—inasmuch as it is purportedly pertinent—their personal inclination toward and passion for the material. As alluded to earlier, while this could well be construed as nothing more than an ostensible hunch, or a gut feeling at best, it should, to my mind, be pinpointed as the key challenge involved in an otherwise creative process—one that aims at conjuring an appropriate match between a performer and a role (or, in the case at hand, a given written text).

In the realm of audiobooks, casting directors need to possess (or, at the very least, to develop) an ability to ostensibly "enhear"—quite literally predict—how a putative aural performance should sound. Their process no doubt begins by reading the text in question while attempting to attain a sense of its overall internal logic and grasp what it is purportedly "all about." Subsequently—and, in certain cases, perhaps even simultaneously—they endeavor to imagine who, among the several hundred actors they work with regularly, might possibly (or, rather, plausibly) best be suited for the job. Howard, for example, expressed to me her tendency to scribble notes to herself as she reads, claiming that she usually comes up with four or five names of potential readers who she believes could be a good fit for the book in question. Eventually, she succeeds in working it down to one name. By her own admission, she does so without having needed to *actually* hear them read that text or have them come for an audition. She thus seems to just *know*—intuitively, "forehear"—that the person she has in mind should be a good match for the particular so-called "needs" of the book she has been tasked with casting. Howard believes it is very much "an instinctive thing that develops over time and experience." In the same vein, Thompson explains that when the choice of which particular audiobook to review is left up to her, she bases her decision "on length, subject, narrator, and author." If the book in question happens to be part of a series or adheres to some overall mythology, she makes a point of finding out whether the narrator may have also recorded previous corresponding titles. This, she claims, can considerably affect one's listening experience—especially if one is already accustomed to having a particular voice embody the overall literary voice of that series or, indeed, that of a leading protagonist.

Conceivably, to replace the voice that one has grown to identify with—and, in many cases, even love and cherish—can yield both oppositions and heated debates, reminiscent of those that surround the ever-changing interpretations and characterizations of icons such as Batman, James Bond, or Doctor Who. In this context, the process of casting an aural performance in itself entails something of a preliminary evaluation of the expected putative performance—that is, ascertaining the potential aesthetic nature of a recording that does not yet exist. To attain a better understanding of the craft of casting aural artifacts can therefore potentially provide one with a deeper wisdom insofar as the manner in which one aesthetically appreciates *any* artwork.

The world of cuisine, to my mind, serves as a good analogy for beginning to understand how casting might work. Consider, for instance, the well-established coupling between apples and cinnamon—which, as celebrity chefs Clarissa Dickson Wright and Jennifer Paterson had once remarked on their *Two Fat Ladies* cooking show, constitutes "a match made in heaven." Arguably, the first person to have conjured up this particular "match" would have, in terms of this study, had to have been sufficiently acquainted with the purported individual internal logic of each ingredient. Put simply, in order to have ostensibly predicted that this match *should* "work"—before having actually tasted the two together—they would have had to have attained not only a rather exhaustive understanding of how apples "work" but also a comprehensive sense of the so-called "workings" of cinnamon. Appropriately, by employing what I would regard as their "informed intuition," that person could in effect determine and conclude what the matching of the two could—and, indeed, *should*—yield. This, I believe, can be conflated with how casting works both in action and in practice.

By the same token, I find that one is able to extend this analogy further by examining the kinds of ostensible "culinary castings" that might initially seem counterintuitive or rather those that can be characterized as requiring an acquired taste. Consider for instance, such phenomena as chocolate and chili, pear and blue cheese, salted caramel fudge, peanut butter and bacon, or pretzel ice cream, to name but a few. Arguably, the mere thought of these combinations can, for some more than others, raise at least one eyebrow. Yet while all these instances might be classified as requiring one's acquired taste, they are all also the resulting matches of one's "informed intuition."

The notion of ostensibly "playing with matches"—aiming, of course, not to get burned—could also be understood by way of, say, attempting to conclude which particular musical performer(s) might potentially be best suited for taking on a so-called "cover version" of a given song or a piece of music. Here, too, one is essentially required to acquaint oneself not only with the internal logic of the song or musical piece but also with the talent and qualifications of the performing artist, thereby allowing for one's "informed intuition" to spring into action.

Now, while the aforementioned *Fifty Shades of Grey* "*a la* Gottfried" was obviously created to elicit laughter, one is sure to come across certain similarly counterintuitive, *real* matches in the realm of the performing arts. Although some may well prove to be pleasantly rewarding surprises, others could well be regarded as flawed casting decisions. When it comes to aural artifact, the challenge with so-called "oppositional" casting seems particularly fascinating. In this context, casting aural performances—as a form of aesthetic "matchmaking" of sorts—is both guided by one's "informed intuition" and rooted in the identification of different kinds of internal logic. The process of deciphering which particular performer is best suited to deliver a certain text—even if this decision follows an interpretation that abides by a new internal logic—and, indeed, the ability to quite literally predict whether or not a performance should be evaluated as aesthetically good, can potentially be applied to different performance-based artistic fields.

As with any other craft, to all intents and purposes, one is surely able to develop and fine-tune the expertise and proficiencies required for making ever better casting choices. Thus, once one is acquainted enough with both the skills and range of a particular performer *and* with the purported internal logic of a certain printed work, one should be able to conclude for oneself whether a certain recording should constitute a rewarding experience. This, to a large extent, is precisely what one does quite naturally with "celebrity" readings. As such, to merely imagine the likes of, say, Jennifer Connelly reading Paul Bowles' *The Sheltering Sky* (1949), Héctor Elizondo delivering John Steinbeck's *The Pearl* (1947), Colin Firth narrating Graham Greene's *The End of the Affair* (1951), Dustin Hoffman performing Jerzy Kosinski's *Being There* (1970), John

Malkovich delivering Kurt Vonnegut's *Breakfast of Champions* (1973), Ian McKellen reading *The Odyssey* by Homer, Alan Rickman performing Thomas Hardy's *The Return of the Native* (1878), Meryl Streep narrating Colm Tóibín's *The Testament of Mary* (2012), or Kate Winslet delivering Emile Zola's *Thérèse Raquin* (1867)—to name but a few that come to mind—can essentially be said to prompt one's "informed intuition" to evaluate their achievements "before the fact" and arguably put forward the question "what could go wrong?." This is explicitly what projects such as Audible's "A-List" Collection seem to count on, as well as many "Audible Original" projects.

To be sure, some of Audible's brief behind-the-scenes clips—gracefully posted online for the benefit of both fans and, indeed, enticing new listeners—prove absolutely fascinating as well as rather illuminating in the context of this study. Hoffman, for instance, is seen quite literally "conducting" himself while reading Kosinski's novel, thus almost rendering the written text as sheet music. Two minutes into the recording, as the camera focuses on his hands, he is clearly seen attempting to find, in real time, the pace or rhythm that the text purportedly embodies—in order to appropriately transform it into a spoken-word performance.[2]

Rosamund Pike's iteration of *Sense and Sensibility* stands out among the various aural iterations the novel has received—the best of which, among those that I have engaged with and consumed hitherto, include the audiobook versions performed by Julie Christie, Glenda Jackson, Kate Winslet, and Juliet Stevenson. It is an absolute delight to witness Pike's transition from narrator to character and to hear her explaining her process:

> I have a sort of strange system of notation that I've developed over time—of indicating to me where the thoughts are going. So, my script for doing these is covered with sort of arrows and directions, and, it's funny, it wouldn't make sense to anybody else, but I can follow it.[3]

Overall, Pike finds,

> When you're listening to something, words go into your head in a very unique way, and you do retain a lot of a novel that you've heard—just as much as you do when you've read. Reading gives you one experience, but listening gives you

---

[2.] See URL: accessed February 10, 2023, https://www.youtube.com/watch?v=qsK1O7QsFFM.

[3.] See URL: accessed February 2, 2023, https://www.youtube.com/watch?v=0YHJ2cJfcLY, 01min45sec–01min53sec

a different one, and makes you start and notice, and respond to different things, and perhaps gives you a perspective that you wouldn't necessarily have thought of. An audiobook gives you something because it suggests voices to you, but what you're picturing is still all your own.[4]

Colin Farrell, in describing his profound experience narrating Joyce's *A Portrait of the Artist as a Young Man* (1916), and Rachel McAdams, in explaining the importance of her having an emotional connection to Lucy Maud Montgomery's *Anne of Green Gables* (1908), provide rather interesting meditations.[5] Similarly, when asked what she likes most about storytelling, Winslet replied,

> Creating voices, creating characters. I absolutely love that because I know it adds so much to the narrative, and I know that it adds a huge amount to the rhythm and the colour of a story—particularly for the listener, especially if it's children. They can conjure up how a character might look just based on whether they have a lisp or not, or whether they have an American accent or a Scottish accent, or an Irish accent, or just a plain old posh English accent. It can make a huge difference to how the listener imagines that character might appear to be, as a person, and *that* for me is wonderful, so, that's my favourite part of storytelling.[6]

All these glimpses into the "making-of" process—allowing one to actually *see* the narrator in action, as they perform for the audience that "isn't there"—are quite fascinating. While they may be well aware of the camera documenting them, they are most certainly not performing for its benefit. This, again, clearly demonstrates the type of delivery that is required of an aural performing artist. Additional examples can be found in various recording sessions that have captured the narrations of Stephen Fry, as well as those featuring Emma Thompson and the cast of Jane Austen's *Emma* (1815) and *Northanger Abbey* (1817).[7] The same holds true when one views Joanne Froggatt recording Emily Brontë's *Wuthering Heights* (1847).[8]

[4.] Ibid., 00min55sec–01min28sec.

[5.] See URL: accessed February 10, 2023, https://www.youtube.com/watch?v=QOk2Bsngp2s; and https://www.youtube.com/watch?v=Z0_YzVbNQPw.

[6.] See URL: accessed February 10, 2023, https://www.youtube.com/watch?v=MiJ-2HtP62g, 01min28sec–02min10sec.

[7.] See URL: accessed February 10, 2023,https://www.youtube.com/watch?v=BzcdY6vyOUk; and https://www.youtube.com/watch?v=nDw54tRVnAM.

[8.] See URL: accessed February 10, 2023, https://www.youtube.com/watch?v=bcQmaSFRxV8.

In the same vein, when commenting on his own *Stories by Heart* (2019)—explicitly identifying the difference between performing this piece live on Broadway as opposed to recording its aural iteration—John Lithgow explains that

> I'm excited to record it for Audible because it's doing it in a very, very different form. It's all […] *audible*. It's not physical. I have to make it absolutely clear to the audience who is speaking when—because there are moments when there are five people on stage, all talking and bickering and overlapping, and you've got to know exactly who's talking at every point.[9]

In promoting the audiobook version of *Macbeth: A Novel* (2011) by A. J. Hartley and David Hewson, the latter explains that "one of the things I really wanted to try with this was to tailor our writings towards an audio audience. I absolutely adore audio. I think it's the most natural and pure storytelling medium that we've got."[10] This clearly demonstrates an astute awareness that aural artifacts adhere to certain *requirements* of their own. To a large extent, all the reflections and insights presented herein prove invaluable for understanding the largely untapped core aesthetics that aural artifacts embody. They all, to my mind, also serve as an indication as to precisely why aural artifacts *should* be aesthetically evaluated.

Ultimately, once one both accepts and adopts the role of institutional procedures in the Artworld, it becomes clear why the understanding of audiobooks as aural artifacts not only *necessitates* an interdisciplinary perspective but also effectively both merits and warrants an aesthetic category of its own. The more one acquaints oneself with the institutional category, the more adept one becomes at classifying, appreciating, and, conceivably, even *creating* these unique artifacts.

***

[9.] See URL: accessed February 2, 2023, https://www.youtube.com/watch?v=XXBuj-144r4, 01min05sec–01min30sec.

[10.] See URL: accessed February 2, 2023,https://www.youtube.com/watch?v=hJbSveEm-Pg, 00min36sec–00min51sec.

APPENDIX

A Note on Definitions

A definition is, by definition, a closed concept. To *define* art, therefore, renders it a closed concept. Yet for American philosopher and aesthetician Morris Weitz, art—as a philosophical construct—appears to lack the necessary and sufficient conditions that are precisely what is required for properly defining it. Drawing on the analytical notion of "family resemblance" put forward by renowned Austrian British philosopher Ludwig Wittgenstein—postulating that one can account for not only the exhibited properties that certain family members might display (e.g., visual similarities) but also their non-exhibited qualities (e.g., a shared DNA)—and similarly utilizing Wittgenstein's application of logical categories for scrutinizing the structure of games, Weitz fails to detect a conceivable constant that appropriately applies to all things art.

Asserting that the introduction of every new artwork can potentially either slightly modify or altogether alter one's overall perception of what counts as art, Weitz concludes that art is, in fact, an "open" concept.[1] As such, not only does art become quite literally undefinable, but also the very notion of theorizing about aesthetic practice is rendered completely redundant, insipid, and futile. Although his argument is not widely supported, it is nonetheless commonly held that Weitz had successfully ruled out the more insidious art theories, which fail to acknowledge, account for, or, indeed, outwardly facilitate art's openness.[2] Ultimately, however, Weitz leaves one faced with a theoretical "dead-end."

It took close to a decade for American philosopher and phenomenologist Maurice Mandelbaum—for whom theorizing about art was not at all far-fetched—to confront and challenge the supposed stalemate imposed by Weitz. Similarly corresponding with Wittgenstein's conception of family resemblances, Mandelbaum argues that in order to get a sense of what art is, attention must be paid

---

[1] Morris Weitz, "The Role of Theory in Aesthetics," *Journal of Aesthetics and Art Criticism* 15, no. 1 (September 1956): 27–35.

[2] Frank Boardman, "Weitz's Legacy," *American Society for Aesthetics Graduate e-Journal* 7, no 1 (January 2015), 1.

to an artwork's *non-exhibited* properties.[3] While he may not allude to Danto directly (despite having published his response to Weitz a year or so after "The Artworld"), Mandelbaum provides a complementary perspective to the remarkable insight that artworks are *not,* in fact, defined by their aesthetic features. In one way or another, theories about art have existed since the dawn of art.

To be sure, most of us hold at least some vague notion or an ostensible personal take as to what art is (or, for that matter, what it should be). Even claiming that art should not be theorized, to begin with—or, indeed, that any attempt to define it effectively goes against everything that art supposedly stands for—is in itself, to all intents and purposes, a theory "about" art. Nevertheless, art—for Danto—not only *can* be defined, but, indeed, most certainly *should*. In this respect, Danto's conception of the Artworld also proved its ingenuity in solving a scandalous conundrum that had, in fact, been mystifying artist, audiences, and scholars for almost half a century, namely, Duchamp's *Fountain*.

On the one hand, the very conception of such an artwork—to say nothing of seriously submitting it for display—could well be construed as pure provocation. Not only were Duchamp's actions unheard of and, indeed, profoundly bewildering, but one might also regard them as a bridge too far. Even over one hundred years later, it may prove rather arduous to try and fathom just how such a plebeian, unsavory, and arguably objectionable object—indeed, one which cannot (and perhaps should not) in any way be regarded as art—still, rather successfully, withstands the rigorous *soi-disant* finely cultured confines of a respectable art gallery. On the other hand, to the surprise of almost everyone involved—and, conceivably, first and foremost to Duchamp's own surprise—the artistic status and identity of *Fountain* incessantly prevails.

Arguably, Duchamp had never intended for that particular piece to be taken seriously. Nor was it necessarily his objective to willfully provoke or agitate. He was, however, quite serious about communicating his disconcertment in light of there being virtually no discrimination insofar as what might count as an artwork. Thus, the fact that *Fountain* was officially granted a stamp of approval—thereby concretizing precisely what Duchamp was essentially calling out—may have ultimately nonplussed the artist well beyond any ripple effect that the work itself had generated. While it may not be so intrinsically deep (or even engaging), and despite its purported defiant shock value, *Fountain*

---

[3] Maurice Mandelbaum, "Family Resemblances and Generalization Concerning the Arts," *American Philosophical Quarterly* 2, no. 3 (July 1965): 219–228.

nonetheless remains a legitimate artwork—which is not only historically important but also profoundly meaningful.[4]

Postulating that artworks are, first and foremost, "about something" (no matter what that "something" may be), it, in turn—for Danto—would have to be "embodied in the object in which the work of art materially consists."[5] As such, a particular artwork's *embodied* meaning effectively abides by, adheres to, and, indeed complies with a certain kind of aesthetic style, conception, or attitude. Madeleine Schechter, for instance—in her fascinating study, bridging modernism and postmodernism by journeying through romantic views on aesthetics, meaning, and truth, and ultimately leading one to Immanuel Kant, Eco, and, indeed, Danto—considers the notion of embodied meaning in respect of such notions as "symbol" and "imagination."[6] Drawing on what she identifies as Danto's inherently Hegelian predilection for what is ultimately an expressionist (rather than a representational or formalist) approach to artistic praxes, she maintains that to perceive of artworks as symbolic expressions that embody *their own* meaning—completely interdependent of both form and content— in effect provides one with a comprehensive understanding of socio-cultural contexts.[7] Thus, as one engages with an artwork, one is effectively required to both interpret and identify what that is purportedly supposed to be about—by ascertaining its putative socio-cultural, philosophical, or, indeed, art-historical contexts. Notwithstanding, the conclusion (as opposed to the assumption) that art *is* embodied meaning, does not, in fact, originate from Danto. Rather, it is an idea at least as old as Aristotle's notion of art being a "materialized" idea, which, in essence, alluded to depicting an abstract concept in a concrete manner. Ultimately, once one finds oneself unable to ostensibly explain that which one wishes to convey, one instead endeavors to *show* it—thereby appealing to one's senses as much as to one's intellect.[8]

Interestingly enough, it was only at a later stage that Danto called attention to the not-inconsequential fact that the original Brillo packaging was in itself devised and designed by a commissioned artist—James Harvey—who had endowed it with a certain kind of aesthetic that predominantly pertains to what

---

[4] Graves, *The New Institutional Theory of Art*, 12–14.

[5] Arthur Danto, *What Art Is* (New Haven, CT: Yale University Press, 2013), 149.

[6] Schechter, *Semiotics and Art Theory: Between Autonomism and Contextualism*, 96–109.

[7] Ibid., 162.

[8] Graves, *The New Institutional Theory of Art*, 85–86.

in Hegelian terms would be identified as the "objective spirit" of 1960s Americana. Whether or not, or the extent to which, Warhol's work actually embodies *that* aesthetic is not necessarily conclusive:

> I don't know what aesthetic properties if any belong to Warhol's *Brillo Box* itself.
> […] Harvey's box was part of popular culture, but it was not a piece of Pop Art
> because it was not about popular culture at all. Harvey created a design that
> obviously appealed to popular sensibilities. Warhol brought those sensibilities
> to consciousness.[9]

At the end of the day, however, since they are arguably lacking any genuine aesthetic interest, prevailing as identical iterations of their nonartistic original counterparts, it seems as though the very existence of these predominantly postmodern products—that is, so-called "conceptual" or "appropriation" artworks such as *Fountain* and *Brillo Box*—makes it all the more arduous to regard them as artworks, to begin with. In other words, they quite poignantly illustrate that art and the aesthetic (which, in its core, is perceptual) not only do *not* necessarily go hand in hand but also that the Artworld could conceivably forego the aesthetic altogether.

A Further Note on Institutional Facts

Consider, for instance, one's natural (or, to some, "God-given") ability to run extremely fast—as opposed to one's demonstrating the same ability amid the confines of an Olympic race. Although one values each instance quite differently, both instances essentially concern the exact same phenomenon. Yet for want of a particular institutional context such as the Olympics, the mere (brute) fact that one simply happens to be an extremely fast runner, is, in itself, of no particular value. Perhaps of no value at all. Of course, one might well be inclined to argue that such an ability *can*, in fact, become considerably useful when, say, securing one's escape and thus extending one's life span in the event of one being chased by a somewhat peckish tiger. (And, in this respect, if one happens to outrun some other potential candidate for the hypothetical tiger's afternoon nosh, then being able to run extremely fast can potentially become even more significant and meaningful). According to Graves, however—drawing on what

---

[9.] Danto, *What Art Is*, 148.

he alludes as Wittgenstein's response to Darwin—survival purely constitutes an innate human necessity, at best. As such, it cannot be construed as something of any concrete value.[10]

In this context, the "brutish" natural world is essentially devoid of meanings and values, which are exclusively institutional constructs. Put simply, everything that happens, simply happens: a lion that devours the cubs of another pride when staking a claim over new territory, for instance, is not avowedly evil. Likewise, a solar eclipse is no more ominous than a rainbow is a sign of hope (or, for that matter, an indication of the whereabouts of a pot of gold, allegedly hidden by an indigenous leprechaun). In the same vein, a tsunami does entail that "Nature" might be "angry"—as nature, to be sure, has no purported will of its own. (And, in that respect—with absolutely no offense to any religious denomination, tradition, or conviction—neither does "God"). Yet once one's cultured societies began to evolve, and as one endeavored to spend one's days doing something more than simply making it through another day without expiring prematurely, one thus began to actively pursue *meaningful* endeavors. For Graves, one's cultural institutions do just that: they are designed to bestow meanings and values on things that, by their nature, have neither—things that merely "are."[11] As such, to celebrate one's ability to be the absolute best at "running extremely fast"— say, among a group of similarly able and trained individuals by awarding one a medal in the Olympic Games—is most definitely a meaningful thing of value.

Now, cast your minds back, if you will, to the infamous scandal that would forever disgrace the 1988 Seoul Olympics: after having won the Men's 100m Final, and, following an inquiry and subsequent confession pertaining to his use of banned substances, Canadian athlete Ben Johnson was disqualified and stripped of his gold medal, which was subsequently awarded to Carl Lewis— who, in turn, was credited with a new Olympic world record. To be sure, the fact that Johnson was, to all intents and purposes, the *fastest* man in that race— and, at the time, indeed, the fastest man in the world—constitutes a rather unequivocal "brute" fact. Similarly unequivocal, however, is the fact that Johnson did not play by the rules. Making matters worse, in what ultimately became one of the most sensational sports stories to date, it was revealed that six of the eight men in that lineup were in one way or another involved with performance-enhancing drugs, including Lewis.

---

[10] Graves, [To See a Sunset and Die], 33.

[11] Ibid.

Ultimately, since one's socio-cultural institutions "institute the facts of the matter"—as Graves puts it—they are thus able to literally *create* undisputed facts.[12] In this respect, the power to hand over Johnson's medal to Lewis could arguably be equated with the power and authority of one's judicial system—that is, a cultural institution—to acquit a person who has already been found guilty.

A Further Note on the Evolution of George Dickie's Theory

Although the Artworld is surely not a physical whereabouts, it nevertheless operates as a virtually palpable, albeit abstract, framework that both establishes and facilitates different artistic praxes, rooted in an inherently human creative process. By prescribing a particular set of parameters—that is, a context—it effectively both articulates and, indeed, defines what can and cannot be included amid its own confines.

Over the years, Dickie's definition of art was subject to quite a few revisions. Commencing with a 1969 journal article—followed by two subsequent revisions in 1971 and 1974 (with the latter, in fact, customarily regarded as Dickie's *first* version)—Dickie essentially attempted to shape his theory as a value-neutral tool for *classifying* artworks. As such, the theory posited that "a work of art in the classificatory sense is (1) an artifact, (2) a set of the aspects of which has had conferred upon it the status of candidate for appreciation by some person or persons acting on behalf of a certain social institution (the artworld)."[13]

While Danto, on his part, may have saluted Dickie for his bravura, it is nonetheless commonly held that this initial definition was not entirely well constructed.[14] In addition to apparently exhibiting an inherently vexing circularity, it also seemed to rub some people the wrong way—or, as Graves puts it, "it appeared to focus upon the wrong sorts of things."[15] The explicit decision to set aside evaluation, for example, provoked no little confusion—having been taken as an assertion that one should altogether discard "bad art" as "not art." Moreover, for a supposedly definitive theory—that should effectively apply to

---

[12] Ibid., 22.

[13] George Dickie, "The Institutional Theory of Art," in *Theories of Art Today*, ed. Noël Carroll (Madison: University of Wisconsin Press, 2000), 94.

[14] Danto, *What Art Is*, 145.

[15] Graves, *The New Institutional Theory of Art*, 19.

all things art—it seemed both limited and restrictive. Indeed, since the Artworld is conceived of as democratic, pluralistic, and all-inclusive at its core, Dickie's proposed definition appeared unnecessarily elitist and presumptuous. (Even in recent times—following the rise, and assumed demise, of postmodernism—elitism is not only customarily frowned upon but might also be identified as some form of academic foul play, for lack of a better term). Most of the reservations it attracted, however, can be discounted as having been based on an inaccurate interpretation of just what it was that his theory sets out to do.

In his second version—which, perhaps jokingly, and with some degree of irony, was titled *The Art Circle* (1984)—Dickie offers a set of five consolidating and inflective clauses, each signifying a different institutional role. Their intrinsic "inter-relatedness," or mutual dependency, is governed by both conventional and non-conventional rules. Together, they effectively form the definition of what art is.[16] Although Graves finds Dickie's wording more precise this time around—arguing that it does not leave one completely uninformed—he also maintains that, for the most part, the definition itself remained, alas, unconvincing.[17]

As far as Dickie was concerned, however, this version constitutes "the single best account of the institutional theory of art."[18] Indeed, despite the purported deficiency in its overall circularity, it would seem as though the fundamental idea that in order to understand each individual clause essentially *necessitates* an understanding of each and every other clause is—to all intents and purposes—one of this theory's utmost important insights. Drawing on Graves—utilizing a rather frequent analogy in philosophy—suffice it to say that it is akin to one's understating of both the moves and the roles of the pieces in a game of chess: that is to say, one cannot entirely comprehend the meanings of "checkmate" or "stalemate" without fully grasping the role of a player's "king," and *vice versa*.

A Further Note on Internal Logic and Aesthetic Appreciation

When interviewed by Melvin Bragg for *The South Bank Show* in 1986, celebrated English comedian John Cleese alludes to his friend and collaborator Marty Feldman, who used to go on at great length about what he used to call the

---

[16] George Dickie, *The Art Circle: A Theory of Art* (New York: Haven, 1984), 80–82.

[17] Graves, *The New Institutional Theory of Art*, 25.

[18] Dickie, "The Institutional Theory of Art," 108n13.

"internal logic of a sketch." Cleese explains that this, for Feldman, entailed that if a sketch happened to feature a bunch of people sitting in dustbins or dressed as carrots and if one were then introduced to a character who is not likewise attired, there would have to be some *explanation* as to why not.[19]

In this context, both Feldman and Graves seem to refer to something that is inherent to a particular sketch or an artwork, which somehow needs to be exhibited. Respectively alluding to some kind of an internal logic, the phrase itself is thus taken to be a "given." As a proper term, however, rather than as a mere *façon de parler*—the wording "internal logic" does not abide by any official or explicit definition. Although one can fairly easily surmise its overall sentiment—perhaps even dismiss it as nothing more than a certain *je ne sais quoi* quality—one need not relegate it to simply a matter of jargon, common sense, or colloquial use. Nevertheless, as this book employs the notion of internal logic as a pivotal—indeed, practical—*evaluative* tool, I find myself obliged to both further articulate and contextualize its particular use herein.[20]

In Graves' publication of NITA, this particular wording evidently appears only once: mentioned almost in passing and employed in respect of his discussion on "really identifying a work of art," which Graves demonstrates through an explanation of Cubism.[21] Albeit in broad strokes, and on what he regards as an "intuitive level," he proceeds to elaborate on the particular "logic" that the Cubist style adheres to.[22] Graves ultimately alludes to some inherent "internal lawfulness," which he explains through a consideration of Picasso's *Three Musicians* (1921):

> It is the institution of Cubism, as an Artworld Big Theory, which tells which facts count, and as what. [...] They are *Artworld* musicians, instruments and dog, not *natural* ones. They abide by different laws than do natural ones. They are synthetic signs for a lawfully ordered reality which can exist *only* in the Artworld institution of Cubism. That is the heart and soul of the Cubist endeavor.

---

[19] See: *The South Bank Show*, ITV/LWT, January 12, 1986, edited and presented by Melvin Bragg.

[20] All things considered, it should also be noted that the very notion of an "internal" could arguably be construed as something of a tautology—since logic, to all intents and purposes, is intrinsically internal. Furthermore, some scholars have even gone so far as to maintain there is fundamentally no such thing as an "external" logic either. See, e.g., V. A. Smirnov, "Internal and External Logic," *Bulletin of the Section of Logic* 17, no. 3/4 (1988): 170–176. These notions, however, can also be negated: See, e.g., Ralph Wedgwood, "The Internal and External Components of Cognition," in *Contemporary Debates in Cognitive Science*, ed. Robert J. Stainton (Malden, MA: Blackwell, 2006).

[21] Graves, *The New Institutional Theory of Art*, 66.

[22] Ibid., 68–69.

> The ten blue and ten white patches, arranged among the black and brown, establish a good deal of that internal lawfulness, by establishing a rhythm and sense of highly-contrastive balance of that particular and synthetic "world" of the "*Three Musicians*". Could that internal lawfulness of the *Musicians'* world be expressed otherwise, as, say, an equation or deductive argument? Picasso raises a bewildered brow, for he knows that there is only one way to be able to identify that particular sense of order, only one way to understand that particular lawfulness. That one way is to actually see it embodied in an artifact, and to this we add that one must see the artifact in the context of the Artworld, in general, and of Cubism, in particular.[23] [emphasis in original].

In this respect, I would argue that in conceiving of the existence of an internal logic, one essentially alludes to some overall organizational rationale, of sorts, which effectively interconnects the abundance of mutually dependent and simultaneously self-contained palpable constituents that inhabit a given cultural institutional system.

When appreciating paintings, for instance, one is required to not only consider the overall internal logic of paintings as paintings, but also account for their place amid the Artworld at large. However, when one sets out to appreciate *specific* paintings—e.g., Raphael's *Madonna and Child with Saint John the Baptist* (1507), Rembrandt's *The Night Watch* (1642), Friedrich's *Wanderer above the Sea of Fog* (1818), Manet's *A Bar at the Folies-Bergère* (1882), or Pollock's *Blue Poles* (1952)—one must ascertain the specific kind of internal logic that invariably applies to each individual work. To be sure, even different paintings by the same artist—supposedly expected to exhibit similar themes or corresponding aesthetic properties—can each adhere to a distinct internal logic of their own: e.g., Picasso's *The Old Guitarist* (1903–1904) as opposed to his *Girl with Mandolin* (1910), *Harlequin with a Guitar* (1917) or *Still Life with Guitar* (1921).

Appropriately, the fact that Leonardo da Vinci's *Mona Lisa*, for instance, is conventionally considered as one of the most important artistic achievements of Western art is, in point of fact, an institutional fact. As such, it is something that one is intrinsically expected to accept "on trust." However, to *really* see the painting—properly identifying and fully appreciating it "as a masterpiece artwork by

---

[23] Ibid., 64.

the institution of Neo-Platonic Renaissance painting in Italy"[24]—one is required to adopt the perspective of a fifteenth-century Italian art seeker.

Ultimately, without an appropriate context to inform one's aesthetic experience, one might, alas, never actually "get" what the commotion surrounding Mrs. Lisa del Giocondo is all about. Indeed, it is not at all far-fetched to assume that when one visits her in the Louvre, arguably armed with "selfie-stick," one customarily experiences the *Mona Lisa* as an unexpectedly small portrait of a somewhat androgynous-looking lady with an oddly enigmatic smile, whose eyes, for whatever reason, appear to follow one around the exhibition hall. This, to be sure, is not a proper aesthetic experience of what that painting actually is.

By the same token, consider, say, one's first-ever encounter with a typical Vincent van Gogh "Cypress" painting: if one happened to conclude that it's not a good painting, asserting something to the effect that it simply doesn't look like an actual tree, one's statement cannot be cast aside as merely another case of "to each their own." Indeed, such a case would reveal that one had not assumed the minimum responsibility of acquainting oneself with even a modicum of the most elementary aspects of the reputed internal logic of the artist's endeavors. Van Gogh's "trees," *in nuce*, are not, in fact, paintings *of* actual, realistic trees. Trying to determine whether or not, or to what extent, the (decidedly non-realistic) "tree" in question happens to look like a *bona fide* tree is, therefore, entirely missing the point. As Graves points out, drawing on Danto, "a person who is ignorant of a particular artistic phenomenon should refrain from passing judgment on it."[25] If, however, one was to duly invest some time and reasonable effort to scrutinize the particular internal logic of the art that one happens to be engaging with—in this case, Post-Impressionism (or, indeed, as some might argue, Expressionism)—one could then begin appropriately evaluating its aesthetic quality. This, again, should illustrate precisely why "beauty" is most definitely *not* in the eye of the "beholder."

A Further Note on Intuition

Numerous interpretations and fascinating insights abound about intuition and what it supposedly is (or, indeed, ought to be)—dating back to both Plato and Aristotle, pertaining to one's ability to see something clearly and apprehend the

---

[24] Ibid., 38.

[25] Ibid., 17.

very essence of things.[26] As it is certainly not my intention to attempt an ostensibly oxygen-deprived deep-dive into this otherwise fascinating topic, and also for the sake of brevity, I shall briefly allude to the essential alluring insights that prove most pertinent to my own investigation.

Drawing on the Greek word for things that are perceived by the senses (as opposed to things that are known by the mind), it was Alexander Gottlieb Baumgarten who introduced the term "aesthetic" in his 1735 Master's dissertation, calling for the establishment of a science of aesthetics—which, as Elizabeth Prettejohn puts it, constitutes "a science that would deal with human perception, something different from the well-established science that dealt with logical knowledge."[27] Greatly inspired by Plato's notion of *noesis*—that is, one's perceptual cognitive capability, effectively alluding to what could be construed as intuition (or, perhaps, what could more colloquially be regarded as one's ubiquitous "sixth sense")—Baumgarten suggested that one possesses a certain kind of sensitive knowing, which he termed *Ars combinationis*. It is, in contrast to one's innate analytical mental faculty—ostensibly "in-charge" of one's power to grasp such things as mathematics and science, and which one employs in order to understand measurable or quantifiable properties—that this so-called "dark faculty," which conceivably both belongs to and resides in one's soul, essentially represents one's capacity to amalgamate, unify, or fuse complex sensuous compounds.[28] This, *in nuce*, is achieved intuitively.

Just as paramount in this context, and conceivably crystalizing the French proverb *les grands esprits se rencontrent*, are Kant's celebrated critiques on concepts such as taste and judgment. Among the variety of influential insights they inhabit, these texts effectively contribute not only to the understanding of

---

[26.] For further reading, consider, e.g., R. E. Allen, *Plato's "Euthyphro" and the Earlier Theory of Forms: A Re-Interpretation of the Republic* (Abingdon, UK: Routledge, 2013); and Carlo Cellucci, *Rethinking Logic: Logic in Relation to Mathematics, Evolution, and Method* (New York: Springer, 2013); Amy L. Baylor, "A Three-Component Conception of Intuition: Immediacy, Sensing Relationships and Reason," *New Ideas in Psychology* 15, no. 2 (August 1997): 188–189; Jerome S. Bruner, *The Process of Education* (Cambridge, MA: Harvard University Press, 1999); Nel Noddings and Paul J. Shore, *Awakening the Inner Eye: Intuition in Education* (New York: Teachers College Press, 1984); Daniel Kahneman, *Thinking, Fast and Slow* (New York: Farrar, Straus and Giroux, 2011); and Iain McGilchrist, *The Master and His Emissary: The Divided Brain and the Making of the Western World* (London: Yale University Press, 2019).

[27.] Elizabeth Prettejohn, *Beauty and Art: 1750–2000*, Oxford History of Art Series (Oxford: Oxford University Press, 2005), 40.

[28.] Nicholas Davey, "Baumgarten, Alexander G(ottlieb)," in *A Companion to Aesthetics*, 2nd ed., eds. Stephen Davies, Kathleen Marie Higgins, Robert Hopkins, Robert Stecker, and David E. Cooper (Chichester, UK: Wiley-Blackwell, 2009), 162.

human perception and the very act of appreciating artworks but also to the evolution of aesthetics as a recognized and essential philosophical field of inquiry.

A Note on the Role of Performance in Aesthetic Theory

Aesthetic theories have routinely asserted that there can be only *one* single work of art. In this context, the medium of the novel itself seems to evoke inherently ontological questions concerning its own status and identity: e.g., what should one consider as *the* work? An author's handwritten manuscript, an original first edition, or perhaps the very idea (or even inception thereof) conjured up in an author's psyche. If, indeed, *the* work itself is singular and unique, it cannot assume more than one so-called "version." As such, a particular given artwork (say, a novel) and the performance thereof (i.e., its aural iteration as an audiobook) simply cannot be considered as one and the same.

Appropriately, when it comes to aesthetically appreciating aural artifacts, one seems to be faced, therefore, with something of an ontological and philosophical obstacle—being essentially required to account for *two* different sets of internal logic, namely, that of the original work *and* that of its aural iteration. To distinguish between a "performance" (i.e., as a singular artwork in its own right) and a "performance *of*" an already existing work (i.e., which is in itself singular and unique) therefore becomes imperative.[29]

If, however, one accepts the so-called classic ontological distinction between "types" and "tokens," then to evaluate a "performance *of*" as an artwork in and of itself would essentially necessitate one to refrain from referring to the original work. Summarily, the "type-token" paradigm identifies a so-called "general law" *contra* its particular concrete instances (i.e., to say, the particular cases demonstrating the praxis of how the general law actually *works*). In effect, one must distinguish between *the* work of art (i.e., the singular type or one particular prototype) and its different concrete manifestations (i.e., its various tokens). As John Dilworth explains it, while they customarily allude to plays, musical compositions, or dance choreographies, "such 'type' views are also common for non-performing arts such as literature and film, and even as applied to

---

[29.] For further reading, see, e.g., David Davies, "Work and Performance in the Performing Arts," *Philosophy Compass* 4, no. 5 (September 2009): 744–745.

apparently particular artworks such as paintings."[30] One might thus be inclined to assume that to aesthetically evaluate audiobooks as the aural performances of already acknowledged literary works, similarly requires one to set aside (indeed, to completely ignore) the original text—thereby focusing solely on the particular aesthetics of the *performed* work.

At the same time, however, Dilworth finds that there inheres a certain "logical feature" in the type-token approach, which ultimately renders any such theory quite futile for fully explaining any case where "a single play performance" in fact consists as "a performance of two *different* plays."[31] Therein, he concludes, is where the deficiency of the type-token–like theories lies. As such, to attain a better understanding of audiobooks as an artistic phenomenon—that is, the products of a distinct aesthetic category that both abides by and complies with its own unique internal logic—one should adopt a completely different approach and a more befitting evaluative tool. In the same vein, Bar-Elli maintains that a performance does not constitute "an independent entity."[32] Rather, it is, in itself, "a type that has many tokens." Explicitly addressing musical works—which, he finds, are essentially "designed, by their very nature, to be performed"—Bar-Elli finds that any performance *necessarily* constitutes a "performance *of*" a given, specific composition.[33]

Interestingly enough, as Jed Rasula points out, Victorian English poet Gerard Manley Hopkins had apparently conceived of poetry "not [as] an honorary term indicating excellence in verse-craft," but rather as "a *composition* meant to be heard for its own sake—that is, *not* as an instance of—or conduit to—something else." [emphasis in original]. In this context, Rasula argues that "the vocalization of a poem, especially a poem 'meant to be heard for its own sake,' is one in which the acoustic dimension literally marks the limits of understanding."[34]

Musical compositions, as far as Bar-Elli is concerned, are constituted by "aesthetic-normative" properties—which, in turn, determine the manner in which a particular composition *must* be realized, and, as such, become relevant

---

[30] John Dilworth, "Theatre, Representation, Types and Interpretation," *American Philosophical Quarterly* 39, no. 2 (April 2002): 201.

[31] John Dilworth, "A Counter-Example to Theatrical Type Theories," *Philosophia* 31, nos. 1–2 (2003): 165.

[32] Bar-Elli, "Ideal Performance," 241.

[33] Gilead Bar-Elli, "Evaluating a Performance," 1; 5; 7–19. See URL: accessed December 19, 2022, https://bar-elli.co.il/greatPerformance.pdf.

[34] Jed Rasula, " Understanding the Sound of Not Understanding," in *Close Listening: Poetry and the Performed Word*, ed. Charles Bernstein (Oxford: Oxford University Press, 1998), 242–243.

both to its aesthetic evaluation and, indeed, very conception.[35] It is on the basis of these so-called "defining conditions" that one would ascertain whether or not—and, indeed, to what extent—one happens to be engaging with two (different) "tokens" of the purportedly "same" performance (type).[36] This, for Bar-Elli, is the idea behind what he perceives as an "intentionalistic performance"—which is ultimately defined by a particular composition's "aesthetic-normative" properties, whose overall system is "so rich and complex" that "many performance-types are instantiated, in practice, by only one token," effectively rendering those properties responsible for "the relevant concept of difference between performances." As such, they not only constitute the very nature and identity of a given piece of music but also determine the guidelines for performing it *correctly*.[37]

It is precisely in this respect that I find that Bar-Elli's approach to directly correspond with the notion of an artwork's embodied meaning, as well as, indeed, its internal logic. His consideration of aesthetically appreciating musical performances seems particularly pertinent to aesthetically evaluating audiobooks *as* artifacts.[38]

To be sure, questions pertaining to the very nature of artistic value—and, indeed, the aesthetic itself—remain a matter for debate among philosophers and art theorists. Some have argued, for instance, that a distinction should be made between the philosophy of the arts and the study of aesthetics, which effectively draws a line between artistic judgments and general aesthetic ones. In other words, to evaluate and appreciate something—that is, employing an aesthetic judgment—does not apply solely to artworks.[39]

According to Stecker, however, "artistic value derives from what artists successfully intend to do *in* their works as mediated by functions of the art forms

---

[35] Bar-Elli, "Evaluating a Performance," 3–4.

[36] Bar-Elli, "Ideal Performance," 229.

[37] Ibid., 236–238.

[38] Consider, for instance, his opposition to Nelson Goodman and his followers, according to whom "there are no erroneous performances of a composition—a performance that is not utterly loyal to the score is not a performance of the composition." According to Bar-Elli, this does not negate possible variations between different performances, the aesthetic quality of which (insofar as one "being better or worse than others") has nothing to do with its being a performance of a particular composition and whose meaning cannot be properly determined if one adopts Goodman's view. Ibid., 228n4.

[39] For further reading, see, e.g., Noël Carroll, *Philosophy of Art: A Contemporary Introduction* (London: Routledge, 1999), 156–159.

and genres to which the works belong" [emphasis in original].[40] Furthermore, as far as Tomáš Kulka is concerned—in what, by his own admission, consists as "part of a longer argument, the gist of which stands in direct opposition to the claim implied by the article's title"—one is certainly able to justify aesthetic value judgments:

> I believe they can be justified within a model built on the idea that works of art are evaluated on the basis of comparisons with their own alternatives, alternatives that can be thought of as unrealized possibilities of the work under consideration. Comparisons with aesthetically inferior alternatives will point to positive qualities of the work, while aesthetically superior alternatives will identify its faults.[41]

Identifying the "neo-Wittgensteinian" approach as its "major competitor," Noël Carroll asserts that the institutional approach places "the significance of social context on the agenda of contemporary philosophy of art."[42] For Stecker—who, as mentioned previously, referred to an early iteration of NITA—Graves' approach most notably teaches one "a method for distinguishing artistic from nonartistic functions artworks," adding in parentheses that one would need to determine the values of these functions independently.[43] Overall, Stecker finds that Graves' innovative take on institutional rules that govern the Artworld at large ultimately renders them responsible not only for purportedly determining which objects do (and, indeed, do not) count as artworks but also for prescribing particular principles for interpretation, as well as establishing certain criteria for artistic value. Thus, he explains, since "artistic value"—for Graves—"invariably comes from within the artworld," it effectively becomes "unique to artworks."[44]

---

[40] Robert Stecker, "Artistic Value Defended," *Journal of Aesthetics and Art Criticism* 70, no. 4 (2012): 357.

[41] Tomáš Kulka, "Why Aesthetic Value Judgements Cannot Be Justified," *Estetika: The European Journal of Aesthetics* 46, no. 1 (2009): 3; 27.

[42] Noël Carroll, "Dickie, George," in *A Companion to Aesthetics,* 2nd ed., ed. Stephen Davies, Kathleen Marie Higgins, Robert Hopkins, Robert Stecker, and David E. Cooper (Chichester, UK: Wiley-Blackwell, 2009), 249.

[43] Stecker, *Artworks: Definition, Meaning, Value,* 262.

[44] Ibid., 259–260.

BIBLIOGRAPHY

Textual Sources—Cited Publications

Addyman, David, with Matthew Feldman, and Erik Tonning, eds. *Samuel Beckett and BBC Radio—A Reassessment*. New York: Palgrave Macmillan, 2017.

Albrechtslund, Anne-Mette Bech. "Book Review: Have, Iben, and Birgitte Stougaard Pedersen. *Digital Audiobooks: New Media, Users, and Experiences*. New York: Routledge, 2016." *MedieKultur Journal of Media and Communication Research* 32, no. 60 (2016): 235–237.

Allen, R. E. *Plato's "Euthyphro" and the Earlier Theory of Forms: A Re-Interpretation of the Republic*. Abingdon, UK: Routledge, 2013.

Almutairi, Zaynab, and Hebah Elgibreen. "A Review of Modern Audio Deepfake Detection Methods: Challenges and Future Directions." *Algorithms* 15, no. 5 (2022): 1–20. Accessed August 25, 2023. https://www.mdpi.com/1999 -4893/15/5/155.

Anscombe, G. E. M. "On Brute Facts." *Analysis* 18, no. 3 (January 1958): 69–72.

Auslander, Philip. "Humanoid Boogie: Reflections on Robotic Performance." In *Staging Philosophy: Intersections of Theater, Performance, and Philosophy*, edited by David Krasner and David Z. Saltz, 87–103. Ann Arbor: University of Michigan Press, 2006.

Bar-Elli, Gilead. "Evaluating a Performance: Ideal vs. Great Performance." *Journal of Aesthetic Education* 38, no. 2 (2004): 7–19.

———. "Ideal Performance." *British Journal of Aesthetics* 43, no. 3 (July 2002): 223–242.

Baylor, Amy L. "A Three-Component Conception of Intuition: Immediacy, Sensing Relationships and Reason." *New Ideas in Psychology* 15, no. 2 (August 1997): 185–194.

Beck, Alan. *Radio Acting*. London: A & C Black, 1997.

Beckett, Samuel. *The Complete Dramatic Works.* London: Faber, 2006.

————. *Three Novels: Molloy, Malone Dies, the Unnamable.* New York: Grove Press, 2009.

Bercovitch, Sacvan. "Deadpan Huck: Or, What's Funny about Interpretation." *Kenyon Review,* New Series 24, no. 3/4 (Summer–Autumn, 2002): 90–134.

————. "What's Funny about *Huckleberry Finn.*" *New England Review* 20, no. 1 (Winter 1999): 8–28.

Bergman, J. Peter. "British Nostalgia/Spoken Word Issues." *Association for Recorded Sound Collections Journal* 13, no. 3 (1981): 131–136.

Bernstein, Charles. *Close Listening: Poetry and the Performed Word.* Oxford: Oxford University Press, 1998.

Boardman, Frank. "Weitz's Legacy." *American Society for Aesthetics Graduate e-Journal* 7, no. 1 (January 2015): 1–9. Accessed October 20, 2022. http://citeseerx .ist.psu.edu/viewdoc/download?doi=10.1.1.936.5760&rep=rep1&type=pdf.

Bosman, Julie. "Publisher Tinkers with Twain." *New York Times,* January 4, 2011. Accessed January 19, 2023. http://nytimes.com/2011/01/05/books/05huck .html.

Brater, Enoch. *The Drama in the Text: Beckett's Late Fiction.* New York: Oxford University Press, 1994.

Bullock, Darryl W. *Florence! Foster!! Jenkins!!!: The Life of the World's Worst Opera Singer.* New York: Overlook Press, 2016.

Cantril, Hadley, and Gordon W. Allport. *History of Broadcasting: Radio to Television.* New York: Arno Press, 1971.

Carson, Erin. "Audiobooks Are Thriving, but Could AI Take Over?" *CNET,* March 19, 2023. Accessed August 24, 2023. https://www.cnet.com/tech/features /audiobooks-are-thriving-but-could-ai-take-over/.

Carlson, Marvin. *Performance: A Critical Introduction.* London: Routledge, 1996.

Carroll, Noël. *Philosophy of Art: A Contemporary Introduction.* London: Routledge, 1999.

————. *Theories of Art Today.* Madison: University of Wisconsin Press, 2000.

Chia, Melissa. "'My comforts! Be Friends!': Words, Music and Beckett's Poetry on the Third." In *Samuel Beckett and BBC Radio—A Reassessment*, edited by David Addyman, Matthew Feldman, and Erik Tonning, 229–248. New York: Palgrave Macmillan, 2017.

Danto, Arthur. "The Artworld." *Journal of Philosophy* 61, no. 19 (1964): 571–584.

———. *What Art Is*. New Haven, CT: Yale University Press, 2013.

Davey, Nicholas. "Baumgarten, Alexander G(ottlieb)." In *A Companion to Aesthetics*, 2nd ed., edited by Stephen Davies, Kathleen Marie Higgins, Robert Hopkins, Robert Stecker, and David E. Cooper, 160–162. Chichester, UK: Wiley-Blackwell, 2009.

Davies, David. "Book Review: *The Performance of Reading: An Essay in the Philosophy of Literature* by Peter Kivy." *Journal of Aesthetics and Art Criticism* 66, no. 1 (Winter 2008): 89–91.

———. "Work and Performance in the Performing Arts." *Philosophy Compass* 4, no. 5 (September 2009): 744–755.

Davies, Stephen, with Kathleen Marie Higgins, Robert Hopkins, Robert Stecker, and David E. Cooper. *A Companion to Aesthetics*. Chichester, UK: Wiley-Blackwell, 2009.

Dean, Roger, and Hazel Smith. *Improvisation Hypermedia and the Arts Since 1945*. New York: Routledge, 1997.

Dickie, George. *The Art Circle: A Theory of Art*. New York: Haven, 1984.

———. *Evaluating Art*. Philadelphia: Temple University Press, 1988.

———. "The Institutional Theory of Art." In *Theories of Art Today*, edited by Noël Carroll, 93–108. Madison: University of Wisconsin Press, 2000.

Dilworth, John. "A Counter-Example to Theatrical Type Theories." *Philosophia* 31, nos. 1–2 (2003): 165–170.

———. "Theatre, Representation, Types and Interpretation." *American Philosophical Quarterly* 39, no. 2 (April 2002): 197–209.

Doyno, Victor A. *Writing Huck Finn: Mark Twain's Creative Process*. Philadelphia: University of Pennsylvania Press, 1991.

Eliot, T. S. "An Introduction to Huckleberry Finn." In *Bloom's Major Literary Characters: Huck Finn*, edited by Harold Bloom, 17–24. Philadelphia, PA: Chelsea House Publishers, 2004.

Engberg, Maria, Iben Have, and Birgitte Stougaard Pedersen, eds. *The Digital Reading Condition*. London: Routledge, 2023.

English, James F. "Teaching the Novel in the Audio Age." *PMLA* 135, no. 2 (March, 2020): 419–426. Accessed 24 August, 2023. https://www.english.upenn.edu/sites/default/files/articles/English%2C%20J_PMLA_Teaching_Novel_Audiobook_Age.pdf.

Gontarski, S. E. *On Beckett: Essays and Criticism*. New York: Grove Press, 1986.

Gordon, Robert. *The Purpose of Playing: Modern Acting Theories in Perspective*. Ann Arbor: University of Michigan Press, 2006.

Graves, David C. "Art and the Zen Master's Tea Pot: The Role of Aesthetics in the Institutional Theory of Art." *Journal Aesthetics and Art Criticism* 60, no. 4 (Autumn 2002): 341–352.

———. "Lir'ot Shki'a Ve'Lamut" [To See a Sunset and Die]. *Odyssey—A Journey through Ideas*, 4 (July 2009): 32–38. Accessed June 20, 2014. http://odyssey.org.il/files/pdf/issue4/10.pdf.

———. "Logic and the Sense of Necessity." *Book of Abstracts*, Presented at the 15th Congress of Logic, Methodology and Philosophy of Science (CLMPS 2015), University of Helsinki, August 3–8, 2015:225. Accessed April 30, 2024. http://philomatica.org/wp-content/uploads/2013/01/CLMPS_LC_book-of-abstracts-29.7.2015.pdf

———. "Reshimat Ha'Makoet" [The Groceries List]. *Odyssey—A Journey through Ideas*, 11 (May 2011): 25–29.

———. *The New Institutional Theory of Art*. Champaign, IL: Common Ground Publishing, 2010.

Gray, Frances. "The Nature of Radio Drama." In *Radio Drama*, edited by Peter Lewis, 48–77. London: Longman, 1981.

Guidall, George. "Letter to the Editor: The Mind's Ear." *New York Times*, December 23, 2011. Accessed August 20, 2022. http://nytimes.com/2011/12/25/books/review/the-minds-ear.html.

Hall, Peter. "Directing Pinter." In *Harold Pinter: You Never Heard Such Silence*, edited by Alan Bold, 19–28. London: Vision Press, 1984.

———. "Interview with Catherine Itzin and Simon Trussler." *Theatre Quarterly* 4, no. 16 (1974/1975): 129–133.

Hancher, Michael. "Learning from Librivox." In *Audiobooks, Literature, and Sound Studies*, edited by Matthew Rubery, 199–215. New York: Routledge, 2011.

Have, Iben, and Birgitte Stougaard Pedersen. *Digital Audiobooks: New Users, Media, and Experiences*. New York: Routledge, 2016.

———. "Reading Audiobooks." In *Beyond Media Borders, Volume 1: Intermedial Relations among Multimodal Media*, edited by Lars Elleström, 197–216. Växjö, Sweden: Palgrave Macmillan, 2021.

Hein, Hilde. "Performance as an Aesthetic Category." *Journal of Aesthetics and Art Criticism* 28, no. 3 (Spring 1970): 381–386.

Hemingway, Ernest. *The Green Hills of Africa.* New York: Charles Scribner's Sons, 1935.

Hibbitts, Bernard J. "Making Sense of Metaphors: Visuality, Aurality and the Reconfiguration of American Legal Discourse." *Cardozo Law Review* 16 (1994): 229–356.

Humphries, Barry. *Handling Edna: The Unauthorised Biography*. Sydney: Hachette, 2009.

———. *More Please*. London: Viking, 1992.

———. *My Life as Me*. London: Michael Joseph, 2002.

———. [Credited as] Dame Edna Everage. *My Gorgeous Life: An Adventure*. London: Macmillan, 1989.

———. [Credited as] Sir Les Patterson. *The Traveller's Tool*. London: Michael O'Mara Books, 1985.

Jacobi, Peter. "Some Midsummer Oddities." *Music Magazine and Musical Courier* 164, no. 8 (September 1962): 42–44.

Kivy, Peter. *The Performance of Reading: An Essay in the Philosophy of Literature.* Oxford: Wiley-Blackwell, 2006.

Knox, Sarah. "Hearing Hardy, Talking Tolstoy: The Audiobook Narrator's Voice and Reader Experience." In *Audiobooks, Literature, and Sound Studies*, edited by Matthew Rubery, 127–142. New York: Routledge, 2011.

Koestler, Arthur. *Insight and Outlook: An Inquiry into the Common Foundations of Science, Art and Social Ethics*. New York: Macmillan, 1949.

Kostelanetz, Richard. *Text-Sound Texts*. New York: William Morrow, 1980.

Leeder, Natalie. " 'None but the Simplest Words': Beckett's Listeners." In *Samuel Beckett and BBC Radio—A Reassessment*, edited by David Addyman, Matthew Feldman, and Erik Tonning, 269–288. New York: Palgrave Macmillan, 2017.

Lorand, Ruth. *Al Tiv'a Shel Omanut* [On the Nature of Art]. Tel-Aviv, Israel: Dvir Publishing House, 1991.

Mai, Kimberly T., with Sergi Bray, Toby Davies, and Lewis D. Griffin. "Warning: Humans Cannot Reliably Detect Speech Deepfakes." *PLoS ONE* 18, no. 8 (2023): 1–20. Accessed August 25, 2023. https://doi.org/10.1371/journal.pone.0285333.

Mandelbaum, Maurice. "Family Resemblances and Generalization Concerning the Arts." *American Philosophical Quarterly* 2, no. 3 (July 1965): 219–228.

McDonald, Rónán. *The Cambridge Introduction to Samuel Beckett*. Cambridge: Cambridge University Press, 2006.

McGovern, Barry "It's a Question of Voices…." In *Samuel Beckett: Three Novels*, read by Barry McGovern. [Appears in the Accompanying Booklet to the Audiobook Box Set], 29–32. RTÉ, RTE271CD, 2006.

McLuhan, Marshall. *Understanding Media: The Extensions of Man*. New York: McGraw-Hill, 1964.

McLuhan, Marshall, and Quentin Fiore. *The Medium Is the Massage: An Inventory of Effects*. New York: Bantam Books, 1967.

McMillan, Douglas, and Martha Fehsenfeld. *Beckett in the Theatre: The Author as Practical Playwright and Director*. London: Calder, 1988.

Mercier, Vivian. "The Uneventful Event." *Irish Times*, February 18, 1956.

Morris, Jeremy Wade, and Eric Hoyt, eds. *Saving New Sounds: Podcast Preservation and Historiography*. Ann Arbor: University of Michigan Press, 2021.

Morrison, Toni. "*Huckleberry Finn*: An Amazing, Troubling Book." In *Ethics, Literature, and Theory: An Introductory Reader*, edited by Stephen K. George, 279–288. Lanham, MD: A Sheed & Ward Book, 2005.

Newman, Andrew Adam. "Expanding the Market for Audiobooks Beyond Commuters." *New York Times*, June 11, 2013. Accessed December 19, 2022. http://nytimes.com/2013/06/12/business/media/expanding-the-market-for-audiobooks-beyond-commuters.html.

Noddings, Nel, and Paul J. Shore. *Awakening the Inner Eye: Intuition in Education*. New York: Teachers College Press, 1984.

Obregon, Juan. "Review: Have Iben, Birgitte Stougaard Pedersen: *Digital Audiobooks: New Media, Users and Experiences*." *MEDIENwissenschaft: Rezensionen\Reviews* Jg. 35 (2018), no. Sonderpublikation, S. 10–11. Accessed August 25, 2023. https://mediarep.org/handle/doc/5406.

Osipovich, David. "What Is a Theatrical Performance." *Journal of Aesthetics and Art* 64, no. 4 (Fall 2006): 461–470.

Parker, James. "The Mind's Ear." *New York Times*, November 25, 2011. Accessed December 19, 2022. http://nytimes.com/2011/11/27/books/review/the-minds-ear.html.

Pavice, Patrice. *Contemporary Mise en Scène: Staging Theatre Today*. Translated by Joel Anderson. New York: Routledge, 2013.

———. *Theatre at the Crossroads of Culture*. London: Routledge, 1992.

Pilling, John. "Changing My Tune: Beckett and the BBC Third Programme (1957–1960)." In *Samuel Beckett and BBC Radio—A Reassessment*, edited by David Addyman, Matthew Feldman, and Erik Tonning, 169–184. New York: Palgrave Macmillan, 2017.

Pinter, Harold. "Writing for the Theatre." In *Various Voices: Sixty Years of Prose, Poetry, Politics, 1948–1998*, by Harold Pinter, 19–24. New York: Grove Press, 1998.

Powers, Katherine A. "Don't Let a Bad Reader Ruin Your Audiobook Experience: Here Are Recordings to Savor—And to Avoid." *Washington Post*, August 5, 2019. Accessed December 19, 2022. https://www.washingtonpost.com/entertainment/books/dont-let-a-bad-reader-ruin-your-audiobook-experience-here-are-recordings-to-savor--and-to-avoid/2019/08/05/0750b980-ae2f-11e9-a0c9-6d2d7818f3da_story.html.

———. "AI Is Coming for Your Audiobooks: You're Right to Be Worried." *Washington Post*, August 16, 2023. Accessed August 22, 2023. https://www.washingtonpost.com/books/2023/08/17/audiobooks-artificial-intelligence/.

Prettejohn, Elizabeth. *Beauty and Art: 1750–2000*. Oxford History of Art Series. Oxford: Oxford University Press, 2005.

Railton, Stephen. *Mark Twain: A Short Introduction*. Oxford: Blackwell, 2003.

Rashkow, Mike. "Ed and Sam Chalpin, His Father the Pop Singer: A Recitation of the Ridiculous." Accessed January 10, 2023. https://spectropop.com /SamChalpin/.

Roach, Helen. *Spoken Records*, 3rd ed. Metuchen, NJ: Scarecrow Press, 1970.

Rubery, Matthew, ed. *Audiobooks, Literature, and Sound Studies*. New York: Routledge, 2011.

———. *The Untold Story of the Talking Book*. Cambridge, MA: Harvard University Press, 2016.

Scannell, Paddy. *Broadcast Talk*. London: Sage, 1991.

Schechter, Madeleine. *Semiotics and Art Theory: Between Autonomism and Contextualism*. Würzburg, Germany: Königshausen & Neumann, 2008.

Schnapp, Jeffrey, and Adam Michaels. *The Electric Information Age Book: McLuhan/Agel/Fiore and the Experimental Paperback*. New York: Princeton Architectural Press, 2012.

Schnapp, Jeffrey, and Kara Oehler. "The First Spoken Arts Record You Can Dance to." *Sensate* 1, no. 1 (March 2011).

Smirnov, V. A. "Internal and External Logic." *Bulletin of the Section of Logic* 17, nos. 3/4 (1988): 170–181.

Snelling, Maria. "The Audiobook Market and Its Adaptation to Cultural Changes." *Springer Publishing Research Quarterly* 37, no. 42 (2021): 642–656. Accessed August 22, 2023. https://www.ncbi.nlm.nih.gov/pmc/articles /PMC8489886/#CR15.

Stecker, Robert. "Artistic Value Defended." *Journal of Aesthetics and Art Criticism* 70, no. 4 (Fall 2012): 355–362.

———. *Artworks: Definition, Meaning, Value*. University Park: Pennsylvania State University Press, 1997.

Stodola, Amy. "Letter to the Editor: The Mind's Ear." *New York Times*,

December 23, 2011. Accessed August 20, 2022. https://www.nytimes
.com/2011/12/25/books/review/the-minds-ear.html.

St. Pierre, Paul Matthew. *A Portrait of the Artist as Australian: L'Oeuvre bizarre de Barry Humphries.* Montreal, Canada: McGill-Queen's University Press, 2004.

Tassin, Algernon de Vivier. *The Oral Study of Literature.* New York: Alfred A. Knopf, 1929: 20

Tracy, Lorna. "Echoes in a Bottle." *Books at Iowa* 8, no. 1 (1968): 24–29. Accessed February 25, 2023. https://pubs.lib.uiowa.edu/bai/article/29024/galley/137519/download/.

Twain, Mark. *The Annotated Huckleberry Finn.* Edited with Introduction and Notes by Michael Patrick Hearn. New York: W. W. Norton, 2001.

———. "How to Tell a Story." In *How to Tell a Story and Other Essays,* 3–12. New York: Harper and Brothers, 1898.

Voigts-Virchow, Eckart. "Paratracks in the Digital Age." In *Intermedialities,* edited by Evelyne Keitel, Gunter Süss, and Werner Huber, 129–139. Trier, Germany: WVT, 2007.

Wedgwood, Ralph. "The Internal and External Components of Cognition." In *Contemporary Debates in Cognitive Science,* edited by Robert J. Stainton, 307–325. Malden, MA: Blackwell, 2006.

Weitz, Morris. "The Role of Theory in Aesthetics." *Journal of Aesthetics and Art Criticism* 15, no. 1 (September 1956): 27–35.

Wittkower, D. E. "A Preliminary Phenomenology of the Audiobook." In *Audiobooks, Literature, and Sound Studies,* edited by Matthew Rubery, 216–231. New York: Routledge, 2011.

Wolfson, Gene. "Using Audiobooks to Meet the Needs of Adolescent Readers." *American Secondary Education* 36, no. 2 (Spring 2008): 105–114.

Textual Sources—For Further Reading

Abbott, H. Porter. "Beginning Again: The Post-Narrative Art of *Texts for Nothing* and *How It Is.*" In *The Cambridge Companion to Beckett,* edited by John Pilling, 106–124. Cambridge: Cambridge University Press, 1994.

Adalaide, Morris. *Sound States: Innovative Poetics and Acoustic Technologies*. Chapel Hill: University of North Carolina, 1997.

Albright, Daniel. *Beckett and Aesthetics*. Cambridge: Cambridge University Press, 2003.

Alburger, James R. *The Art of Voice Acting: The Craft and Business of Performing for Voice-Over*. New York: Focal Press, 2010.

Arnheim, Rudolf. *Radio: An Art of Sound.* Translated by Margaret Ludwig and Herbert Read. New York: Da Capo Press, 1972.

Athanases, Steven Z. "When Print Alone Fails Poetry: Performance as a Contingency of Literary Value." *Text and Performance Quarterly* 11, no. 2 (April 1991): 116–127.

Auslander, Philip. "Against Ontology: Making Distinctions between the Live and the Mediatized." *Performance Research* 2, no. 3 (Autumn 1997): 50–55.

———. "At the Listening Post, or, Do Machines Perform?" *International Journal of Performance Arts and Digital Media* 1, no. 1 (2005): 5–10.

Austin, J. L. *How to Do Things with Words*. Cambridge, MA: Harvard University Press, 1962.

Bader, Rolf. *Sound—Perception—Performance*. Current Research in Systematic Musicology, vol. 1. New York: Springer, 2013.

Baird, Susan G. *Audiobook Collections & Services*. Fort Atkinson, WI: Highsmith Press, 2000.

Barton, John. *Playing Shakespeare*. London. Methuen, 1984.

Beardsley, Monroe. *Aesthetics: Problems in the Philosophy of Criticism*. New York: Harcourt, Brace, and World, 1958.

———. "In Defense of Aesthetic Value." *Proceedings and Addresses of the American Philosophical Association* 52 (1979): 723–749.

Ben-Zvi, Linda. *Drawing on Beckett: Portraits, Performances, and Cultural Contexts*. Assaph Series. Tel-Aviv, Israel: Tel-Aviv University, 2004.

Ben-Zvi, Linda, and Angela Moorjani. *Beckett at 100: Revolving It All*. New

York: Oxford University Press, 2008.

Bernhart, Walter, ed. *Word and Music Studies: Essays on Performativity and on Surveying the Field*. Vol. 12. Leiden, The Netherlands: Brill, 2011.

Bernhart, Walter, and Lawrence Kramer, eds. *Word and Music Studies: On Voice*. Vol. 13. Leiden, The Netherlands: Brill, 2014.

Bernhart, Walter, and Werner Wolf, eds. *Word and Music Studies: Self-Reference in Literature and Music*. Vol. 11. Leiden, The Netherlands: Brill, 2010.

Berry, Cicely. *The Actor and the Text*. New York: Applause, 1992.

―――. *Voice and the Actor*. New York: Wiley, 1973.

Bishop, Nancy. *Secrets from the Casting Couch: On Camera Strategies for Actors from a Casting Director*. London: Methuen Drama, 2009.

Blake, Virgil L. P. "Something New Has Been Added: Aural Literacy and Libraries." In *Information Literacies for the Twenty-First Century*, edited by Virgil L. P. Blake and Renee Tjoumas, 203–218. Boston: G. K. Hall, 1990.

Blanchot, Maurice. *A Voice from Elsewhere*. Translated by Charlotte Mandell. SUNY Series, Insinuations: Philosophy, Psychoanalysis, Literature, edited by Charles Shepherdson. Albany: State University of New York Press, 2007.

Bloor, David. *Wittgenstein, Rules and Institutions*. London: Routledge, 1997.

Bolter, Jay David, and Richard Grusin. *Remediation: Understanding New Media*. Cambridge, MA: MIT Press, 1999.

Brecht, Bertolt. "The Radio as an Apparatus of Communication." In *Brecht on Theatre: The Development of an Aesthetic*, translated and edited by John Willett, 51–53. New York: Hill & Wang, 1977.

Brinker, Menachem. *Estetika Ke'Torat Ha'Bikoret* [Aesthetics as the Theory of Criticism]. Tel-Aviv, Israel: Broadcast University Library, Published by the Ministry of Defence, 1982.

Brockmeier, Jens, and Donal Carbaugh, eds. *Narrative and Identity: Studies in Autobiography, Self and Culture*. Amsterdam: John Benjamins, 2001.

Bull, Michael, and Les Back, eds. *The Auditory Culture Reader the Auditory Culture Reader*. 2nd ed. London: Routledge, 2015.

Burchfield, Robert. *The Spoken Word: A BBC Guide*. New York: Oxford University Press, 1982.

Burkey, Mary. *Audiobooks for Youth: A Practical Guide to Sound Literature*. Chicago: American Library Association, 2013.

Burnham, Douglas. "Immanuel Kant: Aesthetics." In *The Internet Encyclopedia of Philosophy*, edited by James Fieser and Bradley Dowden. Accessed December 12, 2022. http://www.iep.utm.edu/kantaest/.

Cahill, Maria, and Jennifer Moore. "A Sound History Audiobooks Are Music to Children's Ears." *Children and Libraries* 15, no. 1 (Spring 2017): 22–29.

Calder, John. "Notes." In *Malone Dies*, by Samuel Beckett. Read by Sean Barett. Unabridged. Naxos Audiobooks, NA531912D, 2004.

———. "Notes." In *Molloy*, by Samuel Beckett. Read by Sean Barett and Dermot Crowley. Unabridged. Naxos Audiobooks, NA729212D. 2003.

———. "Notes." In *The Unnamable*, by Samuel Beckett. Read by Sean Barrett. Unabridged. Naxos Audiobooks, NA533712D, 2005.

Cantril, Hadley, with Hazel Gaudet, and Herta Herzog. *The Invasion from Mars: A Study in the Psychology of Panic*. Princeton, NJ: Princeton University Press, 1940.

Çarkıt, Cafer. "Evaluation of Audiobook Listening Experiences of 8th Grade Students." *Educational Policy Analysis and Strategic Research* 15, no. 4 (2020): 146–163.

Carroll, Noël. *Beyond Aesthetics*. Cambridge: Cambridge University Press, 2001.

———. "Essence, Expression, and History: Arthur Danto's Philosophy of Art." In *Danto and His Critics*, edited by Mark Rollins, 118–145. Chichester, UK: Wiley-Blackwell, 2012.

Catliff, Suzy, and Jennifer Granville. *The Casting Handbook: For Film and Theatre Makers*. New York: Routledge, 2013.

Cellucci, Carlo. *Rethinking Logic: Logic in Relation to Mathematics, Evolution, and Method*. New York: Springer, 2013.

Chapman, Siobhan, and Christopher Routledge. *Key Ideas in Linguistics and the Philosophy of Language*. Edinburgh: Edinburgh University Press, 2009.

Clark, Ruth Cox. "Audiobooks for Children: Is This Really Reading?" *Chil-*

dren and Libraries 5, no. 1 (2007): 49–50.

Cohn, Ruby. *A Beckett Canon.* Ann Arbor: University of Michigan Press, 2005.

Cole, Toby, and Helen Kirch Chinoy. *Directors on Directing: A Source Book of the Modern Theatre.* London: Macmillan, 1963.

Cottingham, John. "Intuition and Genealogy." In *Intuition, Theory, and Anti-Theory in Ethics,* edited by Sophie Grace Chappell, 9–23. Oxford: Oxford University Press, 2015.

Cowan, Joseph L. "Wittgenstein's Philosophy of Logic." *Philosophical Review* 70, no. 3 (July 1961): 362–375.

Critchley, Simon. "Who Speaks in the Work of Samuel Beckett?" *Yale French Studies* no. 93 (1998): 114–130.

Crook, Tim. *Radio Drama: Theory and Practice.* London: Routledge, 1999.

Cusic, Don. *The Poet as* Performer. Lanham, MD: University Press of America, 1991.

Danto, Arthur. *The Abuse of Beauty.* Chicago: Open Court, 2003.

———. *After the End of Art: Contemporary Art and the Pale of History.* Princeton, NJ: Princeton University Press, 1997.

———. "Art and Meaning." In *Theories of Art Today,* edited by Noël Carroll, 130–140. Madison: University of Wisconsin Press, 2000.

———. *Beyond the Brillo Box: The Visual Arts in Post-Historical Perspective.* Berkley: University of California Press, 1992.

———. *Embodied Meanings.* New York: Noonday Press, 1994.

———. "From Aesthetics to Art Criticism and Back." *Journal of Aesthetics to Art Criticism* 54, no. 2 (Spring 2006): 105–115.

———. *The Transfiguration of the Commonplace.* Cambridge, MA: Harvard University Press, 1983.

Davies, David. *Art as Performance.* Oxford: Blackwell, 2004.

———. *Philosophy of Performing Arts.* Malden, MA: Wiley-Blackwell, 2011.

Davies, Paul. "Three Novels and Four *Nouvelles*: Giving up the Ghost Be Born at Last." In *The Cambridge Companion to Beckett*, edited by John Pilling, 45–66. Cambridge: Cambridge University Press, 1994.

Davies, Stephen. "A Defence of the Institutional Definition of Art." *Southern Journal of Philosophy* 26, no. 3 (Fall 1988): 307–324.

———. *Definitions of Art*. Ithaca, NY: Cornell University Press, 1991.

———. *Philosophical Perspectives on Art*. New York: Oxford University Press, 2007.

Dell'Antonia, K. J. "Does 'Reading' an Audio Book Count?" *Motherlode* (blog), *New York Times*, August 31, 2012. Accessed October 19, 2022. http://parenting.blogs.nytimes.com/2012/08/31/does-reading-an-audio-book-count/.

———. "When Audio Books Do and Don't Count for School." *Motherlode* (blog), *New York Times*, September 7, 2012. Accessed October 19, 2022. http://parenting.blogs.nytimes.com/2012/09/07/when-audio-books-do-and-dont-count-for-school.

Dickie, George. *Art and the Aesthetic: An Institutional Analysis*. Ithaca, NY: Cornell University Press, 1974.

———. "Art and Value." *British Journal of Aesthetics* 40, no. 2 (1998): 228–241.

———. "Defining Art." *American Philosophical Quarterly* 6, no.3 (1969): 253–256.

———. "A Tale of Two Artworlds." In *Danto and His Critics*, edited by Mark Rollins, 111–117. Chichester, UK: Wiley-Blackwell, 2012.

———. "Wollheim's Dilemma." *British Journal of Aesthetics* 38, no. 2 (1998): 127–135.

Drakakis, John. *British Radio Drama*. Cambridge: Cambridge University Press, 1981.

Eleveld, Mark. *The Spoken Word Revolution "Redux."* Naperville, IL: Sourcebooks MediaFusion, 2007.

Esslin, Martin. *The Theatre of the Absurd*. New York: Anchor Books, 1961.

Euritt, Alyn. *Podcasting as an Intimate Medium*. Oxon: Routledge, 2022.

Felton, Felix. *The Radio-Play: Its Technique and Possibilities*. London: Sylvan Press, 1949.

Fischer-Lichte, Erika. *The Routledge Introduction to Theatre and Performance Studies*. London: Routledge, 2014.

Furniss, Graham. *Orality: Power of the Spoken Word*. New York: Palgrave Macmillan, 2004.

Godlovitch, Stan. *Musical Performance: A Philosophical Study*. London: Routledge, 1998.

Goehr, Lydia. *The Imaginary Museum of Musical Works*. Oxford: Oxford University Press, 1994.

Goldberg, RoseLee. *Performance Art: From Futurism to the Present*. London: Thames & Hudson, 1989.

Gontarski, S. E. *The Edinburgh Companion to Samuel Beckett and the Arts*. Edinburgh: Edinburgh University Press, 2014.

Goodall, Jane. *Stage Presence: The Actor as Mesmerist*. London: Routledge, 2008.

Goodman, Nelson. *Languages of Art: An Approach to a Theory of Symbols*. Indianapolis, IN: Bobbs-Merrill, 1968.

Goody, Jack. *The Interface between the Written and the Oral*. Cambridge: Cambridge University Press, 1987.

Graham, Gordon. *Philosophy of the Arts: An Introduction to Aesthetics*. London: Routledge, 1997.

Halperin, Chaim. *Kri'a Omanutit: Clalim Ve'Targilim* [Artistic Reading: Rules and Exercises; Literal Translation from the Original Hebrew. Main Title Could Alternatively Be Translated as *Elocution*]. Tel-Aviv, Israel: Tel-Aviv University's Theatre Department, 1969.

Hampshire, Stuart. "Logic and Appreciation." In *Aesthetics and Language*, edited by William Elton, 161–169. Oxford: Basil Blackwell, 1954.

Hinsliff, Gaby. "Ignore the Purists—Listening to a Book Instead of Reading It Isn't Skiving or Cheating." *Guardian*, December 29, 2022. Accessed August 25, 2023. https://www.theguardian.com/commentisfree/2022/dec/29/listening -reading-audiobooks-podcasts-generational-shift.

Holt, Jim. "Two Brains Running." *New York Times*, November 25, 2011.

Accessed May 3, 2022. http://nytimes.com/2011/11/27/books/review/thinking
-fast-and-slow-by-daniel-kahneman-book-review.html.

Huwiler, Elke. "Radio Drama Adaptations: An Approach towards an Analytical Methodology." *Journal of Adaptation in Film and Performance* 2, no. 2
(2010): 129–140.

Jesson, James. "A Library on the Air—Literary Dramatization and Orson
Welles's Mercury Theatre." In *Audiobooks, Literature, and Sound Studies*, edited by Matthew Rubery, 44–60. New York: Routledge, 2011.

Kahn, Douglas, and Gregory Whitehead. *Wireless Imagination: Sound, Radio and the Avant-Garde.* Cambridge, MA: MIT Press, 1992.

Kahneman, Daniel. *Thinking, Fast and Slow*. New York: Farrar, Straus and
Giroux, 2011.

Kaufman, Leslie. "Actors Today Don't Just Read for the Part: Reading IS the
Part." *New York Times*, June 29, 2013. Accessed May 3, 2022. http://nytimes.
com/2013/06/30/business/media/actors-today-dont-just-read-for-the-part-read-
ing-is-the-part.html.

Kimber, Marian Wilson. *The Elocutionists*: *Women, Music, and the Spoken
Word*. Urbana: University of Illinois Press, 2017.

King, Nicola. *Memory, Narrative, Identity: Remembering the Self.* Edinburgh: Edinburgh University Press, 2000.

Kivy, Peter. *Antithetical Arts: On the Ancient Quarrel between Literature and
Music*. Oxford: Clarendon Press, 2009.

———. *Philosophies of the Arts*. Cambridge: Cambridge University Press,
1997.

———. "What Makes 'Aesthetic' Terms Aesthetic?" *Philosophy and Phe-
nomenological Research* 36, no. 2 (1975): 197–211.

Kleege, Georgina. "Aurality." In *Further Reading*, edited by Matthew Rubery
and Leah Price, 206–212. Oxford: Oxford University Press, 2020.

Koestler, Arthur. *The Act of Creation*. London: Hutchinson, 1964.

———. "The Tree Domains of Creativity." In *Challenges of Humanistic Psychology*, edited by J. F. T. Bugental, 31–40. New York: McGraw-Hill, 1967.

Kozloff, Sarah. "Audiobooks in a Visual Culture." *Journal of American Culture* 18, no. 4 (1995): 83–95.

Kozlowski, Michael. "Audiobook Trends and Statistics for 2020." *Good e-Reader*, June 20, 2020. Accessed August 25, 2023. https://goodereader.com /blog/audiobooks/audiobook-trends-and-statistics-for-2020.

Kunzel, Bonnie, with Joyce Saricks, Kaite Mediatore Stover, and Neal Wyatt. "Selecting Audiobooks: Towards a Core Collection of Narrators." *Reference & User Services Quarterly* 51, no. 2 (Winter 2011): 97–104.

Kuzmičová, Anežka. "Audiobooks and Print Narrative: Similarities in Text Experience." In *Audionarratology: Interfaces of Sound and Narrative*, edited by Jarmila Mildorf and Till Kinzel, 217–237. Berlin: De Gruyter, 2016.

Lee, Linda. "Audiobooks: Taking the World by Storm." *White Paper*. Written in Partnership with Zebralution. Frankfurter Buchmesse, Guest of Honour Canada, October 14–18, 2020. Accessed December 13, 2020. https://www .dosdoce.com/wp-content/uploads/2020/09/Audiobooks-Taking-theWorld -by-Storm.pdf.

Lewis, Peter. *Radio Drama*. London: Longman, 1981.

Lind, Richard. "The Aesthetic Essence of Art." *Journal of Aesthetics and Art Criticism* 50, no. 2 (Spring 1992): 117–129.

Lodato, Suzanne M., and David Francis Urrows, eds. *Word and Music Studies: Self-Reference in Literature and Music*. Vol. 7. Leiden, The Netherlands: Brill, 2005.

Marchetti, Emanuela, and Andrea Valente. "Interactivity and Multimodality in Language Learning: The Untapped Potential of Audiobooks." *Universal Access in the Information Society* 17, no. 2 (2018): 257–274.

Mathien, Thomas, and D. G. Wright. *Autobiography as Philosophy: The Philosophical Uses of Self-Presentation*. Abingdon, UK: Routledge, 2006.

Mcenaney, Tom. "Forgotten Histories of the Audiobook: Tape, Text, Speech, and Sound from Esteban Montejo and Miguel Barnet's *Biografía de un cimarrón* to Andy Warhol's *a: A Novel*." *Journal of Musicology* 36, no. 4 (2019): 437–463.

McWhinnie, Donald. *The Art of Radio*, London: Faber, 1959.

Mediatore, Kaite. "Reading with Your Ears: Readers' Advisory and Audio Books." *Reference & User Services Quarterly* 42, no. 4 (Summer 2003): 218–232.

Nudds, Matthew, and Casey O'Callaghan. *Sounds and Perception: New Philosophical Essays*. Oxford: Oxford University Press, 2009.

Oliver, Douglas. *Poetry and Narrative in Performance*. New York: McMillan, 1989.

Ong, Walter J. *Orality and Literacy*. London: Routledge, 2002.

Padberg-Schmitt, Britta. "Increasing Reading Fluency in Young Adult Readers Using Audiobooks." *Children's Literature in English Language Education* 8, no. 1 (2020): 31–51.

Peters, John Durham. *Speaking into the Air: A History of the Idea of Communication.* Chicago: University of Chicago Press, 1999.

Piette, Adam. *Remembering and the Sound of Words: Mallarmé, Proust, Joyce, Beckett*. New York: Oxford University Press, 1966.

Rizzuto, Ana-María. *Freud and the Spoken Word: Speech as a Key to the Unconscious*. New York: Routledge, 2015.

Rosenberg, Patsy. *The Need for Words: Voice and the Text*. London: Methuen, 1993.

Rubery, Matthew. "Play It Again, Sam Weller: New Digital Audiobooks and Old Ways of Reading." *Journal of Victorian Culture* 13, no. 1 (January 2008): 58–79.

Rudin, Jen. *Confessions of a Casting Director: Help Actors Land Any Role with Secrets from inside the Audition Room*. New York: It Books, 2013.

Saricks, Joyce G. *Reading on…Audiobooks: Reading Lists for Every Taste*. Read on Series, edited by Barry Trott. Santa Barbara, CA: Libraries Unlimited, 2011.

Schechner, Richard. *Performance Studies: An Introduction*. 3rd ed. London: Routledge, 2013.

Schnapp, Jeffrey. "The Book of the Now." Accessed October 22, 2022. http://wearethemasses.bandcamp.com/track/the-book-of-the-now.

Searle, Judith. *Getting the Part: Thirty-Three Professional Casting Directors Tell You How to Get Work in Theater, Films, Commercials, and TV.* New York: Limelight Editions, 1995.

Shokoff, James. "What Is an Audiobook?" *Journal of Popular Culture* 34, no. 4 (2001): 171–181.

Singh, Anisha, and Patricia A. Alexander. "Audiobooks, Print, and Comprehension: What We Know and What We Need to Know." *Educational Psychology Review* 34 (2022): 677–715.

Smith, Marc Kelly, with Joe Kraynak. *Take the Mic: The Art of Performance Poetry, Slam, and the Spoken Word*. Naperville, IL: Sourcebooks MediaFusion, 2009.

Snyder, Stephen. "Arthur Danto's Andy Warhol: The Embodiment of Theory in Art and the Pragmatic Turn*." Leitmotiv: Topics in Aesthetics and in Philosophy of Art* (2010): 135–151. Accessed October 17, 2022. http://ledonline.it /leitmotiv/Allegati/Leitmotiv-2010-0-Snyder.pdf.

St. Clair, Justin. *Sound and Aural Media in Postmodern Literature: Novel Listening*. New York: Routledge, 2013.

Stecker, Robert. "Do All Valuable Artworks Possess Aesthetic Value?" *Annales Philosophici* 1 (2010): 83–90.

Sterne, Jonathan. *The Audible Past: Cultural Origins of Sound Reproduction*. Durham, NC: Duke University Press, 2003.

———. *The Sound Studies Reader*. London: Routledge, 2012.

Strauss, Valerie. "Is Listening to a Book 'Cheating?'" *Washington Post*, July 31, 2016. Accessed August 25, 2023. https://www.washingtonpost.com/news /answer-sheet/wp/2016/07/31/is-listening-to-a-book-a-cheating/.

Thompson, John B. "The Remarkable Rise of the Audiobook." *Logos* 32, no. 2 (2021): 10–19.

Wedgwood, Ralph. "The Meaning of 'Ought.' " In *Oxford Studies in Metaethics,* vol. 1, edited by Russ Shafer-Landau, 127–160. New York: Clarendon Press, 2006.

Weiss, Allen S. *Experimental Sound and Radio*. Cambridge, MA: MIT Press, 2001.

West, Sarah. *Say It: The Performative Voice in the Dramatic Works of Beckett*. (Faux titre, 352). Amsterdam: Rodopi, 2010.

Willingham, Daniel T. "Is Listening to a Book the Same Thing as Reading It?" *New York Times*, December 8, 2016. Accessed August 25, 2023. https://

www.nytimes.com/2018/12/08/opinion/sunday/audiobooks-reading-cheating
-listening.html.

Wittgenstein, Ludwig. *Philosophical Investigations*. Translated by G. E. M. Anscombe. Oxford: Blackwell, 1958.

———. *Tractatus Logico-Philosophicus*. Translated by D. F. Pears and B. F. McGuinness. 1921. Reprint, London: Routledge/Taylor & Francis e-Library, 2002. Accessed June 19, 2020. http://aramdhon.staff.uns.ac.id/files/2011/10 /wittgenstein_tractatus_logico_philosophicus__routledge_classics_.pdf.

Yanal, Robert J. "The Institutional Theory of Art." In *The Encyclopedia of Aesthetics*, edited by Michael Kelly, 508–512 [1–7]. New York: Oxford University Press, 1998.

———. *Institutions of Art*. Pittsburgh, PA: University of Pittsburgh Press, 1994.

Young, Jordan R. *Acting Solo: The Art of One-Man Shows*. Beverly Hills, CA: Moonstone Press, 1989.

———. *The Beckett Actor: Jack MacGowran, Beginning to End*. Beverly Hills, CA: Moonstone Press, 1987.

Audiobooks & Sound Recordings

Alda, Alan. *Things I Overheard While Talking to Myself*. Read by the Author. Unabridged. Random House Audio, 2007.

Auslander, Shalom. *Foreskin's Lament: A Memoir*. Read by the Author. Unabridged. Penguin Audio, 2007.

Beckett, Samuel. *MacGowran Speaking Beckett*. Performed by Jack MacGowran. [Made under the Personal Supervision of Samuel Beckett]. Claddagh Records, CCR3CD, 1966.

———. *Malone Dies*. Read by Sean Barret. Unabridged. Modern Classics. Naxos Audiobooks, NA531912D, 2004.

———. *Molly*. Read by Sean Barret and Dermot Crowley. Unabridged. Modern Classics. Naxos Audiobooks, NA729212D, 2003.

———. *Molloy/Malone Dies/The Unnamable*. Performed by Cyril Cusack. Directed by Howard Sackler. Caedmon Records, TC 1169, 1963.

———. *Three Novels.* Read by Barry McGovern. RTÉ, RTE271CD, 2006.

———. *The Unnamable.* Read by Sean Barret. Unabridged. Modern Classics. Naxos Audiobooks, NA533712D, 2005.

———. "*...the Whole Thing's Coming out of the Dark.*" Created for German Radio. Produced for the "Intermedium" Media Art Biennale. BR Radio Drama and Media Art/ORF/DLR/Kunsthalle Wien/ZKM Karlsruhe.

Bell, Lake. *Inside Voice: My Obsession with How We Sound.* Pushkin Industries, 2022. Accessed August 31, 2023. https://www.pushkin.fm/audiobooks/inside-voice.

Benét, Stephen Vincent. *The Devil and Daniel Webster.* Read by Alec Baldwin. [DVD Bonus Feature, Recorded Exclusively for the Criterion Collection.] Spine #214, 2003.

Bennett. Alan. *The Complete Talking Heads.* BBC Worldwide, 2015.

Bergman, Ingmar. *The Passion of Anna.* Read by Elliott Gould. [DVD Bonus Feature in the "The Ingmar Bergman Special Edition."] MGM, 2004.

Brooks, Albert. *2030: The Real Story of What Happens to America.* Read by Dick Hill.. Tantor Audio, 2011.

Coogan, Steve. *Easily Distracted.* Read by the Author. Unabridged. Random House Audio, 2015.

Cleese, John. *So, Anyway...* Read by the Author. Unabridged. Penguin, 2014.

Cross, David. *I Drink for a Reason.* Read by the Author, and Featuring the Voices of John Benjamin, Krsten Schall, and Robot, with Musical Guests Les Savy Fav and Yo La Tengo. Hachette, 2009.

Dench, Judi. *And Furthermore.* [As Told to John Miller]. Read by Samantha Bond. Unabridged. With Preface Read by Judi Dench. Orion, 2010.

Fassett, Jim. *Strange to Your Ears: The Fabulous World of Sound.* Columbia Masterworks, ML 4938, 1955.

Humphries, Barry. *Handling Enda.* Read by the Author. Orion, 2010.

———. [Credited as] Dame Edna Everage. *My Gorgeous Life.* Read by the Author. Dove Audio, 1993. [Digitally Remastered by Phoenix Books, 2014].

———. [Credited as] Sir Leslie Colin Patterson. *The Traveller's Tool.* Read by the Author. Bolinda Audio, 2011.

Eric Idle, [The Story of] *The Quite Remarkable Adventurea of the Owl and the Pussycat*. [Musically Scored]. Written and performed by Eric Idle. Based on the poems, drawings, and writings of Edward Lear. Music and Lyrics composed by Eric Idle and John Duprez [sic.]. Dove Music, 1997.

Kosinski, Jerzy. *Being There* (1970). Performed by Dustin Hoffman. Audible, 2012.

MacGowran, Jack. Interviewed by Liam Nolan. Excerpt. (circ. 1966).

Marshall McLuhan, Quentin Fiore, and Jerome Agel. *The Medium Is the Massage with Marshall McLuhan*. Produced by John Simon. Conceived & Co-ordinated by Jerome Agel. Columbia Records, 1968.

Pinter, Harold. *Various Voices: Prose, Poetry, Politics: 1948–1998*. Read by the Author. Faber/Penguin Audiobooks, 1998. [Two Audiocassettes].

Python (Monty). "Soundtrack for the Lonely." [DVD Bonus Feature; "Collector's Edition" of] *Monty Python's the Meaning of Life* (1983). Universal, 2003.

Springsteen, Bruce. *Born to Run.* Read by the Author. Simon & Schuster Audio, 2016.

Tap, Spinal. [Band Members; In-Character]. "Commentary." [DVD Bonus Feature; "Special Edition" of] *This Is Spinal Tap* (1982). MGM, 2000.

Twain, Mark. *Adventures of Huckleberry Finn.* Read by Jim Donaldson. Trout Lake Media, 2012.

———. *Adventures of Huckleberry Finn.* Read by Eric G. Dove. Dreamscape Media, 2013.

———. *Adventures of Huckleberry Finn.* Read by William Fortier. Trout Lake Media, 2011.

———. *Adventures of Huckleberry Finn.* Narrated by Grover Gardner. Audio Book Contractors, 1994.

———. *Adventures of Huckleberry Finn.* Read by John Greenman. Sheba Blake Publishing, 2021.

———. *Adventures of Huckleberry Finn.* Read by Don Hagen. Gildan Media, 2010.

———. *Adventures of Huckleberry Finn*. Narrated by Michael A. Harding. Providence Publishing, 2022.

———. *Adventures of Huckleberry Finn*. Narrated by B. J. Harrison. B. J. Harrison, 2008.

———. *Adventures of Huckleberry Finn*. Read by Chris Hendrie. Chris Hendrie, 2011.

———. *Adventures of Huckleberry Finn*. Narrated by Lee Howard. Page2-Page, 2019.

———. *Adventures of Huckleberry Finn*. Adapted and Read by Garrison Keillor. HighBridge Audio, 1996.

———. *Adventures of Huckleberry Finn*. Read by Mike McShane. Harper-Collins, 1994.

———. *Adventures of Huckleberry Finn*. Read by Shamrock McShane. Shamrock McShane, 2022.

———. *Adventures of Huckleberry Finn*. Read by Alan Munro. Trout Lake Media, 2015.

———. *Adventures of Huckleberry Finn*. Read by Michael Prichard. Books on Tape, 1977.

———. *Adventures of Huckleberry Finn*. Read by Roberto Scarlato. Lukeman Literary Management, 2019.

———. *Adventures of Huckleberry Finn*. Read by Mark F. Smith. [LibriVox, "Version 2," Catalogued: 2007-07-12].

———. *Adventures of Huckleberry Finn*. Read by Stephen L. Vernon. A. R. N. Publications, 2015.

———. *Adventures of Huckleberry Finn*. Read by Elijah Wood. Audible, 2014.

———. *The Adventures of Huckleberry Finn*. Performed by Matt Armstrong. Matt Armstrong, 2011.

———. *The Adventures of Huckleberry Finn*. Read by Thomas Becker. In Audio, 2003.

———. *The Adventures of Huckleberry Finn*. Read by Tim Behrens. Books in Motion, 2011.

————. *The Adventures of Huckleberry Finn.* Dramatized. Read by Jason Damron. ABN, 2012.

————. *The Adventures of Huckleberry Finn.* Read by Parzaan Dastur. Audible, 2018.

————.*The Adventures of Huckleberry Finn.* Read by Denny Delk. Cherry Hill Publishing, 2012.

————. *The Adventures of Huckleberry Finn.* Narrated by Norman Dietz. Recorded Books, 1980.

————. *The Adventures of Huckleberry Finn.* Read by William Dufris. Tantor Media, 2008.

————. *The Adventures of Huckleberry Finn.* Read by Robin Field. Mission Audio, 2011.

————. *The Adventures of Huckleberry Finn.* Read by Patrick Fraley. Audio Partners, 1999.

————. *The Adventures of Huckleberry Finn.* Abridged. Presented by Geoffrey & Eden Giuliano. Icon Audio Arts, 2020.

————. *The Adventures of Huckleberry Finn.* Read by Tom Parker. Blackstone Audio, 2014.

————. *The Adventures of Huckleberry Finn.* Read by Garrick Hagon. Naxos, 2007.

————. *The Adventures of Huckleberry Finn.* Read by Johnny Heller. Listen2aBook.com, 2015.

————. *The Adventures of Huckleberry Finn.* Read by Richard Henzel. Richard Henzel, 2010.

————. *The Adventures of Huckleberry Finn.* Read by Dick Hill. Brilliance, 1992.

————. *The Adventures of Huckleberry Finn.* Read by Theo Holland. American Renaissance Books, 2018.

————. *The Adventures of Huckleberry Finn.* Read by Jim Killavey. Jimcin Recordings, 1980.

————. *The Adventures of Huckleberry Finn.* Read by Sam Kusi. Lauscher Audiobooks, 2024.

———. *The Adventures of Huckleberry Finn*. Abridged. Read by Jack Lemmon. Simon & Schuster, 2000.

———. *The Adventures of Huckleberry Finn*. Read by Nathan Osgood. SNR, 2023.

———. *The Adventures of Huckleberry Finn*. Read by Robin Miles. Thomas Nelson, 2020.

———. *The Adventures of Huckleberry Finn*. Read by Sharon Plummer. Strelbytskyy Multimedia Publishing, 2020.

———. *The Adventures of Huckleberry Finn*. Retold from the Mark Twain original. Read by Rebecca K. Reynolds Oasis Audio, 2019.

———. *The Adventures of Huckleberry Finn*. Abridged. Read by Kerry Shale. Penguin, 1997.

———. *The Adventures of Huckleberry Finn*. Read by Lawrence Skinner. Audioliterature, 2018.

———. *The Adventures of Huckleberry Finn*. Read by Matthew Taylor. In *10 Essential Pieces of Literature*. MustRead, 2019.

———. *The Adventures of Huckleberry Finn*. Abridged. Read by Trevor White. Audible, 2012.

———. *The Adventures of Huckleberry Finn*. Abridged. Read by Will Wheaton. Phoenix Books, 2014.

———. *The Adventures of Huckleberry Finn*. [*With Lectures for Use as a Study Guide*]. Narrated by Kevin O'Brien. Kevin Obrien, 2022.

———. *The Adventures of Huckleberry Finn*. [*An A+ Audio Study Guide by Kirsten Silva Gruesz, PhD*]. Narrated by John O'Connell. Hachette Audio, 2006.

———. *The Complete Tom Sawyer & Huckleberry Finn Collection*. Read by Henry Adams. Author's Republic, 2019.

———. *Huckleberry Finn*. Retold by Anna Kirwan. Read by Bob Karper. Real Reads, 2009.

———. *Huckleberry Finn*. [*Readings from the Stories and from*]. Adapted and performed by Will Geer. Folkways Records, FL 9769, 1961.

————. *Huckleberry Finn*. The Campbell Playhouse. Produced by Orson Welles and John Houseman. CBS, March 17, 1940.

————. *Mark Twain Collection: The Adventures of Tom Sawyer, Adventures of Huckleberry Finn, and a Connecticut Yankee in King Arthur's Court*. Unabridged. Narrated by Jim D. Johnston. Combray Media, 2018.

————. *Stories of*. Read by Walter Brennan and Brandon De Wilde. Caedmon Records, TC 1027, 1956.

Wright, Steven. *Harold*. Simon & Schuster Audio, 2023.